MANTLE OF CHRIST

William George Taylor, foundation superintendent 1884–87, and again 1889–93 and 1898–1913. By courtesy of the Wesley Central Mission.

MANTLE OF CHRIST

A HISTORY OF THE SYDNEY CENTRAL METHODIST MISSION

DON WRIGHT

University of Queensland Press

First published 1984 by University of Queensland Press
Box 42, St Lucia, Queensland, Australia

© D.I. Wright 1984

Typeset by University of Queensland Press
Printed by The Dominion Press-Hedges & Bell, Maryborough, 3465

Distributed in the UK, Europe, the Middle East, Africa, and the Caribbean
by Prentice Hall International, International Book Distributors Ltd,
66 Wood Lane End, Hemel Hempstead, Herts., England

Distributed in the USA and Canada by Technical Impex Corporation,
5 South Union Street, Lawrence, Mass. 01843 USA

Cataloguing in Publication Data

National Library of Australia

Wright, D.I. (Donald Ian), 1934—
 Mantle of Christ.

 Bibliography.
 Includes index.

 1. Central Methodist Mission (Sydney, N.S.W.) —
History. 2. Methodist Church — Missions — New South
Wales — Sydney — History. 3. City Missions — New
South Wales — Sydney — History. I. Title.

266.719441

Library of Congress

Wright, Don, 1934 Oct. 22—
 Mantle of Christ.

 Bibliography: p.
 Includes index.
 1. Sydney Central Methodist Mission—History.
I. Title.BV3660.N6W74   1984   287'.19441   84-2222

ISBN 0-7022-1739-5.

Contents

Illustrations

Preface

For more than one hundred years the industrial city has confronted the Protestant churches with their most dangerous threat and their major missionary challenge. In the second half of the nineteenth century they gradually began to appreciate their lack of contact with the industrial workers who were becoming the main inhabitants of those cities. Some spoke as if those workers had once been linked to the church and had fallen away; in fact, most had never belonged, but this had not been realized while a significant church-attending middle class remained. As it moved out to the suburbs, the poverty of the church's understanding of the urban workers was laid bare and the realization grew that the cities were as much a mission field as Asia or the Pacific. The old forms of religion, purely spiritual in content, and often rural in orientation, had little relevance to the situation.

Protestant churches responded in different ways to this challenge. In the United States, the development of a new theology — the social gospel — underpinned the growth of the institutional church. In England and Australia, it was more a matter of marrying a new humanitarianism to the old evangelical gospel. The most interesting example of this development was the Wesleyan Methodist "Forward Movement" which gave birth to the Methodist central missions. At the heart of the central mission concept was a worshipping, evangelizing congregation which also sought to minister to the bodies and minds of its inner-urban host population. This new dimension made the central mission a more powerful force in the life of the "downtown" areas of the great industrial cities in which they were placed.

While the central mission concept undoubtedly originated in the work of the Rev. Charles Garrett of Liverpool, dating from 1875, one of the most interesting examples of this form of church developed in Sydney, originating at the York Street church in 1884, but at 210 Pitt Street since 1908.

The outside observer is most likely to be conscious of the host of service agencies which crowd around the mission; children's homes, homes for the aged and homeless, hospitals, Life Line, a sheltered workshop, and others. It is the argument of this study that the essential characteristics of the Sydney Central Mission is its combination of the traditional spiritual life of the church (expressed through worship, prayer, and evangelism) with Christian humanitarianism in such a way that the philanthropic activity is seen to be the logical outworking of the church's inner life. The two aspects are inseparable, the obverse and the reverse of the one coin.

It could be said (with Jacques Ellul, *The Meaning of the City*) that the Christian view of the city is that it was the creation of Cain, the world's first murderer, who sought in it a place where he might escape from God and from himself. Yet it is destined to become the "City of God", the "New Jerusalem". The agency of the transformation is the redemptive power of Christ, ministered through His church. The Sydney CMM has always seen itself as an important part of that process as it sought, in the words of one superintendent, "to cast the mantle of Christ over Sydney".

The history of the mission has been one of struggle. Born out of the failure of the York Street Wesleyan church, it was beset by difficulties: by the doubts of a Conference which failed to understand the new work and by the unwillingness of New South Wales Methodists to support it financially before it became established. Its most important struggle, and one which forms a major theme in this book, has been the struggle to preserve its own nature. The mission and the city have been in conflict: as the mission has sought to redeem the city, so the city has sought to secularize the mission and to rob it of its uniquely Christian character.

The Sydney CMM has also made its own mistakes. It will be argued in this book that the most serious of these was the consequence of its firm grounding in the essentially practical and conservative English tradition which led it to content itself for much of its first three-quarters of a century with what were essentially "ambulance" functions: healing the broken members of society but not seeking to change radically the society which broke them, except as what might be done through the conversion of individual men and women. In this it was remaining loyal to its individualistic Protestant heritage. It was slow to take up that aspect of the "whole Gospel" which taught that society, as well as people, had to be changed, that Christ came as Emancipator as well as Redeemer. Initially this aspect of the potential work of the CMM received only sporadic attention, but over the last quarter-century of its history it has been more prominent.

The nature of the argument has determined the form of its presentation. Because spiritual and philanthropic activities are so closely interlinked, it has been necessary to hold them together in the story. It would have been easier for both author and reader to separate them, but it would have meant abandoning the attempt to illustrate a key aspect of the mission's history. There have also been a number of interesting characters associated with the CMM over the years, whether among its superintendents, its sisters of the people, or men like Charlie Woodward. Because this is the history of the mission, it has been impossible to do them full justice. They feature here only in so far as they contribute to the life of the CMM.

Some readers, and especially some closely associated with the mission itself, may feel a measure of disappointment that certain people and service agencies have not been mentioned. This is not intended to be a "bricks and mortar" chronicle of the CMM. It seeks to understand the life and work of the institution and it necessarily selects those incidents, people, and activities which most assist in reaching that understanding and which enable us to see the mission in its Sydney and Australian context. Again, because it is interpretative, the account proper ceases several years before the date of writing, though a brief epilogue has been added to update the purely factual material. It is simply impossible to provide a clear perspective on work which is still in train and the outcome of which is not yet evident. To try to provide it would be to move from history into prophecy, an area beyond the competence of the present author.

This work leaves unanswered many questions about the relationships of the CMM to the Methodist church and to its host society, Sydney. This is partly the result of the records which survive and partly the result of the particular blinkers which I, in company with all other historians, wear. The intention of the work is to add a further dimension to the understanding of Protestantism in New South Wales to those already given us by such writers as David Bollen, Walter Phillips, and Richard Broome.

There is another value in writing the history of the Central Methodist/Wesley Central Mission at this time. The central mission concept was undoubtedly one of the most significant contributions of the Methodist church to religious development. Now that the Methodist church has ceased to exist in Australia, it is desirable that this aspect of the nation's religious history be assessed. Presumably too, the successor church, the United Church in Australia, would wish to understand so important an aspect of its own inheritance.

Acknowledgments

I gratefully acknowledge help given in the writing of this book. The Superintendent and Officers of the Wesley Central Mission willingly gave me free access to the archives of the mission, without making any demands in return. I have also received much help from Rev. Eric Clancy and his staff of volunteers at the Uniting Church Archives, Clarence Street, the staff of the Mitchell Library, and the Inter-Library Loans Service of the Auchmuty Library (University of Newcastle). A number of people associated with the mission allowed me to interview them, often at considerable length; Dr Keith Suter, formerly of the WCM staff, helped in a variety of ways and Mr Athol Ford did much to help me to become acquainted with some of the mission institutions. Revs. Gordon Moyes, Eric Clancy, and Alan Walker read all or part of the typescript and made helpful suggestions as well as saving me from a number of inaccuracies. Each also provided me with encouragement along the way. The final version of the typescript was prepared by Robyn Gay and Lynne Turner. Thanks are also due to the University of Queensland Press for publication. My wife, Janice, accepted my absences from home, made it easier for me to find the long periods of time needed to write, and prodded me into many improvements of presentation. Responsibility for factual accuracy and for the interpretation lies with the author alone.

1
Context

The last quarter of the nineteenth century saw organized Christianity in deep trouble in the major centres of population throughout the Western world. Mankind had long lived in cities, but nowhere, in either ancient or medieval world, had they posed the problems for organized religion that they were to pose at the latter end of the nineteenth century. Never before had there been anything like the industrial revolution which had affected life so dramatically in England, Europe, and the U.S.A. This brought in its wake the new industrial city, a far less friendly host to religion than previous rural or urban centres of population had been.

The city began to influence life in a way that had not occurred before. Not only did it increase its share of the national population, it began to dominate the economy and to reorient the lifestyle of its citizens. It was the centre of modern economic and industrial development, the place where the enormous powers of organization and centralized wealth were wielded most strongly and were most in need of restraint. The city, as Josiah Strong pointed out, was also where human relations were the most complex and where the maladjustments of society created the worst frictions.[1]

The growth of industrialism saw the increasing division of labour and the consequent reduction of the worker from skilled artisan, responsible for a product and with pride in his workmanship, to unskilled labourer dependent on machinery and performing only a single function in a chain process. He became a mere wage-earner whose work provided neither physical nor intellectual stimulation. Indeed, it was more likely to dull mind and body through its repetitiveness.

Writing about nineteenth century Liverpool, Margaret

Simey argued that this change in status disturbed the working classes far more than bad housing, to which they were used, and made them sullen and hostile towards their social superiors.[2]

By the late nineteenth century, the industrial worker was fast becoming the main inhabitant of the great cities of the western world. In earlier times, merchants and shopkeepers had lived on the premises where they carried on their business in the major thoroughfares of the city. The development of industry had made this impossible. Warehouses replaced homes. Inner-city land became too expensive for the residences of the middle and upper classes. At the same time, improved means of public transport enabled those with comfortable incomes to flee to the more attractive suburbs. Industrial workers, unable to afford even the relatively low fares involved, and needing to remain within walking distance of their place of employment because of their long hours of work, had no alternative but to remain in the inner city.

The tenth U.S. census found an average of sixteen people in every dwelling-house in New York City,[3] while the *Sydney Morning Herald* of 2 January 1884 reported on the filth of the London slums. In her study of nineteenth century England, K. J. Heasman also painted a graphic picture of the state of habitation in the London slums, all too often created in what had once been "good areas" as those of higher income moved out and were replaced by the poor in the now heavily subdivided properties.[4]

Physically and intellectually, every major industrial city showed the reality of the "two nation" theory, with the poor crowded into dingy, jerry-built structures around the factories and wharves where they worked, while those with some means lived in relative comfort and cleanliness further out. The division was often made worse by the congregation of foreign immigrants in the city areas: in England, the Irish; in the U.S.A., Europeans of various nationalities; in Australia, people from all parts of the British Isles. While there are many graphic portrayals of the lot of the poor, undoubtedly the most graphic, and the most influential at the time, was the Rev. Andrew Mearns's *The Bitter Cry of Outcast London.*[5]

The nature of the industrial city posed a serious problem

for the Protestant wing of the Christian church.[6] The plain message of the 1851 Religious Census in England was that a large proportion of the population never attended worship and, since the lowest attendances were in London and the large manufacturing towns, it was clear that many absentees were workers.[7] Whatever some churchmen may have felt later, it is apparent that the church did not lose the working classes at some stage of the nineteenth century: it simply never had their loyalty. Migrants from rural areas often failed to renew religious contacts in the city, sometimes because the cities were inadequately provided with churches, and sometimes because they quickly realized that the people with whom they now mixed did not go to church as their rural peers had. In his biography of S. F. Collier, George Jackson reports that whereas the famous Oldham Street chapel in Manchester, opened by Wesley himself, had attracted a congregation of sixteen hundred in the late eighteenth century, a hundred years later it "lay derelict" and drew only fifty to one hundred.[8]

Nor was the situation different on the other side of the Atlantic. A religious census at Pittsburgh and Allegheny in 1888 revealed that business, professional, and salaried men made up more than 60 per cent of the membership of the Protestant churches although they comprised less than 10 per cent of the male population of the two cities. Though many held this situation to be natural, as the Christian virtues of honesty, industry, and thrift often led to material prosperity, not everyone took so kindly a view of the links between capital and Protestant Christianity. Samuel Gompers, of the American Federation of Labor, claimed that working men had come to look upon church and ministry "as the apologists and defenders of the wrongs committed against the interests of the people simply because the proprietors are possessors of wealth". There was considerable anger among the workers of a Chicago businessman who gave for a theological college $100,000 "saved" by cutting their wages.[9] Samuel Loomis, an early student of the problem, summed the situation up well: "Now city churches of the Protestant order are usually attended and sustained by persons of means and intelligence. It makes a man prosperous to be a Christian.

The Protestant city churches are, therefore, to the laborer, the churches of the capitalist. He will have nothing to do with them."[10]

The demands made on the church by the working classes of the new industrial cities were different in important ways from those made by the old rural society. I. A. Abell's account of urban Protestantism in America points out that whereas rural dwellers, and even the old urban middle class, were prepared to support a purely spiritual religion, the poorer folk of the new cities were not. They expected the church to champion their industrial demands for a more just and equitable social and economic order in the long term, whilst providing in the short term agencies for their spiritual and moral welfare. The growing solidarity of labour, with its spirit of democracy (fostered in the union, lodge, club, and saloon) also posed a problem for the Protestant churches.[11]

The Protestant theological tradition had always concerned itself primarily with the spiritual regeneration of the individual as an individual. This meant that it was inadequate in at least two ways to deal with the problems of the industrial working class. The separation of the realms of body and spirit, and the attribution of religious value to spirit alone, with its concomitant concentration on fitting men for the perfect society of heaven, led to the neglect of temporal welfare except as the result of individual acts of philanthropy springing from the consciences of individual men and women. Furthermore, until late in the nineteenth century the idea of social salvation was hardly seen as relevant, and might even appear to be a distraction from the true work of the church. Some social reform might spring from the regeneration of individuals, but Protestants had forgotten the gospel concept of the Kingdom of God as the new social ideal to be realized on earth. It would take time for them to evolve a more adequate social theology and until they did they would lag behind the Catholics in their approach to the working class.[12]

In the late nineteenth century, there were still some who considered social inequality the will of God and thought that the poor had as many blessings as the rich, but others had begun to feel that existing conditions of poverty were not in keeping with the tradition of the churches. Even those committed to the separation of spirit and body might come to doubt whether people sunk deep in misery and degradation could be reached on the spiritual level if they were not first given material help.

The Wesleys had started orphanages, at first for the children of members but later for others as well. Elizabeth Fry started the Nightly Shelter for the Homeless Poor in 1819, a movement which had mushroomed by the 1860s. David Nasmith began his city mission movement in Glasgow in 1826 and then spent the rest of his life founding a total of forty-five such institutions in the U.K. and a further thirty-six in the U.S.A. and Canada. Where they survived, these often became major organs for social and evangelical work, though, after its early years, the London City Mission seems to have confined its activities to evangelical work. The method was the same everywhere: the city was divided into districts to each of which a working-class missionary was appointed to do house-to-house visitation. They read the Scriptures and prayed with people, invited them to the mission hall, to social gatherings, mothers' meetings, or a ragged school. In London a mission magazine was published.

There were many other societies with similar or more specialized aims: Rev. Baptist Noel's hostel for ex-prostitutes in the 1830s; the Rescue Society (1853); the Field Lane Institution (1841) with a ragged school and refuges for the destitute. T. C. Young's New Cut Mission at Lambeth (1877) had a Sunday school, clubs for men and women, soup kitchens, and a brass band. Young won election to the local Board of Guardians and the Southwark Borough Council so that he might draw the attention of the authorities to the problems associated with poverty. Mrs Rayward's London Bible and Domestic Mission (1857) used biblewomen for evangelical and social work and introduced the first paid social workers, while the Rev. William and Mrs Pennefather, who played an important part in early attempts to coordinate the social work of evangelicals, introduced the deaconess system to England on the model of the German Lutherans.[13]

The obvious common factor about all these missions was that none of them was the work of the church — or even a church — as an institution. All were extra-institutional

developments begun by individuals or small groups with
whatever support they could muster from like-minded
Christians. It was a surprise when such activity led occasionally to political action as in 1850 when, as a result of the
London City Mission's survey of cheap accommodation in
London which revealed that apart from that provided by the
Evangelicals there were only the "ill-regulated and often
insanitary common lodging houses", Shaftesbury introduced
a bill laying down minimum standards for lodging houses.
The problem was that many Evangelicals were socially conservative and thought poverty was ordained by God and
hence could not be eliminated by reconstructing the social
and economic order. Sin was the fundamental cause of
human misery and personal conversion its only effective
remedy.[14]

The situation in the U.S.A. was similar. W. A. Muhlenberg
founded the Church of the Holy Communion in New York in
1845 with free pews and "novel benevolent adjuncts", while
in the early 1870s Thomas K. Beecher established at Elmira
(New York) a church well equipped for social service and
which, among other curiosities, provided free baths for the
unclean. But, generally speaking, the mission stations which
began to be opened in the "downtown" areas of major cities
after 1852 were operated outside normal church structures.[15]

Eventually the concept of private charity was bound to
lead to something bigger than itself. By the end of the
century, the picture had changed substantially in both North
America and Great Britain. This period saw the rise of the
"social gospel" which rested on the premise "that Christianity was a social religion, concerned, when the misunderstanding of the ages was stripped away, with the quality of human
relations on this earth. Put in more dramatic terms it was a
call for men to find the meaning of their lives in seeking to
realise the Kingdom of God in the very fabric of society."
The development of this new vision of the Gospel had
occurred under the pressure of the positive, organic, and
developmental forms of thought arising in Europe and elsewhere at this time, forms which made the traditional evangelical approach seem less appropriate and which demanded a
shift from saving individual men to saving society.[16]

The theoretical aspects of this development were more obvious in North America than in Britain. This was hardly surprising in view of the speed with which the industrial revolution occurred there and the completely impersonal nature of the gigantic corporations which resulted. C. H. Hopkins's work on the rise of the social Gospel emphasizes the significance of the movement which perhaps began with the Christian Labor Union of Boston (1872) and developed through the Church Association for the Advancement of the Interests of Labor (1887) and the Open and Institutional Church League (1894). The Revs. Frank Mason North, Josiah Strong, Samuel L. Loomis, Charles Stelzle, Elias B. Sanford, Walter Rauschenbusch, and Washington Gladden were only the most famous of a substantial group of writers and workers in the field. Such bodies and men sometimes supported strikes and, while mainly interested in action through trade unions and the like, sometimes supported government intervention in the interests of the workers, the compulsory arbitration of industrial disputes, and even the socialization of public utilities.[17]

Charles Stelzle recognized the city as the centre of the modern economy and industrial development. He saw a concentration of forces there challenging the church: business dishonesty, competition, and greed had to be fought. The influence of social conditions on the poor must be recognized. For those living in slums and tenements and working long hours in insanitary factories, "no future hell can be worse than the hell in which they now are". The church's ministry had to be directed to the needs of the people and not merely designed to win them to itself. Speaking at a Social Service Congress in Ottawa in 1914 he criticized heavily the "smug, self-satisfied middleclass" which lacked the courage to tackle the problems of industry and the city honestly. The "call of the new day to the old church" was to apply the principles of Jesus fearlessly to existing social and economic conditions.[18]

Theological change led rapidly to practical developments, especially in the form of the "institutional church" which became an agency seeking to minister to the whole person within a social context rather than an individual one. If such churches could reach only limited numbers of people, for them at least they might secure the values which the social gospellers wished to secure for all. From another perspective, the institutional church was also an attempt to win back ground lost by the Protestant denominations when they had deserted the increasingly working-class "downtown" areas of the large cities in their pathetic determination to take the easy way out and follow middle-class money to the suburbs.

Probably the first great institutional church in the U.S.A. was William S. Rainford's St George's Episcopal Church in New York which from 1882 abolished pew rents and inaugurated nearly continuous weekday use of the property in a programme designed to meet the needs of the surrounding areas. Fifteen years later it had an annual budget of $60,000, four assistant pastors, four deaconesses, and specialists in charge of industrial and athletics departments. Like other institutional churches in the 1880s, it was involved with kindergartens, gymnasium classes, boys' and girls' clubs, libraries, dispensaries, open forums, an employment service, study classes, popular lectures, sewing and cooking schools, penny banks, games rooms, soup kitchens, and various other social amenities. Such churches were a far cry from the inadequate mission halls of earlier decades.[19]

In England, despite some social work at St Mary's, Whitechapel, by William Chamneys from 1837, by William Cadman at St George's, Southwark, from 1847, and at C.H. Spurgeon's South London Tabernacle from 1853, the beginning of the true institutional churches is usually placed in the 1880s.

Heasman argued that the motive force behind the "Forward Movement" in the British churches was the publication, in October 1883, of Andrew Mearns's pamphlet *The Bitter Cry of Outcast London*. Without doubt Mearns, a Congregationalist, focussed attention on the impact of social conditions on spiritual life and his work may be described as environmentalism of the most uncompromising kind. The church had dreamt of the coming millenium but had failed to notice the deteriorating conditions of the poor, the widening gulf between them and the churches, or the "terrible flood of sin and misery" which was gaining on the churches every day.

The Congregational Union called other free churches to a conference to discuss the relationship of their work to the needs of the poor and, though no common plan was formulated, the various denominations were made more sensitive to the needs of the poor and each acted in its own way. The Congregationalists opened disused chapels as halls where the homeless might find shelter and some food. But the Wesleyan Methodist development of the "Central Mission", which used a hall as the centre for religious activity and then carefully organized around it a planned and controlled range of social services, provided the most thorough and orderly response. In London, the model was the Rev. Peter Thompson's East End Mission (1885). He acquired two small music halls and a public-house ("Paddy's Goose") as his centre, and as well as doing religious and philanthropic work educated his people in citizenship and himself took an active part in local politics. The most famous of the London missions was Hugh Price Hughes's West End Mission (1887) which had the full range of activities found in the American institutional churches: an employment bureau, an enquiry office for those needing advice, a "Poor Man's Lawyer", a guild for crippled children, and "Sisters of the People" (established by his wife) to work among the poor.[20]

Yet some modification of Heasman's thesis is needed, for the first Central Methodist Mission (CMM) anywhere in the world was undoubtedly founded by the Rev. Charles Garrett in Liverpool in 1875.[21] The Pitt St chapel had existed from the time of the Wesleys but, by the 1870s, was left desolate and largely empty in the slums of "the black spot on the Mersey". Garrett's mission arose from the failure of a Moody campaign to touch the unchurched. From the start, he was fortunate to have the help of five lay missionaries. He introduced most of the features later to be so prominent elsewhere: a business-like approach, a Sunday school, homes for destitute children and aged people, a Shoeblack Brigade, a Labour Bureau, a scheme to assist prospective emigrants, and cocoa rooms to attract men away from public-houses. His philanthropic work was an adjunct to his evangelistic preaching which remained fully faithful to orthodox Wesleyan Arminianism. His weaknesses were an obsession with alcohol and a belief that while the church should perform an ambulance function for the victims of society, rectification of the causes of the problem was the province of the state.

Although the practical aspect was more evident than the development of a new theology in England, the latter was not entirely absent. Hugh Price Hughes was able to comprehend both aspects to some extent, which probably explains why he was regarded as the leader of the Forward Movement though his practical contribution was not greater than that of Garrett, Thompson, or S.F. Collier of Manchester. He realized that "we have practically neglected the fact that Christ came to save the Nation as well as the Individual, and that it is an essential feature of His mission to reconstruct human society on the basis of justice and love."[22]

This desire "radically to reconstruct the existing organisation of society on the basis of righteousness and the comradeship of brotherly love rather than merely palliate existing social evils by charitable help" was even more prominent in the thought of J. Scott Lidgett, the most prominent English Wesleyan Christian Socialist at the end of the century.[23] But Lidgett, whose words must certainly be seen as a criticism of the early phase of the Forward Movement, was a thinker rather than an activist and his immediate impact was negligible.

In religious terms, the Forward Movement sprang from a "quickening of heart and purpose which created the readiness to act". It involved "a revival of the spirit of evangelism in the early Methodist form" and a readiness to move away from traditional methods and accept what appeared to be divine guidance into new paths.[24] But this was not the only perspective. Entirely new circumstances had created an environment foreign to the Christian religion, a situation hardly less strange than that which existed when the early church took its first tentative steps beyond its Judaic boundaries into the gentile world. Just as Peter was forced to a radical re-examination of his position by the vision which led him to visit Cornelius at Joppa (Acts, chap. 10), so the economic and social developments of the nineteenth century industrializing world forced Protestantism to reassess the validity of its own presentation of the Gospel.

The old evangelism had relied on a degree of religious knowledge among the people which was lacking among the new city dwellers and it was therefore inadequate for the salvation of the city. The church must not represent an absentee God and future Heaven, but the Kingdom of God here and now. It must be concerned with every interest of the community and equipped to render every necessary service which could not be rendered better by other means.[25] The result was a genuine reinterpretation and development of Protestant tradition.

Physically, Sydney enjoyed many advantages over the great cities of the northern hemisphere, but its environment was subject to decline in the period 1870-90 and, for many, it was an unpleasant place in which to live.

During the 1860s and 1870s, both city and suburbs were subject to rapid population growth, though the latter grew the faster. In the 1880s, while the suburbs mushroomed, the city population grew only marginally. The nineties saw a slowing down in suburban growth and virtual stagnation in the city.[26] (See table 1.)

Table 1 Sydney City and Suburban Population Growth, 1860-1900

Census Date	Sydney Population	Suburban Population	Metropolitan Population
1861	56,840	38,949	95,789
1871	74,560	63,210	137,776
1881	100,152	124,787	224,939
1891	107,652	275,631	383,283
1901	111,255	369,721	480,976

Source: From note 26.

Variations within the trends were evident. In 1870, the city as a whole was marginally deficient in higher status white-collar jobs and had a slight overrepresentation of petty entrepreneurial and unskilled workers. Yet, while the eastern wards held a higher proportion of professionals than any suburb, the western wards were firmly at the other end of the social scale. This oldest settled part of the city already contained most of the largest factories and workshops as well as food-and-drink-processing plants. In her study of life and work in late nineteenth century Sydney, Shirley Fisher argues that George Street, the dividing line between Gipps and Brisbane wards to the west and Bourke and Macquarie to the east, was a real dividing line in terms of status and function.[27] There is no doubt that the population of Gipps and Brisbane was essentially working class: timber and metal workers, wharf labourers and seamen.

The environment of Brisbane ward (in which stood Wesleyan Methodism's York Street Church) had been deteriorating for some time. The development of Darling Harbour had transformed the nearby streets as bond stores, shipping offices, and warehouses (the "speciality" of York Street) sprang up in place of the older buildings. "Homes" were often jerry-built and inadequate like Garrett's Building, off Clarence Street, which had ten two-roomed, two-storeyed terraces facing each other within a 34-foot allotment – 10 feet on either side being devoted to the buildings (the rooms were 10 feet square and 7.5 feet high), 4.5 feet on either side was yard space, and there was a lane 5 feet wide in the centre for entry. As all the sewage flowed into this lane, it had to be planked over to make it "navigable".[28] The situation of the inhabitants of these and other slums was well expressed by an Anglican clergyman in 1894: "The poor of our great city parishes have scarcely any real homelife. The . . . little buildings are over-crowded with babies and children. Where shall the young find rest and recreation but out in the streets? And from the streets the only hospitable doors open to them are the hotel and the vile dancing saloon."[29]

With the removal of many family groups, Brisbane ward's population declined 35 per cent over the period 1871-91, although the number of inhabitants per building increased to 7.2 (higher than any suburb and second only to Bourke ward). In terms of inhabitants per room, Brisbane ward and Botany North were at the top with 1.2 against a city average of 1.0 and a suburban average of 0.9.[30] Thus, despite its declining population, Brisbane ward was becoming ever more slum-like. Sometimes the very attempt to clear slums made the congestion worse. If no alternative accommodation were provided, those whose homes had been demolished simply moved in with their neighbours since they could not afford fares and had to live within walking distance of their employ-ment. For such, Sydney conditions were clearly very bad and neither absentee landlords, health authorities, city council, nor Parliament appeared particularly interested in their problems. Another significant characteristic of the district was the concentration of common lodginghouses there. In 1890 Sydney had a substantial floating population of dock and seasonal workers, seamen, migrants, and unem-ployed who lived in these cheap, low-grade, boardinghouses, many of the worst of which were to be found in Brisbane ward.[31]

In view of these population changes, it was as expected as it was significant that the percentage of Methodists in the city proper dropped from 5.4 to 4.4. between 1871 and 1891, while that in the suburbs rose from 8.8 to 9.1. Even in 1871, Brisbane ward had one of the lowest concentrations of Methodists (4.1 per cent) and this must have declined in the next twenty years.[32]

If the lot of those who were forced to continue to live in areas like Brisbane and Gipps wards was so bad at home, it was not much better at work. Here as overseas, the status of industrial workers was largely eroded in the period 1870—1890 as increasing mechanization transformed them from skilled craftsmen into mere machine-minders and effected their alienation from the employer and from society at large. Many factory workers were little more than day-labourers and suffered periodic bouts of unemployment, a situation which seemed beyond the capacity of the primitive capitalism of the time to cope with. Long hours were the norm, even for women, as N.S.W. did not follow England and Victoria in passing an Early Closing Act until the 1890s. The habits of Sydney shoppers, which made the streets so lively and colourful at night, also kept the drapers, grocers, confec-tioners, chemists, hairdressers, and others open for twelve hours or more a day for wages that were generally low. Physical conditions were improving in some of the larger, recently rebuilt factories but the women in dressmaking establishments, jam factories, and the like often suffered hardship. Sexual harassment seems to have been a constant problem for the young woman anxious to keep her position.[33]

The Sydney poor had not been entirely neglected. Religious and charitable individuals had taken some interest in their well-being. Nathaniel Pidgeon, a Wesleyan cabinet-maker and lay preacher had, from 1850, given his entire time to city mission work. He frequently preached salvation in Kent, Clarence, and Sussex Streets, at Millers Point, and in the parks and back streets, sometimes singing from place to place to gather a crowd. There was a fiery vehemence about his preaching which offended the cultured but appealed to the "lowest" elements of the city's degraded society who, no doubt, derived from it an excitement which their colourless lives otherwise denied them.[34]

From mid-1862, the Sydney City Mission existed for this same work. It both gained and lost from being inter-denominational and also seems to have contributed to its own early weakness by failing to take up philanthropic work seriously — a surprising omission given its later heavy emphasis in that area.[35]

Primarily philanthropic agencies, like the Benevolent Society of N.S.W., had a much longer history but fall almost outside the scope of our present interest, despite the fact that they were founded and maintained by men of genuine Christian conviction. In the case of the Benevolent Society, it was true that one of the tests to determine whether a person was a member of the "deserving poor", and therefore entitled to assistance, was willingness to submit to at least a measure of evangelical persuasion, but the unspecific nature of its religious objectives meant that it was hardly likely to be seen as other than a purely charitable society by the community at large.[36]

In the eighties and nineties, Sydney was notorious for its larrikin "pushes", street gangs of youths ranging from four-teen to twenty-five years (but with a few as young as ten years) who indulged in a wide variety of antisocial behaviour, from relatively harmless jibes at well-dressed citizens to verbal harassment of women and, ultimately, to genuine criminal behaviour like bashing, gang-warfare, murder, and rape. Such "pushes" had existed as far back as the fifties and sixties but reached their peak in organization and influence in the late eighties and early nineties, then gradually declined around the turn of the century.[37]

Youths from all levels were involved in the pushes, though working-class lads were most prominent and some thought that the genuine antisocial behaviour was confined to them. Of course, that view may have been founded on nothing more solid than middle-class distrust of working-class social mores. Sydney was genuinely worried by the activities of these youths and speculated extensively on their origins and on possible cures for the problem. Postulated origins included eating too much meat, drinking too much alcohol, lack of parental control, and bad housing conditions. The projected cures sometimes included better housing and recreational facilities, but were often simplistic, depending on tougher police action. Recent research suggests that a more complex approach is necessary to both questions.

It was no coincidence that the period of rapid urbanization and industrialization corresponded with the rise of urban larrikinism and that the worst larrikin areas in Sydney — the Rocks, Woolloomooloo, Millers Point, Pyrmont, parts of Balmain and Leichhardt — were all what American urban sociologists call "zones of transition" which showed the greatest concentrations of poverty, bad housing, family dis-integration, physical and mental diseases, and were areas of lodginghouses, homeless men, and sexual vice.

The tedium of the factory, and the basic insecurity of the unskilled worker in an immature colonial capitalist society, where alternate cycles of boom and bust seemed natural and inevitable, certainly assisted the development and helped to account for the evident antagonism towards those perceived, from their superior dress, as belonging to the upper levels of society. The near-total lack of recreational facilities in such a 'zone of transition" and the failure of organized religion to make any significant impact there would seem to complete the picture.

The decline of larrikinism attracted far less attention than its rise, but explanations varied from the use of corporal

punishment, to the arming of the police (1884), to McLachlan's "improved educational standards, the extension of
unionism, and the greater array of organised entertainments
available to working class youths — films, sports' facilities,
boys' clubs — rather than to any fundamental change in the
nature of unskilled labour in industry."[38] This last explanation seems like a polite way of saying that working-class boys
were being acclimatized to middle-class mores. The significance of this in the story of the Sydney CMM will appear
later.

This is not the place for a detailed history of early Methodism in N.S.W., but a very brief resume is needed to provide
background for the establishment of the CMM.[39]

Methodism started in Australia through the class meeting.
One of the characteristic features of the denomination, this
was a weekly meeting for prayer, praise, and testimony with
the object of building members up in their faith and keeping
them together as an identifiable unit. Until near the end of
the nineteenth century, regular attendance each week at the
class meeting was the official test of membership. It is
uncertain whether the first Australian class meeting was the
one conducted by Thomas Bowden in his home in Princes
Street, Sydney, on 6 March 1812, or one led by Irish ex-
convict, Edward Eagar, at Windsor at about the same time.
Priority has usually been given to Bowden's meeting, but
some doubt must remain. Such meetings soon led to a
request for an ordained clergyman from England and Samuel
Leigh arrived in Sydney on 10 August 1815 to take charge of
a tiny cause meeting in a rented cottage at the corner of
Essex and Gloucester Streets in The Rocks. Leigh opened
Australia's first Wesleyan chapel in Castlereagh on 7 October
1817. Sydney's first, in Princes Street, came only in 1819,
by which time the cottage referred to above was proving too
small and inconvenient. A second was built in Macquarie
Street in 1821.

This seems to have been the extent of Sydney's Wesleyan
provision for over two decades. Eighteen thirty-nine was the
centenary year of Methodism and an appeal was launched to

enable a new and larger chapel to be built on a site better related to the main centres of population than either Princes Street or Macquarie Street. Problems in finding an appropriate site, and with the builders, delayed its opening until 14 February 1844. This was the church known affectionately in Methodist circles as "old York Street" and which was forty years later to become the CMM.

By 1846, York Street had 570 members, 591 Sunday school scholars, 18 local preachers, and 35 class leaders. The congregation continued to increase rapidly and galleries had to be added in 1848. The York Street church was well situated in the midst of a prosperous business and professional area at a time when such people lived where they worked and when the total lack of trams and the relatively few ferries made suburban living too inconvenient for most. The strength of nineteenth century Wesleyan Methodism lay among the "petty bourgeois" and "most of the regular attenders were either small business owners or skilled tradesmen".[40] The prosperous days of York Street continued for more than a quarter of a century, until 1871, with the

Centenary Chapel and Mission House, "Old York Street". From Colwell, *Illustrated History of Methodism* (1904).

"floodtide of prosperity" occurring in the period 1866—71, just before the rot set in.

The best service at York Street was always in the morning. It was unusually liturgical for an Australian Wesleyan service, since it regularly followed Wesley's abridgement of the Anglican service of Morning Prayer. The choir was well balanced and of high quality, while the organ was powerful and the preachers the best available to N.S.W. Wesleyanism. It was no wonder that the warmly ecclesiastical cedar pews were crowded week by week with middle-class family groups. These features, and the Corinthian pillars outside, which made the facade more like that of a bank or a post office than a church, gave the place an air of permanence and stability which eventually proved deceptive.

York Street's importance to Wesleyan Methodism was much greater than the sum total of its choir, congregation, preachers, and Corinthian pillars. It was unquestionably the "mother church" of N.S.W. Methodism. It was there that the Wesleyans among the many immigrants to these shores would first hear the "grand old Gospel truths" in a new land far away from home. From York Street they would be filtered out to churches near and far throughout the colony, or even in neighbouring colonies. The first Australian Wesleyan Conference had been held there, and after a separate N.S.W. Conference had been established it was always at that site until its demolition. Thus all the great connexional institutions had been born there. It was a place for historic decision making and therefore dear to those who made and lived under those decisions. "Old York Street" was yet more. It regularly drew within its walls those country Wesleyans who came to Sydney on business or holiday. By being part of a great congregation and by hearing the best preachers, they could receive inspiration beyond what was available in their little local churches. York Street, with its central presence in the heart of the capital city of the colony, was performing a truly "cathedral" function for Wesleyanism.

In view of this, it was a serious blow to Methodism throughout N.S.W. when York Street went into rapid decline in the early seventies, despite the appointment of men of recognized preaching ability like George Martin and J.G. Middleton.

The urban decline of Methodism drew comment on 14 November 1871 at a Sydney District meeting but, while demographic change was accepted as part of the explanation, more emphasis was put on the people's concern with business and entertainment, inadequate pastoral visitation, and the need for Sydney ministers to meet more regularly for "spiritual intercourse and prayer".

In later years, W. G. Taylor sometimes pushed this argument even further, holding that the whole problem was due to the church's "unfaithfulness and backsliding". The true evangel had ceased to be proclaimed. Methodism in the 1870s had become "the church at Ephesus" referred to in *Revelation*, for its evangelical fire had degenerated into formalism.[41] Taylor's answer was that of a man for whom evangelism was the entire raison d'etre of the Methodist church and who was deeply disappointed at its neglect.

An interesting attempt at an answer to the city problem began to be formulated during 1873. On 8 August, in the Hay Street chapel, twenty-eight representatives of city and suburban circuits met to consider the formation of a Wesleyan City Mission in accordance with a resolution of the Melbourne Conference of 1872. A committee of six ministers and twelve laymen was established and on 11 August it was decided to engage an accredited local preacher as a city missionary, though some favoured the appointment of a minister as soon as possible. The scheme was to supplement existing circuit work, not replace it, and the missionary was to engage in house-to-house visitation in neglected parts of the circuit for five hours daily and three on Sunday as well as hold cottage meetings and outdoor services with the help of other lay preachers. Thomas Crisford was appointed to the work on 17 September 1873 and the Wesleyan Lay Mission came into being. For the time, its activities were confined to neglected parts of York Street, Bourke Street, and Chippendale circuits. In commenting upon this development, the *Christian Advocate* argued that the evangelization of the neglected classes at home was no less important than overseas missions, especially as major social changes were impending which excited considerable apprehension. The work would also release the latent talent of the urban lay preachers who lacked the opportunities of their rural brethren.

In his first year, Crisford visited more than 2,380 families of whom only 84 were Wesleyan and even they were "comparatively lost to us".   Many were persuaded to attend services and 9 joined various churches while two females were taken to the Refuge and help was given to several families in distress.   Crisford's diligence could hardly be faulted, but 9 converts in a year was doing nothing to turn the tide in favour of the church and his efforts merely emphasized the problems involved in making fruitful contact with the working classes.

By October 1876, there was no further mention of the Lay Mission in the report of the Sydney District Meeting.[42]   Even earlier than this, in January 1875, the York Street Quarterly Meeting had specifically refused to give £50 towards the cost of a clerical missionary in the Sydney circuits.[43]   In the absence of any explanation, it must be assumed that the earlier attempt was failing by that time and that the York Street folk, already struggling, could see no point in further exertion in that direction.

By 1882, the *Wesleyan Advocate* (successor to the *Christian Advocate and Weekly Record*) had accepted the view that great cities were moral battlefields and that Methodism would be judged by its ability to cope with the vast mercantile, social, intellectual, and moral forces concentrated there. Wesleyans had become "too respectable" and if they would not do God's work of salvation He would remove it from them.   After all, the Salvation Army was only doing the work of "aggressive, conquering Methodism".[44]

But Methodism was not the only denomination in trouble at this time.   When Dr James Jefferis moved to Sydney from Adelaide in 1877 to take charge of the Pitt Street Congregational church, he told those who met to welcome him that throughout the Empire city churches "naturally and almost necessarily decrease in strength as their age increases", because of the movement of population out from the centre. He warned them that, despite his reputation, they could expect no increase in their congregation and that he would be satisfied to avoid decline.   He intended to pay attention to the poor and young, but even that would not bring increase.[45]   Under his care, Pitt Street, better located than

York Street, if those who advocated the move from York to Elizabeth Street (see chapter 2) were correct, did decline, though not as disastrously as York Street had done.[46]

Even the Anglicans were experiencing trouble in the seventies and early eighties and F. B. Boyce later recorded his anguish at the failure of his church to deal effectively with the situation created by the removal of the well-to-do and his plans for dealing with both the human and economic situation.[47]

In the early seventies significant new developments occurred in the city. During 1882, the YMCA began Sunday evening services in the Opera House, with the general approval of the denominations. Members went into the streets beforehand to invite "wandering youth, but not the larrikins of the city" to the service which often drew five hundred, mostly in the eighteen to twenty-five years age group. According to Phillips, in his study of Protestantism in late nineteenth century N.S.W., these services continued until October 1885 when they were transferred to the newly opened YMCA hall, though the *Advocate* stated correctly that they closed down at the end of May 1884 because a new lessee raised the rent to £10 a night. The YMCA could not afford this, but an "infidel" lecturer did, thus bringing every theatre in the city under rationalist control.[48]

More important was the arrival of the Salvation Army. This organization had been well known in England for some time but the first attempt to found it in Sydney in late 1880 had failed, unlike a slightly earlier attempt in Adelaide. Its Sydney career began on 2 December 1882 when Captain Tom and Mrs Sutherland, Sister Mary Ann Cox, and Lieutenant Alex Canty "armed with flag, tambourine, cornet and drum . . . joined Tom Mundiman in declaring war on the sins of Sydney". Six hundred people attended the opening meeting in the Protestant Hall. Thereafter the Army marched straight into the larrikin strongholds where it struck immediate trouble and pitched battles sometimes occurred. A second corps was formed in Newtown on 1 April 1883 and a third in Newcastle on 12 May 1883, the former running into some criticism because it operated close to six existing Protestant churches.   Wherever it went, the Army's band caught the attention of the crowd and drew numbers to its meetings.   The *War Cry*, the first Australian issue of which was published from Sydney on 24 March 1883, was a further effective means of spreading an intensely evangelical message cast in popular terms.[49]

The Army did not pass unnoticed by Methodists. Between 10 June 1882 and 4 August 1883, the *Advocate* published at least two dozen references to its work. Some of these were only passing comments, others comprised as much as two columns of solid material   There were several extensive editorials.   The *Advocate* disliked the Army's "extreme sensationalism" and its total lack of interest in "Christian culture", but it reacted positively to its novel evangelical methods and thought that "were they modified and used by some of our Churches they would soon result in the inflow of a new life".   The paper recognized the strong similarity between the Army and "aggressive Methodism", especially over the use of "the power of personal testimony". It also noted with appreciation that "the Salvation Army uses the language of the people among which it labours, and this is another cause of success".   Perhaps the most significant comment published was in a "Brief Note" which appeared on 24 February 1883: "The Salvation Army, under the leadership of Captain and Mrs. Sutherland, is carrying on a campaign in the school rooms of York Street church on several nights in each week".[50]

Of course, this reflected the problems which the Army was having with accommodation, but it also reflected its ability to at least mount a campaign at the very spot at which Methodism was failing and from which it was considering withdrawal.   The evidence suggests that neither the York Street Wesleyans nor the Conference immediately drew the appropriate conclusion.

Despite the efforts of individual churches and churchmen, the Sydney Christian scene was bleak in the 1880s. It has been estimated that if 50 per cent of Sydney's inhabitants were regular church-goers in 1880, only 40 per cent were by 1890, no doubt partly because those who did attend were moving out to the suburbs, while those who moved in, migrants from the English working class, did not. Others, of course, still used the church for the *rites de passage* of birth, marriage, and death.

As well as this, the church in Australia had been under strong attack from the secularists since about 1870, though the eighties was the period of most intense opposition. If the secularist "preachers" could not yet attract the "respectable", they could gather the working classes. It was not so much that they accepted the antireligious teaching as that secularist attacks on institutional religion blended with their own doubts about an organization which had not yet learnt to cope with the new concepts of industrial society and trade unionism. The church still saw conversion as the primary answer to all problems — social, spiritual, and economic.[51]

It was difficult to blame the clergy. They were not equipped to meet the conditions which confronted them. The need to show that Christianity was both reasonable and relevant was new and strange. In the case of the Methodists, at least, there were additional problems. Most of the clergy were country bred and the struggle to cope with the industrial city was a real difficulty, especially as few members of the Sydney work-force seem to have been recruited from rural areas.[52] Furthermore, the strictly applied itinerancy system meant that no minister stayed in one circuit more than three years and this posed an almost insuperable burden in coming to terms with the new urban conditions.

2
Foundations

The Methodist propensity for introspection and self-blame meant that the permanency of York Street's problem was not immediately recognized and 1871 saw the building of a new parsonage in connection with the Princes Street chapel. By 1878 the situation was clearer and the York Street trustees had resolved to sell that property (valuable as a warehouse site) and were planning a new church with a Sunday school and parsonage in a position more central to the residential population, as well as a new church in Princes Street. At the 1878 Conference it was argued that the large population which still existed west of the York Street church could not be induced to attend "a respectable place of worship" and that the new church should be built in Elizabeth Street, near Liverpool Street, to cater for the people who still lived in that part of the city. Conference agreed, subject to further investigation and final approval by its Executive Committee. That was never given — the reason is not recorded — and only the new Princes Street church went ahead. York Street limped aimlessly along, bringing strength and inspiration to none and frustration to those who battled to maintain its organizational existence. A continuing need for reunions and like meetings to cover the debts indicated the weakness of the colony's once premier Wesleyan circuit.[1]

Worldly logic was on the side of those who believed that the change should have been made while there was a favourable opportunity for the sale of the old site and the purchase of a new one. Those who opposed this view had little more than sentiment and nostalgia on their side, though there was force in the view that Methodism needed a central city presence and some doubt whether the Elizabeth Street site would have effected a permanent cure had the same modus operandi been employed.

Just before the Salvation Army was launched in Sydney, actually during August, September, and October 1882, there was a series of special evangelical services held at York Street in the effort to achieve revival. The preachers were the best Wesleyan Methodism could offer. A platform replaced the pulpit, there was a retiring offering instead of the regular collection, and the services were freer in form than usual, though the choir still insisted on rendering an anthem. Workers went out into the streets before the services to bring people in. The congregations were "encouraging" but "not crowded", though some said they were double normal. The *Wesleyan Advocate* concluded that if York Street always used a freer form of evening service it would win a response from those who promenaded the streets on Sunday evenings. There was no point in regretting a lost pastorate, they must do what was possible in its place. The choir should give up anthems and sing melodies popular with nonmusical people.

Despite this, at the Sydney District meeting in October, the York Street congregation was described as "enfeebled" and unable to support two married ministers as in the past. The January Conference agreed and appointed one married and one single man.[2] The evangelical services had achieved nothing of permanence, despite the fillip given to the congregation when they actually took place. Permanent revival seemed beyond the hope of York Street and the end near.

Wesleyan Methodism was struggling to find an answer to the York Street dilemma. It had one more false trail to follow before it found a real solution. The 1883 Conference decided to station there a "topical preacher" who excelled in "smart sentences" and arresting titles in the hope that he would gather a crowd through his discussion of a range of current issues in the light of the gospel. The man chosen was the Rev. John Osborne, formerly of Newcastle, where he had been very popular — sufficient to justify the view that he might carry off the York Street situation.

That something went seriously awry with this scheme is evident, but it is difficult to say precisely what, as there is nothing from Osborne and his supporters while Taylor tells us simply that Osborne filled the church within a month and emptied it again before the next Conference when he was subject to discipline and retired.[3]

The *Evening News* of 23 April 1883 outlined a sermon in which he reportedly argued that the Catholic church was "mainly good" and not very different from Protestantism. On the four nights, 17—20 July, the president of the Conference, Rev. W. Moore, chaired a special District meeting at York Street to investigate aspects of Osborne's doctrine, with special reference to the Catholic question, as well as his general mode of preaching and conduct in the circuit. Ultimately the inquiry accepted the soundness of his teaching but regretted that "his method of presenting these truths [was] at times so inexact as to produce the impression in the minds of some that he [was] erroneous in doctrine". In the "Catholic sermon" he had been "so unguarded in his statements as to appear to advance doctrines not in harmony with our standards".[4]

Having received this shot across his bows, Osborne might have been expected to take some care. However, when Archbishop Roger Vaughan died in August he made matters worse by attending the Requiem Mass. After further criticism at the January 1884 Conference, he resigned to begin a "Christian platform" in the Protestant Hall, to which he took a number of his York Street supporters. By April he was publicly accusing Wesleyan Methodism of "mysticism", lack of originality, the assumption that its doctrines were infallibly true, and anti-intellectualism. He eventually ended as a free-thought lecturer.[5]

There are several inexplicable aspects to this incident. It is strange that Osborne preached such a daring sermon so early in his tenure and that he failed to anticipate the church's hostile official reaction. Even more puzzling is the sudden discovery that his manner of preaching left so much to be desired when he had been chosen for his particular task on the basis of style and his work must have been known to his ministerial brethren.

Osborne's personal qualities and fate are not the present concern. York Street clearly suffered a heavy blow as a result of the incident. The ailing church had briefly received an influx of new blood and some intellectual stimulation, though possibly of a dubious kind. Before it had had time to reorganize itself, or even to rejoice, there had been an explosion which had rocked it to its foundations. The departure of Osborne took away a further portion of its already dwindling membership.

The Conference of 1884 was faced with a dilemma: having disposed of Osborne, what was it to do with York Street? There was before it a recommendation, fully supported by the rump of the York Street Quarterly Meeting, to sell the property and use the money to expand the work of the church in the ever-growing suburbs. The proposal varied from that of 1878, but the arguments were the same. A handful of people — the congregation was less than thirty in the morning and about fifty in the evening, with an official membership of seventeen or eighteen — could not struggle on against the odds trying to maintain a moribund organization and tying up a valuable site which could be realized on to the genuine advantage of the church at large. The counter-arguments sprang from sentiment, history, and some understanding of the importance of a church in the central city as a "standard bearer". The issue was decided on 22 January.[6]

The trend of the discussion was clearly towards sale when, suddenly, it was completely diverted by a dramatic intervention of profound significance for Sydney and Australian Methodism. W. G. Taylor's own possibly overcoloured recollection makes the point well:

> That Nestor of the Conference, George Hurst, a rugged old conservative . . . sprang to his feet, crying out in righteous anger, "Sell it, sell it? Never, God helping us, never!" . . . With arm outstretched and voice thrilled with a pathos and a penetration that was irresistible, the grand old man pleaded for yet another attempt to save alike our historic pile and our connexional honour . . . saying "Brethren, is Methodism bankrupt? Have we quite lost our historic evangelistic fervour? Have we no men among us of the old school — revivalists, evangelists, missioners — call them what you will — one of whom can be put in charge of the old place?"

The sight of the white-haired old supernumerary pleading

for the church where he had begun his own Australian ministry in 1859 moved his brother ministers to a response which sprang more from their emotions than their intellects. In answer to Hurst's last question, someone suggested the name of William George Taylor, whose whole ministry had been one of persistent revival. No sooner was the name mentioned than others took it up, probably without understanding how well Taylor fitted the role Hurst had cast but hoping — they hardly dared believe — that he might provide the answer for which they were so desperately searching.

Taylor was uneasy about this proposed appointment. There were two reasons for this: an understandable unwillingness to leave his present circuit (the Glebe), where he was in the midst of a "blessed revival", to go to a rundown church, and a genuine doubt about his own health. He decided to play the second card. That night he visited his doctor and his circuit steward. The doctor obligingly certified that Taylor could not stand the strain of York Street for six months, while the steward, unwilling to lose so good a minister, organized a petition and wrote to Conference saying, "If you appoint Mr Taylor, pray order his coffin, for he will be bound to need it in a few months". Whether as the result of genuine guidance, or from unwillingness to bow to such transparent pressure, or because it simply did not know what else to do, Conference remained unmoved. The well-loved Dr Kelynack urged Taylor to "try to take this vote as the call of God to you" while Hurst pointed out sensibly that since Conference had given Taylor a task of extraordinary difficulty it should support him in every way possible and also give him a free hand to experiment: "If he wants to kick out the panels of the pulpit, let him kick them out". From any angry York Street steward, Taylor received neither encouragement nor commiseration: "The Conference has made a mistake. We have tried everything and have failed. The building ought to have been sold. Personally I accept no responsibility. If Mr Taylor can get his bread and butter, well and good, if not, he will have to go without it."

Only Hurst emerges from the scene with much credit. Little more than a year from his grave, and in the forty-fifth year of his ministry, George Hurst saw no need to cultivate a popularity he had never cared about. Conservative that he was, he had no vision of a great "Forward Movement", but he did have a very clear vision of the responsibilities and opportunities of the church in the future and he realized that the "commonsense" sale of York Street would mean the denial of the former and the loss of the latter so far as the only significant metropolis in N.S.W. was concerned. He was one of those veterans who held that evangelism and revival were the chief, if not the only, tasks of the church.. If he knew much about Taylor, and he may not have, for at forty the latter considered himself "too junior" to take much part in the affairs of Conference, Hurst must have approved the choice.

By his appeal, cast in terms which would have made its rejection seem like a denial of the Methodist past, Hurst made it difficult for Conference to act otherwise than as it did. But it is unlikely that Taylor was sent to make any bold new departure for Christ and the church. Such a step was beyond the imagining of most members of the Conference who sought only the effective application of well-tried evangelistic methods to save a moribund church. They sought not expensive new innovations, but the means to enable an indebted church to pay its way. Above everything else, Conference wanted to be saved the embarrassment of having an empty church at the heart of Methodism. Taylor was sent to York Street as a last forlorn hope. He was expected to fail and he knew it. It was that which made the appointment particularly galling to him.

Who was William George Taylor, the man sent to take up appointment as superintendent minister of the York Street Wesleyan church in April 1884?[7]

Born on 18 January 1845 in Knayton in the North Riding of Yorkshire, Taylor matured in the emotional atmosphere which then prevailed in north-country Methodism. Converted at twelve in a class meeting by an old minister who knelt beside him, arm around the lad as he told him of the promises of Christ, while the whole meeting prayed for the boy's soul, young William began his own evangelical career at fifteen and always regarded preaching that did not seek an immediate verdict for Christ as "a mere wasting of a great opportunity". Early witnesses leave no doubt that even in his youth he practised "evangelism served up red hot". It was no surprise that he decided to train for the ministry.

Eventually he was sent to Australia where his ministry began in 1871. One of the things which stands out about him is the speed with which he acclimatized to his new and very different environment. Even his later visits to England in no way indicated any nostalgic desire to return permanently. There can be no doubt that his was an Australian ministry in the fullest sense of that term.

Before York Street, Taylor ministered successively in Brisbane, Warwick, Toowoomba, Manning River, and Glebe and was accompanied everywhere by revival. His work at the Glebe illustrates the point perfectly. Within two months of his appointment, Taylor had organized a fortnight's mission. Invitations had been sent to every home to attend midweek services. On several evenings, thirty or forty men and women marched through the streets around the church singing and giving brief addresses at street corners. More than a hundred professed conversion and attended a final service when Taylor gave a half-hour of advice to the "awakened" and an hour was spent listening to testimonies from both old and new converts. The service concluded with the sacrament of the Lord's Supper.[8] Over the entire two years of his ministry, the Glebe saw extensive institutional development with the formation of a Ladies' Benevolent Society, a Temperance Society, a Juvenile Missionary Society, and a Young Men's Society. A circuit missionary was also employed.

Tall in stature, with a magnificent voice, an evangelist to the core, fervent rather than eloquent, he had an impressive but entirely unaffected pulpit manner and an attractive personality. A co-worker wrote of him: "Mr Taylor's delivery of his sermons is distinguished by no great intellectual flights, rather does he strive to reach the hearts of his hearers by the simple, plain gospel uplifting of Jesus Christ . . . Mr Taylor's soul is linked on to the great dynamic force of the Holy Spirit".[9] If Conference had thought about it, Taylor was the kind of man who might have seemed appropriate to the struggling York Street cause. As it was, it had appointed him almost without thinking about it.

More than two months passed between Conference and
Taylor's actual taking up of his appointment. At the time,
Taylor admitted that he trembled at the prospect before him
and that he prayed much as he made his plans for York
Street. Those plans were revealed at a welcome social to
Taylor and his colleague, Frederick Boyer, on 17 April.[10]
They involved monthly evangelical services on Sunday nights
with "numerous addresses and much singing" after an earlier
open-air service and the distribution of handbills in the
streets. A similar plan would be followed every Friday night.
Men who worked in the city but lived elsewhere and who
wished to assist with this could eat in the Princes Street
schoolroom. Notices inviting sailors to services were to be
placed in all ships in the port each Friday and York Street
was to provide the parade service for Methodist sailors from
the British fleet. He hoped to send visitors to the scores of
common boardinghouses each Sunday morning to invite their
occupants to worship. He wanted ladies to visit the homes of
the people on a regular basis. In the long run, he looked for a
ragged school, a young men's club, and a weekly temperance
meeting. The president of Conference had promised help
from the theological students at the Stanmore College, but
Taylor also sought those whose singing might boost his outdoor services. He was probably well aware of a major revival
in England of "the old Methodist practice of singing bands
parading the streets, and thus drawing the people to the
services".[11] His own activity at the Glebe suggests this, and
in any case, Boyer had only arrived from England the year
before and could have advised him on the current practice
there.

This was a straightforward evangelical programme, but one
which took notice of the special features of the area in which
he was working: in particular, the sailors and the transitory
young men of the boardinghouses. Sydney was a very busy
port and York Street was well placed to service the sailors
and already had attached to it a supernumerary minister,
Rev. S. Wilkinson, who was interested in that work. Likewise,
it has already been noted that it was in the midst of a district
containing a very large number of boardinghouses of various
grades.

A consideration of his early work backs up this view of Taylor's programme. On 13 April, he opened with a sermon entitled "the Secret of a Successful Ministry" and followed up with "Does God Really Forgive Sin?" and "the Story of a Wanderer's Life" Always there was the "after-meeting" of Methodist tradition, where the conviction of sin was driven home and penitents helped to faith. So traditional was this that Taylor later regarded his innovative open-air service as the real beginning of his new "Central Methodist Mission". Planned to begin on 27 April, this service was washed out by pouring rain and did not get under way until 11 May when 400 attended to hear a variety of addresses and be led in singing by Boyer, who was perched on a "gospel chariot" with an American organ.

These early services were more successful than Taylor had dared hope. He estimated 250 at the first on 13 April (the *Wesleyan Advocate* said 300) and 50 at the after-meeting. Best of all, there were almost always converts. Nothing pleased him more than improvement in the Tuesday night class meeting — still the official test of commitment for a Wesleyan — and his brief diary entry for 13 May reveals his emotion on that occasion: "A grand class meeting. 20 present. Nearly all new converts. 18 spoke. O how my heart

Rev. W.G. Taylor's CMM Tuesday evening class meeting. By courtesy of the Uniting Church Archives.

did dance for joy!"[12]   Such events led him to decide quickly
that there were already signs of revival at York Street.   This
conclusion was based more on that faith and hope which is so
essential a part of the evangelist's make-up than on evidence,
but it was a conclusion that would prove amply justified.

No doubt some of the early good attendances were the
result of support from well-wishers in neighbouring circuits,
but there was more to it than that.   From the beginning
Taylor had the backing of the *Wesleyan Advocate* which
urged workers from the YMCA's Opera House services to go
and help at nearby York Street when their own service
collapsed.   The editor foresaw no great difficulty in transferr-
ing the congregation.   Almost every week, the *Wesleyan
Advocate* urged help for Taylor's work and it also sought
funds from throughout the colony for the renovation of
York Street.   When criticism of Taylor appeared in the
Queensland *Christian Messenger* later in the year, the
Advocate leapt to his defence, urging that his methods were
those of "eminently successful" connexional evangelists in
England and that Taylor was entitled to support and cooperation for his "zealous and persistent efforts" under great
difficulty.   Consistent help came from the Newington
students who were available Friday night and Sunday afternoon and evening.

From the beginning Taylor tried to make his workers part
of a team by holding workers' conferences to plan and share
experiences.   The first was on Monday, 28 April at 7.45 p.m.
Rain interfered with this, but forty attended.   Incomplete
arrangements were made for the visitation of ships in the
harbour and for the open-air work, but Taylor still required
at least six men to visit the better class boardinghouses with
tickets of invitation, a dozen ladies for house-to-house
visitation, and three or four people to conduct a Sunday
school.   Perhaps it was then that he first made use of the map
found in the back of his diary.   It was a map of Sydney with
the boundaries of the York Street circuit clearly marked.
The circuit was divided into segments and each was allotted
to a worker.   Taylor was not one to fail for lack of organization, but he was following a pattern already set by the
Sydney City Mission.

On 25 July, his second workers' conference drew 180 workers and new converts to tea and "many more" to the meeting which followed. At that stage, a large number of boardinghouses and ships were being visited every Sunday morning and many private homes were also visited by the women. More offers of help were received at the meeting. This meeting was sufficiently successful for the *Sydney Morning Herald* to report it and to note that in three months thirty thousand handbills and tracts had been distributed by Taylor's workers. Money was harder to get. An appeal in the *Advocate* brought him one donation of £25 and seventeen others totalling £35.

This period also saw the introduction of a Saturday night consecration service for Christian workers. It involved "praise, prayer, testimony and exhortation [following] each other in quick succession". Those from other circuits as well as his own were welcome to prepare themselves for the work of soul-saving the next day. This service will be discussed in detail later.[13]

Such steady progress would have satisfied most men, but not Taylor. The period 24 August—2 September saw a "ten days mission to the masses", with daily meetings, including special meetings for young men, for women, and for business-men, and one in which the message was presented entirely by means of music. Large posters were put up in the city and 15,000 of the already well-known CMM "shocking pink" handbills were distributed. Almost every house, common lodginghouse, and ninety "better class" establishments and every ship in port were visited. The preparation was thorough, the execution excellent (despite the fact that the *Sydney Morning Herald* noted that some small boys disturbed the first service by hawking books in the aisles!), and the harvest was seventy-eight professed converts (one lad, four-teen females, sixty-three men, including seven sailors). The only surprising element was that when an unnamed man offered to pay all expenses if Taylor would go on for a month, the latter declined on the ground that the strain was too great. He preferred to return to his "ordinary arrange-ment of three evangelical services a week".[14] It is more than likely that the explanation lay in those fears about his health which had troubled him on his appointment to York Street. He had been working very hard in the five months spent at the CMM.

When Taylor reviewed his first year's work, he expressed considerable delight at the help he had received from a number of unexpected sources near and far. Overall, in the period from 13 April 1884 to 13 January 1885, 539 persons had "expressed anxiety about salvation". Taylor was too experienced to claim them all as genuine converts. Indeed, he had faced a considerable problem in that professional beggars had quickly decided that an expression of anxiety about their salvation was a good way to secure sympathy and help at the mission. Experience had made his helpers discriminating and they refused to assist those not considered genuine. Over nine months there had been an increase of ninety-seven members in the church and York Street was on the way to becoming a "centre of spiritual power".

Not all had been plain sailing in those early months. Taylor's determination to "capture the kerbstone" had given offence to some within the church and on three occasions his methods had been criticized at the monthly Sydney preachers' meetings. His street work also led him into direct confrontation with the secularists then so common in Sydney. This confrontation lasted for twelve months and seems to have ended only after a drunken sundowner fought one of the secularist fraternity in support of the CMM while Taylor sang "Jesus! the Name High Over All" at the top of his voice and hundreds were attracted to the scene by cries of "the parson's having a fight!".

Taylor must have been pleased at the need which confronted the 1885 Conference to set up a committee to find ways of providing adequate accommodation at York Street. That was certainly a more pleasant problem than had confronted the previous Conference. Unfortunately there is no indication of George Hurst's view on the new problem and its cause.[15]

In the back of Taylor's diary for the early days is a list of the names and addresses of 788 persons who sought salvation at services during his first sixteen months at York Street. No occupations are given so the social structure of the converts cannot be analyzed. However, about one hundred more men than women were converted. While a substantial number of converts came from the country, other colonies, overseas, or were sailors, the great majority were from the city and many were from the streets around the CMM or from the inner suburbs. These facts indicate that the mission was at least partially achieving its purpose. They also show why it could not build all its converts into its own structures.[16]

The eighteen months following April 1885 saw steady progress but no new or dramatic developments at York Street. A series of free "social evenings for the people" was held at Princes Street in July 1885 in the hope that they would not only provide a legitimate and harmless form of entertainment but would also encourage more to attend the Sunday services. A temperance society, a mutual improvement association, and a Bible class were formed, but these were all typical nineteenth century church organizations. A lay minister was appointed for a time (until he became a candidate for the ministry) and Taylor wanted to start a working men's club, but was prevented by lack of funds. He held that those who made their money in the city but lived elsewhere were responsible for the care of the poor.

There was a brief experiment with a service for the coloured citizens of Sydney (on the initiative of the latter) but it broke down quickly. In 1886 there was a further ten-day mission in cooperation with several other city and inner-suburban circuits which was a partial success and which led in turn to the establishment of a Wednesday lunch-hour service, though this does not appear to have worked very well.

Through it all, the number of workers increased, many of the best of them having been York Street converts. Sixty common lodginghouses were visited every Sunday morning and a CMM worker visited the Central Police Court cells daily. Taylor was especially pleased with the response of sailors to his work for them and wished he could afford a full-time seamen's missionary. He argued that the wealthy merchants who employed these men should have some care for their salvation. The only surprise in this period came in November 1885 when Taylor, having been present at a midnight supper for prostitutes, and though ready enough to conclude that the Methodist church at large should assist with their rescue, did not appear to regard it as a work particularly suited to the CMM.[17]

The 1885 Conference had to face up to the problem of the now inadequate accommodation at York Street and had before it a proposal for the conversion of the property into a connexional trust with the object of erecting "commodious premises" on the site. This appears to have aroused some discussion about the role and state of Methodism in the city and, in particular, the role of the York Street church. The editor of the *Wesleyan Advocate*, Rev. Paul Clipsham, devoted considerable space to the issue in the editorial and other columns of the paper.

On 14 March 1885 Clipsham compared the position of Methodism in Sydney with its position in other great cities overseas and argued the need to use methods which would attract people into the churches: free seats, the chance to hear "strong, racy talk", and variations in the mode of conducting the service. A few weeks later (25 April) he stressed the church's double function: not only was it a place for quickening the Christian culture of "believing, loving hearts", it really existed for those outside and should look after "the poor, the hopeless, the ignorant, the vicious, the profligate". It had a reformative role in politics, business, and society and by fulfilling its role in the secular world it would win people to the faith. The *Advocate* also drew attention to the value of some relaxation of the itinerancy rule in city work, as illustrated by Charles Garrett's long stay in Liverpool.[18]

The 1885 Conference consented to the transfer of the York Street property to a connexional trust so that the old church could be removed and a new connexional premises erected. These buildings would consist of warehouses on the ground floor front and basement, connexional offices, committee rooms and caretaker's home on the first floor, with rooms for tea meetings, a workers' club, and reading rooms above. At the rear was to be a church to seat fifteen hundred, fitted with a rostrum for public meetings, and open pews. This was remarkably similar to a project started sometime earlier at Oldham Street, Manchester, for the renewal of a valuable but run-down Methodist inner-city site there. Old

York Street church did not close its doors until November 1886, when a nostalgic final service was held.[19]

In view of Taylor's own request to be relieved for a year on health grounds and to be permitted to go to England to look at mission work there, the 1887 Conference decided to drop plans to use the large Protestant Hall while the York Street property was unavailable and to use only the Princes Street church. It appointed only one minister to the circuit. In sharp contrast to the concern shown over the emptiness of York Street three years earlier, it was now taking an enormous risk with the congregation gathered with so much difficulty. Taylor was aghast, believing that both workers and congregation would be scattered.

His fears were partly, though not entirely, fulfilled. Princes Street was not sufficiently central to be an effective single centre of activity and a disused Primitive Methodist chapel in Kent Street had to be hired for evening services at a rental of £2/5/- per week. Payments fell behind and by the end of 1887 the Wesleyans were under notice to quit unless they paid weekly. A Seamen's Mission, which had worked effectively under H. D. Gilbert since July 1886, suffered badly and Gilbert's salary was three months in arrears. Taylor's successor, J.A. Bowring, struggled to maintain the programme. Open-air services seem to have remained strong, due to the continued contribution of the mission's brass band, formed in February 1886 and led by Mr J. Huegill, despite criticisms from those who considered it always inappropriate. If the church congregations dwindled, and this was unavoidable since Kent Street could hold only 200, at least the band of workers remained active. This made it at little easier than it might otherwise have been to reassemble a congregation once the new Centenary Hall was opened in 1888.[20]

The cavalier attitude of the 1887 Conference to the problem of temporary accommodation reflected its continuing uncertainty about the future of York Street. Clearly, despite the decision already taken about the buildings, and a recommendation from the Sydney District Synod in favour of a connexional CMM in York Street, the overall level of commitment in Wesleyan circles to the central mission concept was low. It was not even accepted that a mission existed de facto, if not de jure. Taylor's work during the period 1884–87 was not well understood and his mission was seen as no more than ad hoc, an experiment that might or might not be continued as Conference saw fit.

The retiring president, Rev. Dr R. Sellors, specifically counselled against taking a course merely because it was popular at the time and suggested that the ordinary churches were adequately equipped and willing to deal with the working classes. Such powerful opposition led Conference to remit the question to the Executive Committee of the Church Sustentation and Extension Society and the District Synod meeting for further consideration.[21]

Bowring, who had been unstinting in his efforts to maintain the CMM, had his spirits dashed by the 1888 Conference. He raised the resolutions passed at the 1887 Conference, urged the creation of a connexional CMM, and sought the reappointment of Taylor to the work. Support was limited and criticism strong. Rev. George Brown was appalled that they had no city church to provide for the better class of people to which visitors "who are offended with brass bands and Sankey hymns could go . . . If they gave up that grand new building altogether to the lower classes they would drive away the better classes". There were others besides Taylor who had special evangelical gifts and should be allowed to develop them.

J. E. Carruthers argued sensibly that the relative success of Taylor's work had committed them. York Street should follow the pattern of Hugh Price Hughes's West London Mission, with a cultured address in the morning, one to working men in the afternoon, and an evangelical service at night. Carruthers sought the appointment of Taylor and his more scholarly friend, Rev. E. J. Rodd, to the mission. The doubters were sufficiently strong to prevent the establishment of a CMM for another year by a 38/28 vote. To make matters worse, Taylor was appointed to William Street where he was sufficiently in competition with York Street to make it likely that he would draw some of the supporters away.[22] He himself must have wondered why he had bothered to investigate the workings of city missions while he was in England.

Centenary Hall, York Street. From Colwell, *Illustrated History of Methodism* (1904).

June 1888 saw Paul Clipsham open up a new campaign on the mission question. The situation could hardly be worse in the near-empty city churches. Little had been done to counteract the "exceptional godlessness" of both high and low, the majority of whom were "either indifferent to religion or grossly wicked". More open-air services, as well as indoor services which taught the Gospel at a level appropriate to those they were designed to serve, were needed. Hughes's mission pointed the way. Conservative Methodism, with its stereotyped approach, had to give way to the new methods of the "Forward Movement" if the people were to be brought in from the streets. Special men must be set aside for special work. The 1888 Conference decision to use the (Australian) Centenary Thanksgiving Fund it had set up for "the inauguration of systematic mission work among the masses of Sydney, and the establishment of Home Mission stations in the country districts" logically implied the For- ward Movement with its organized mission agencies, bright services, and systematic evangelism. If Methodism were to renew its youth, Australia must keep in step with the mother church in Britain.

In October—November the battle for the York Street CMM was being fought on two fronts, in the *Advocate* and at the Sydney District Synod, and was given some further impetus by the opening of Centenary Hall.

At the Synod, Taylor had a committee appointed, with himself as convenor, to formulate resolutions relating to the establishment of a CMM in York Street. These resolutions covered everything that Taylor and his supporters wanted, except his own appointment as superintendent, and attempted to defuse the opposition of critics by urging the appointment of Rev. J. H. Fletcher and Dr Kelynack as morning preachers. A provisional Connexional Committee was set up to act until Conference could finally determine the question. Clipsham described the York Street develop- ment as a "stupendous undertaking" the like of which had not been attempted by any church organization in the southern world. A little prematurely, he congratulated the Methodist church on its earnestness and faith and spoke of the financial responsibilities implied by the charitable institutions which would cluster around the church and he hoped it would develop branches in the suburbs and become "a blessing to every circuit and to every church". While there is no direct evidence, it is impossible to avoid the conclusion that Taylor and Clipsham were cooperating. Even an account of the opening of Centenary Hall provided an occasion to refer to Taylor's earlier work at York Street and the opportunities given by the new buildings. Some of the speakers at the meetings supported the mission cause and when Taylor spoke at a love-feast he urged people prepared to work to give their names to Bowring "who would need all the help he could get to carry on the future mission work there".[23] The supporters of the Forward Movement were already behaving as if they had won the last battle.

Their confidence was not misplaced. After yet one more thrust from Clipsham, and after considerable discussion on 30 January 1889, Conference passed the resolutions brought forward from the Sydney meeting, though without committing itself definitely to the appointment of a second minister. The last battle was fought on the following day, 31 January, over the appointment of Taylor. Some thought he should be left at William Street. Others thought that an Englishman should be brought out to do the job. The jealousy of Taylor was understandable if reprehensible, but the cultural cringe was not, for Taylor was English born and trained and had just spent twelve months there looking at the methods used in English missions. Nationalism was of slow growth in Wesleyan circles, despite its rapid spread in the community at large. Eventually the sensible thing was done and Taylor's name was put down.

Later, Taylor was asked to address Conference on his study of the English Forward Movement. He portrayed it as the solution to most of the problems of English church life and seemed especially impressed by the work of Garrett in Liverpool and Collier at Manchester. To have a successful mission, the workers had to be fully consecrated and filled with enthusiasm to save men body and soul, as well as possessed of "sanctified commonsense". Converts must be given an immediate share in the work, missioners a free hand, and good use must be made of music to attract the masses.

If these principles were kept in mind, the success of the English Forward Movement could be transferred to Sydney.[24] He plainly intended to proceed as he had done in 1884—87.

Taylor now had his mission and only had to make it work. There were plenty who were prepared to seize upon the least sign of weakness or of failure, or who had other hopes and plans they would have liked to push forward. One clerical critic, Rev. H. Mack of Redfern, implied that Taylor was straining after "spiritual novelties" and that the Forward Movement was only what had always been called "the work of God". The secularists could crowd Centenary Hall immediately with high class secular music and worldly teaching, or the Salvation Army with "big drums" and other "sensational appliances". It was wrong to use an orchestra to attract people. Reliance should be on the power of God and the aim should be not to fill empty churches but to promote the spiritual work of God without the aid of any histrionic agency. Effort should be concentrated on "the sacred work of preparation for the pulpit" and the mission should not seek to draw strength away from other city and suburban Methodist churches.[25]

Such a statement implied certain misconceptions and offered gratuitous insults which might have offended a man less sure of his purpose than Taylor. He had encountered similar criticisms of the English missions and seems to have attributed them to the fear that the missions might lead the church into financial difficulties. In the presence of such "mother Grundies", and with limited human help and resources, Taylor had the daunting task of implementing a concept which it had taken Conference five years to accept and which many of his supporters had regarded hitherto as no more than experimental.

Taylor frequently claimed that the Sydney CMM was the first in the world. All subsequent superintendents have repeated that claim, but without any independent justification. The foundation of the Sydney mission may be dated from either 13 April 1884 (Taylor's first service) or 11 May 1884 (the first open-air service at the Town Hall corner). It is unreasonable to postdate it to April 1889, the inauguration of the connexional CMM. This makes it the second

CMM and, probably, the third truly "institutional" parish church anywhere.

The first CMM was, without question, that begun in Liverpool by Charles Garrett in 1875. Taylor himself makes it clear that he was in touch with Garrett when he went to York Street and he stated that his original plan of campaign was based on that used in certain large English cities. On one later occasion he also wrote that when Garrett went to the empty Pitt Street (Liverpool) church he "became the father of the modern Forward Movement". Liverpool was organized as a CMM and doing the work of one nine years before Sydney, though it is possible that Taylor was the first to use the name. Unfortunately, his enthusiasm for his own work at York and Pitt Streets led him later to forget his debt to his "dear old friend and personal adviser".[26] The point is of concern to the historian alone.

3
Early Years

Taylor's programme for the connexional mission must have seemed incredibly ambitious. His well-tried pattern of evangelism would continue, backed by the work of a musical department, an evangelists' home, one for "sisters of the people", and another for "fallen and friendless women" as well as an adult Bible class, a workingmen's and a boys' club, a literary association, a savings bank, and a servants' registry office. The seamen's mission would continue and free breakfasts would be offered to the poor. Two to three thousand pounds a year might be needed to run the programme and much of this would have to come from beyond the mission itself since it would serve Methodism within the whole of N.S.W.[1]

There was little wonder that Taylor's conservative critics thought the CMM could only grow strong at the expense of surrounding circuits. Time would prove these critics wrong, but that was not obvious at first. David Bollen has argued that in the nineteenth century the Methodists of N.S.W. sought revival with more persistence and determination than any other denomination.[2] Hindsight suggests that they should have welcomed the CMM as a major contribution towards their goal, but many were not able to recognize the supreme importance of the city in the church's struggle for survival or in its task of extending the Kingdom of God on earth. Others simply found it hard to adjust to new methods and new organizations.

Taylor prepared for the inauguration of the connexional mission with an extensive advertising campaign on city billboards and in the daily papers. Workers prepared spiritually at a consecration service on the Saturday night and an early morning prayer meeting on the Sunday. Men were prominent in the Sunday congregations, though mainly from the middle rather than the working classes. At a public meeting Taylor stressed that the mission was for those who did not worship elsewhere and would not be made strong at the expense of other circuits. The Hon. Ebenezer Vickery, a layman who had caught Taylor's vision, spoke of the CMM as a centre of Christian activity and life which would influence the colony to its furthest limits. At special services for women and young men it was appropriate to speak at length about the sisters' and evangelists' homes. The gift or promise of about £800 suggested reasonable support for the new venture.[3]

For the next four years, the ordinary work of the CMM, worship and evangelism, proceeded steadily. From the start there was a Sunday afternoon adult Bible class conducted by a lay member of the CMM Committee, W. Davies, and a Saturday evening consecration service and workers' conference. Three class meetings were held every Monday though, after some time, they combined once each month to provide the inspiration of a larger meeting. This foreshadowed a much later development in this aspect of the mission's life. There were weekly services in Moorecliff hospital, religious instruction in Fort Street Model School, and four open-air services each week. By the end of the year, one hundred and fifty had "passed through" the Bible class, whatever that might mean, three to four hundred regularly attended the morning service and twelve to fifteen hundred the evening service, rather more than had gathered in the old church before it had been knocked down and the congregation scattered. It was claimed that much of the congregation was new, a gain to Wesleyanism, and that the strength of the surrounding circuits had not been sapped. The large debt on the hall ensured continuing financial weakness.[4]

Special efforts included a "great field day" in the Domain on 9 November 1889. There were few converts throughout the day, but back at Centenary Hall in the evening, after a traditional Methodist love-feast, Taylor turned the whole meeting into an "enquiry room" and twenty-three professed conversion. There was also the 1890 Anniversary, held over the Easter weekend, which included an all-night prayer vigil and communion leading to the Friday services and an all-day workers' conference leading to another love-feast on the Monday. This was perhaps a first attempt to make the CMM the focus of a truly Christian Easter festival.[5] It was not persisted with thereafter, though it is interesting to note that since 1979 a very similar preparation for Good Friday has been reinstituted as part of a regular programme of prayer nights.

Those who had still regarded the CMM as a risky experiment when it reopened in 1889 should have been satisfied by this time, especially as 4 May 1890 saw the opening of the new Balmain Central Mission in direct imitation.[6] Conference had been convinced of the value of the model and intended to build cautiously on it as English Wesleyanism had done in London and elsewhere. Further recognition of the success of the CMM came on 5 August 1890 when the *Evening News* gave two columns to an account of its work. The whole article was very favourable, whether in reference to the "thoughtful" morning service, the music, or the lack of class distinctions. The paper allowed Taylor a bigger evening congregation (up to two thousand) than he had as yet claimed for himself (fifteen hundred). There were complimentary references to his organizing capacity and the manner in which he handled his 150 (mainly voluntary) workers. This notice was a recognition that the CMM was beginning to make its mark on the life of the city. Such publicity was good for the Wesleyan church generally, but did not cause Taylor's critics to give up entirely. Occasional letters appeared in the *Advocate* objecting to the emphasis on the evening service or declaring the morning service "a failure".[7]

Congregations remained good thereafter, with the body of the hall often almost full in the morning while the evening attendance was frequently over fifteen hundred. The most interesting feature of the evening congregation was the estimate that two-thirds or more were "artisans and young men who but for the Mission would not be found within a church". Converts continued in a steady stream, but church membership grew only slowly as many returned to other denominations, to the suburbs, the country, or their ships. The CMM was, as Taylor had predicted, a depot or staging post, not a settled pastorate. This made it hard to follow up and keep in touch with converts and reduced the satisfaction and the effectiveness of the work. But it did mean that the mission was helping rather than hindering other churches. Even more clearly, the evidence shows that the CMM was reaching further down into society than had previously been done. It may not have been reaching many at the very bottom, despite occasional reports of the conversion of men whose only address was the Domain, but the gains were significant. Figures merely indicate the level of evangelical effort, not its quality, but those for 1890 are impressive: 14 meetings of the committee, 2,502 meetings conducted (averaging 48 per week, by the end of the year 60 per week), 13,338 visits to homes, ships, lodginghouses, hospitals, gaols (averaging 256 per week), 434 converts, not to mention the philanthropic effort which went on pari passu with the evangelical.[8]

Early January 1892 saw an Oecumenical Christian Convention held at Centenary Hall. The crowds and enthusiasm were enormous — on the evening of Thursday, 7 January there were said to be four thousand in the hall and overflow meetings (in the various rooms and warehouses attached). Whether the capacity of the building was really up to this cannot now be known. The following evening three thousand attended an open-air service and one hundred converts were claimed.[9] The size of the crowds was aided by the interdenominational cooperation, but Taylor was in the forefront of the convention, as befitted the city's leading evangelical minister, and much of the success was undoubtedly his.

Apart from this sign of the growing influence of the York Street Mission, the previous year had seen "enquiries" increase to 586, growing class meetings, and an increasing percentage of mission converts among the York Street workers. But such good works could not protect Taylor against the jealous and there were discussions at the 1892 Conference about the legality of continuing his appointment beyond three years. In the event, he was appointed to the

"Central Mission" rather than the "York Street Circuit". Worse still, Conference, while greeting the CMM report "by an outburst of hearty cheering", refused Taylor the help of an unmarried minister, so that he actually asked them to move him, despite his commitment to the work, since to continue without help would cause his complete breakdown.[10]

Two special aspects of the "ordinary work" of evangelism and worship require some additional discussion: worker preparation and music.

Saturday evening workers' conferences and consecration meetings were a feature of CMM life even in the 1884-87 period. This continued after the connexional mission had been established. One worker described the inaugural Sunday as beginning at 7.30 p.m. on the Saturday evening. There is also an early account from a visitor who found 150 from all parts of the city there one "cold bleak Saturday night". Some were former drunks, some were once "easy-chair Christians" but all participated in a forty-five minute service which was divided into three fifteen-minute segments devoted respectively to scriptural quotations, reports of good work in any circuit, and "red hot" testimonies. The visitor found it "impossible to describe the enthusiasm, the earnestness, and gladness of the meeting". A second account fifteen months later, in December 1890, found Taylor forced to use the large hall for space and expressed the view that every church should hold such a meeting weekly or send its workers to the CMM. During September 1892, when Taylor introduced a series of fifteen-minute addresses on "How to Deal with Anxious Souls", the *Methodist* expressed an editorial view that "these services have much to do with the character and success of the efforts of the following day".[11]

The CMM was nurtured in a spirit of prayer — half nights, whole nights, and, on occasion, much longer periods of prayer. Tuesday, 26 November 1889 may serve as an example. The meeting lasted from 10.00 p.m. to 5.00 a.m. with two hundred and fifty present at the start and two hundred at the conclusion. (A similar exercise six months later drew four hundred.) Various brethren, lay and clerical, led for an hour each and the form varied to include prayer, praise, exposition, exhortation, and testimony. "The prayers were short, scriptural and full of force" so that the place "became a very heaven below". Not all approved, but it could hardly be denied that the practice had been followed within the church since the first century and certainly by Wesley himself.[12]

An unusual prayer incident occurred in October 1891 when Taylor, with "holy daring", as the *Advocate* put it, organized a ten-day prayer meeting. The decision to hold this astounding event was taken at the end of an emotionally charged midweek staff prayer meeting and was greeted with sheer amazement by those not present on that occasion. There were four daily sessions between 7.00 a.m. and 10.00 p.m. separated by meetings for praise and testimony. There were often several hundred present. Taylor later claimed that the mission received its "Pentecost of grace and influence" between 11.00 a.m. and 12.00 noon on the second Tuesday, though it is not clear precisely what he meant by that untestable expression. The series was closed by a "grand Harbour prayer meeting" when three hundred prayed on the sea and at Middle Harbour, no doubt the dramatic equivalent of a sunrise Easter service or a television session live from Bondi Beach.[13]

Taylor's own later writings make it clear that he regarded the consecration service, especially, as the "power-house" of the CMM. For him, it was the Saturday night meeting which made the Sunday evening service "so great a time of blessing and grace". The prayer meetings grew out of the fact that "early in the history of the Mission it was borne in upon the mind of the workers that if we wished to secure Pentecostal results we must be prepared to adopt Pentecostal methods".[14]

There was nothing unusual about the mission's enormous stress on prayer and consecration as the basis for its evangelical work, nor can it be denied that its preoccupation was appropriate. Christians will readily accept the need to seek divine assistance for such work and for the worker to align himself entirely with the will of God. More sceptical readers will tend to the opinion that the workers were simply "firing themselves up" psychologically for their work. The fact remains that the method was both appropriate and effective. Prayer built up the corporate life of the congregation and provided (by whatever means) the dynamic for its operation as an evangelical cell in the difficult environment of central Sydney.

Taylor was a singer of some ability and was keenly aware of the potential role of music in the life of the church. He insisted that choirs sing simple renderings of Gospel songs rather than elaborate anthems. A brass band was introduced during his first period to assist in gathering a crowd for the street services and in leading the marchers back to York Street church. Although he admitted himself originally opposed to brass instruments, he had quickly come to the conclusion that the band was a valuable and unexceptionable means of attracting people to hear the Gospel and that it had ample precedents in England.[15]

In 1889, before taking up his York Street appointment again, he advertised for and appointed a musical director, W. I. B. Mote. His aim was not merely to establish choir work firmly, but to build up an orchestra along the lines of that used by Hugh Price Hughes at West London. The history of church orchestras, at least in the village churches of England, was much older than the Forward Movement. Kitson Clark comments that "probably something was lost . . . in the sacrifice of the old raucous village orchestras and choirs, who [sic] definitely produced the music of the people, in favour of an organ and a certain number of men and boys in surplices which had a dangerous tendency towards gentility".[16] While the *Advocate* was inclined to take the same view as Kitson Clark, not everyone did, and some saw the orchestra as "an histrionic agency". Innovators must expect criticism and Taylor did not complain. Ultimately he won through by force of the inescapable fact that his method worked. After all, he had been sent to York Street to succeed.

The oldest of the "special branches" of the mission's work, the Seamen's Mission, was firmly established well before the inauguration of the connexional mission, but the following three years saw its activities expand. The most important extension was the opening in August 1889 of a Seamen's Institute, with its headquarters in the Princes Street church. This seems to have been well patronized. The object was to provide a room where sailors could seek refuge from the temptations of the hotel and the brothel and where they could spend the day, or evening, in cheerful surroundings, reading, writing letters, or playing games. Once a week there was an evening entertainment and they were always invited to the Sunday services.   At 9.30 a.m. there was a parade service for Methodist "blue-jackets" (though the actual date at which it started is not clear).   Frequently more than a hundred seamen attended the Sunday evening service as well. A year later, a small boat, "The Seamen's Friend" was christened for the use of the missionary and his helpers.[17]   There was never any doubt about the central purpose of the Seamen's Mission and the CMM was proud of its sailor converts even if it were hard to keep track of them and if their lives as Christians were bound to be perilous.

One other aspect of CMM life which was to assume considerable importance over the years must be introduced here, the Evangelists' Training Institute.   Taylor was conscious from the beginning of his need for dependable assistance with home visitation and street work.   Young men were available, but they were raw, untrained, and in need of assistance.   For this reason, one Saturday night in April 1889, two flats at Centenary Hall were dedicated to this work.   The young men (there were three to begin) were boarded without charge, but were expected to look after their own quarters.   Their mornings were spent studying theology with the Rev. J. Oram, literary subjects with Rev. J. Colwell, and Bible study and Christian methods with Taylor.   In the afternoons they visited homes and hospitals, while the evenings and Sunday were devoted entirely to evangelical work.   Within their first twelve months, they had conducted special missions at Pyrmont, Penrith, and Princes Street, and another year later had assumed full responsibility for Princes Street and were conducting missions as far afield as Queanbeyan.   They also gradually undertook work on the ships and wharves, in factories, and among the cabmen and warehouse caretakers of the city.[18]   Since it was only later that Taylor indicated in writing that his real object with the institute was to equip young men to pass the candidature examinations for the ministry, as well as to gain their assistance in the day-to-day work of the mission, we cannot be sure that he had this object in view from the start. However, it is probable that he did, given the theological element in their education. Many of his early evangelists became clergy. All provided a cheap, readily accessible, and responsive work-force for the less pleasant aspects of mission work and in return got a useful, if limited, education.

Like every other church before and since, the CMM relied heavily on women. Its Ladies' Sectional Committee of fifty ran a weekly mothers' meeting, to which the poor women of the western parts of Sydney were originally attracted through an enormous tea given to four hundred and fifty of them.[19] This was invaluable as an educational occasion for women who knew little about hygiene, cooking, and home care, or child-rearing. It was also an important social occasion for those whose lives were confined to filthy homes and the "pub". Similar work had been carried on in England for years. This same committee would later be important in establishing the first Methodist children's home in N.S.W.

The most significant work of the Ladies' Sectional Committee in this period related to something entirely new for Australian Methodism and of great importance to the work of the church: the inauguration of the "sisters of the people". The Catholic church had a long history of setting young women aside for full-time work in its various orders of sisters, whether to work in schools or hospitals, or to engage permanently in prayer and meditation. Protestantism had hesitated, probably because it was unwilling to follow the example of Rome, and because it did not like the vows of perpetual chastity which seemed a natural, and perhaps necessary, part of sisterhoods. The break had been made in Germany and the movement had spread to England in the 1850s. Anglicans in Australia had been talking about a sisterhood for some years before the CMM began but had done nothing. Taylor himself, while at the Glebe, had seen the need for one within Methodism and had sown the seed, but no one had been sufficiently interested to encourage its germination. In English Methodism, sisters had been employed for some time in T. B. Stephenson's Lambeth Children's Home, but that was a special case. The real beginning was at West London under Hugh Price Hughes, or rather his wife, who seems to have been the originator of the work. There, "sisters of the people" had been an important part of the mission's work almost from the beginning. Taylor had seen the sisters in action during his 1887–88 visit to England and had been impressed.[20] His "plan" for the Sydney CMM, revealed when he returned to York Street in April 1889, had included this item, but for a year nothing was done. Other matters were given higher priority and claimed not only his attention but all the available funds for the first fourteen months. But the stated plan had not been forgotten, either by Taylor or a young Grafton woman.

A few weeks after the release of Taylor's plan in 1889, he had received a letter from young Laura Francis of Grafton saying, "Is that [sister's] home ready? I want to come in as one of the Sisters". For her, his plan had appeared to be the call of God. But Taylor was busy with his Evangelists' Training Institute and told her that it would be a year or two before he could act on the sisters' home. Twelve months later, another letter from Grafton told him that the now-impatient Laura Francis would join the Salvation Army if her own Methodist church would not give her the opportunity for service which she wanted. This time it was Taylor who felt the divine call and he read the letter to his evening congregation and promised to engage Laura Francis if they would cover her costs for a year. They did and gave £76. Taylor now had to do what he should have done first: approach his Connexional Committee. The response seems to have been one of amusement: ' What are you going to do with the young woman when you get her?'' However, Ebenezer Vickery immediately promised a three-storey house (with six bedrooms) rent free for two years as a sisters' home provided it was furnished without charge on the general funds. Not too much should be made of this act of generosity, as housing was undoubtedly hard to let at satisfactory rentals during the depression and some necessary repairs and appointments were made by various firms without cost to Vickery. His assistance was crucial to the

CMM, but he was unlikely to have lost by it. Now he had the house, Taylor turned to his wife and her Ladies' Committee for help with the furnishings and they provided them within a fortnight. The opening of the home (4—5 August 1890) seems to have provided enough funds to operate it for the first year.[21]

Taylor's initial plan was to allow "young ladies of leisure" who were doing little real work for Christ to come into residence, perhaps only for a few months, and to work in the homes of the people, the hospitals, and the mission meetings then to go their way again. By the time it opened, he had realized that such a procedure would be of little value to the CMM and he was obviously hoping that his efforts would create a supply of "godly women" to work in the various city circuits. Taylor was no women's liberationist and he believed that the normal and natural sphere of service for woman was in the home "where she should have absolute power", but he claimed (without argument, which might have proved difficult) that it was Christianity which had raised the social and intellectual status of woman and had given her to man as "man's equal, man's helpmeet, man's counterpart". Catholic sisterhoods had done great work all over the world and there was room within Methodism for similar orders, though without any vows beyond those which any Christian woman might take. By this time, he saw their duties as including the visitation of the poor and sick, reading and praying with the sick and dying, trying to rescue "fallen women", giving temperance pledges to inebriates, helping at CMM services (especially among women and children), and arranging cottage services. The four who were received at the opening of the home (Mary Bibby, Laura Francis, Emily Gannon, and Ada Atkin) were consecrated in a service which had at least some of the major marks of the Wesleyan Ordination Service and they donned a "habit" which was described as "distinctive . . . not conspicuous . . . in every way becoming".[22]

The relative lack of public criticism in a church which, only six years before, had looked with disfavour on John Osborne for his untimely support of the church of Rome was surprising. But, for some, the portent was clear. Methodism was heading "Romewards". "An Observer of the Signs of the

Times" wrote to the editor of the *Maitland Mercury* that this was "the edge of the wedge", it was "doing evil that good may come". The next step would be "auricular confession", prayers for the dead, and purgatorial fines (a "goldmine" for the Methodist clergy). Much of the trouble came from using the word "sister", but Taylor argued that this had warmth and friendship in it whereas the alternatives, "Bible woman", "lady evangelist", or "deaconess" were all "too stiff and unhomelike". It would be folly to reject a good word just because the Catholics had chosen it. Despite this, perhaps only a man of Taylor's standing within the Wesleyan church could have got away with the name and innovation, even though it could be argued fairly that the female diaconate "savours of Romanism only in so far as Romanism savours of the New Testament". The Catholics may have modified it in unwarranted ways, but the Protestants had been just as unwarranted in ignoring it altogether to that point.[23]

Taylor was never short of recruits or funds for this work and within two or three months they had added gaol visitation and school instruction to their tasks. By the end of 1891 their number had risen to ten and Vickery had lent a larger and more suitable house in Crown Street, Woolloomooloo. By then, they were conducting special circuit missions in their own right (there had been more than a hundred converts at one), one was regularly assisting the Chippendale minister, another conducting regular services among the Chinese, and yet another was about to become the first missionary sister in New Guinea. Taylor had every right to be proud of his sisters.[24]

The continuing value of this work may be gauged by looking forward over the career of Laura Francis, the young Grafton woman who had forced Taylor's hand over the sisters' home. She stayed with the CMM six years, mainly involved in rescue work among women, then went to New Zealand as matron of a girls' rescue home. After that she took similar work in New York and in England and participated in the Welsh revival. When she returned home it was to become travelling evangelist for the CMM throughout N.S.W. In her declining years, she returned to hospital visitation and died in Waddell House on 1 December 1946 when the CMM had long passed its Diamond Jubilee.[25] Laura Francis was one of the two truly outstanding women of CMM history. (The work of the other, Deaconess Noreen Towers, is discussed later in the book.)

Taylor's attitude to the sisters of the people is interesting. He had seen their value in England but was prepared to let them wait on other, more vital, aspects of his work — the Seamen's Mission and the Evangelists' Training Institute, for example. His initial view of their function was circumscribed by a typically nineteenth century view of what was appropriate work for women. Yet he was prepared to let their role expand rapidly as the sisters showed their extraordinary resourcefulness and usefulness. With their work in the homes of the destitute and among fallen women, not to mention the preaching role which they rapidly assumed, they became the shock troops of the CMM and within two years of their inauguration they had proved correct Taylor's forecast that the opening of the sisters' home was likely to assume historic proportions.

The Pleasant Sunday Afternoon (PSA) movement will be discussed in detail later, though it began in this period. This was another project, along with the idea of a Saturday night concert, which Taylor had picked up from Hugh Price Hughes in London. Again it took twelve months to act on his plan, and the first PSA was not held until Sunday, 20 April 1890 when seven hundred "working men and their wives" (with men outnumbering women by five to one) listened to Taylor's lecture on the question "Why do not Working Men go to Church?" and voted to continue the movement. These services were freer in form and interested the men enough to bring many back to the evening service when conversions could take place. Typically, a young man so converted one week was out on the street helping at the open-air service the next Sunday. Other early topics included "Bad Times and How to Mend Them", "Legalised and Permitted Social Evils or Foul Blots upon our City Life", "The Englishman's Sunday" and "The Battle of Life". Numbers held up well with six to eight hundred often present. This continued

fourteen months after the inauguration of the PSA.[26] The
free concert on Saturday evening was never introduced,
perhaps because it would have interfered with the consecration service, which was considered to be of crucial importance. Instead, a midweek concert series began on Wednesday,
30 July 1890 with the object of drawing away young people
from "questionable pleasures". Eleven hundred attended,
most of them unchurched members of the inner-city working
class.[27] The size of the audience may reflect the lack of
public entertainment of any quality available in Sydney at
the time. The nature of the audience for this and the PSAs
suggests that both these gatherings provided effective means,
in the short term at least, of making contact with people, and
especially men, outside the normal ambit of the church.

That a church like the CMM would be caught up in general
philanthropic work was inevitable. Some "inquirers" early
became regulars at the penitential stool so they might receive
assistance. The great strike brought enormous suffering to
Sydney's manual workers and Taylor stepped into the
breach, recognizing the duty of Christian people to give aid
whether they approved of the strike or not. He also began in
1890 the practice of a Christmas Day "feast" for several
hundred poor, as well as the distribution of groceries, lollies,
and the like. His report for 1890 indicates that during that
year substantial quantities of food and clothing were distributed and money given to 452 needy people. Help was given
only to the "deserving poor". Even more interesting is an
apartment register, dated 1890, in which he recorded the
address, proprietor's name, details of accommodation, and
cost for sixty-nine lodginghouses, apparently in the attempt
to meet the need of those of limited means who enquired
after board.[28] All this was a small beginning to a very great
work which was to ensue.

It was out of this general philanthropy that Taylor's
limited work for the unemployed in this period sprang. On
7 February 1890 he attended a meeting of the unemployed
in the Temperance Hall and spoke of the real distress among
the working men of Sydney at the time, though he accepted

the view that drink was the root cause of the poverty of many. He was included in a deputation to the minister for public works, Bruce Smith, on 11 February, but that tough conservative would give no ground and advised the deputation to appeal to the public for funds for charitable relief. It was a view typical of nineteenth century conservatism and deserving of condemnation, but Taylor remained silent. In April he opened an employment agency at 83 Clarence Street, mainly with the intent of making known vacancies in the country. The *Daily Telegraph* published an article about his agency but its location appears to have made it a last resort and it placed only 147 people in employment in 1890. It was abandoned as a separate agency, though help continued to be given ad hoc. On 1 February 1891, Taylor again spoke out against unemployment and its consequent misery, sweating and drunkenness (which was still linked in his mind) and on 19 June he urged the Parkes government to establish labour bureaus in country districts to relieve the city of the abnormal pressures of unemployment so rife at that time, though such a measure would have been cosmetic only in its effects. He was included in a deputation to the premier.[29]

Linked with Taylor's general interest in the working man of Sydney was his opening of a free reading and writing room at Centenary Hall in about August/September 1889. This sought to make some provision for men from the neighbouring boardinghouses whose only alternative source of entertainment, or place where they could write a letter, was the hotel. Taylor's room was successful for a time, and was visited by "hundreds" of working men weekly during 1889, an average of thirty-five letters a day being written there. Eventually it became the resort of "loafers" who stole books and brought lice with them, driving out the men for whom it was intended. Taylor closed it briefly in mid-1890, destroyed the vermin, and reopened it as a workingman's club room with a fee of one shilling a quarter to keep out the undesirable.[30]

The serious and well-publicized larrikin problem may have been linked with the lack of facilities available to the youth of Sydney. That Taylor was concerned about it is certain. He appears to have had contact with a number of larrikin pushes and to have become aware of their procedures. His location in the west of the city where a number of the pushes operated made such contact natural. One of his priorities on his return to the CMM in 1889 was to tackle the youth question, both in general terms and specifically in relation to the larrikin. His Young Men's Sectional Committee met on 30 May 1889 to form a subcommittee to investigate starting both a literary and debating society and a boys' club, the object of the latter being "to provide harmless amusement and educational classes for the roughs of the city and to pave the way for higher influences". The work was to be left entirely to the young men of the CMM and such suburban supporters as they could muster.[31]

The contemporary record, which differs substantially from Taylor's own later recollections, suggests that a committee of sixty young men made arrangements for the opening meeting at least a fortnight in advance. Success greatly exceeded expectations and York Street was blocked well before 7.00 p.m. by "a crowd of lively and noisy but good-humoured boys" and police help was needed to control them. Eight hundred attended the tea and listened to Taylor's outline of his plans and to some homely advice. More boldly, the president of the club, a Mr Caldwell, managed to hold their attention for some minutes "whilst in homely terms he preached to them Jesus" — no mean feat. The very real and practical problem which arose from this was that the committee rooms at Centenary Hall which had been set aside for the club's use were quite inadequate and further action had to be delayed until two citizens' meetings (one chaired by the governor, Lord Carrington, and attended by the colonial treasurer and a number of other politicians) had been held to discuss the question. New rooms were found at 83 Clarence Street for what had now broadened out into a truly interdenominational boys' club to cover the entire district from Centenary Hall to Millers Point. Taylor had talked over the new club with the Boys' Brigade leaders who had a similar venture at 390 Sussex Street and there was to be no competition between the two. By the time the new

quarters had come into operation, a problem which was to
bedevil the club had already shown up: despite the large
committee (now said to be seventy), only about twenty were
really interested in working for the club and this could mean
an effective nightly presence of only three or four leaders,
totally inadequate to manage a large group of rough lads
scattered over three large rooms. There was also a potential
problem in the £275 rental for the premises, not to mention
the cost of furniture, gymnasium equipment, books, and
games. The whole made a heavy burden for the CMM with
its small and uncertain budget.[32]

There was later confirmation of the temporary success of
the club in a *Sydney Morning Herald* article by "Thelemiste"
(27 December 1889) which indicated that it had three
hundred members and an average nightly attendance of fifty.
Those eligible, on payment of threepence a month, were boys
from ten years up. There was a class studying for the civil
service examination while Thursday evening was given over
to entertainment. Order was well, but not rigidly, kept and
relations between the boys and the committee were good.
But Taylor and the assistant secretary, A. W. Anderson, were
both troubled by the lack of help from the young men of the
church and regarded the real work as being done by six or
eight only. While Taylor was pleased with the attendance of
forty or fifty lads at an informal Sunday evening service, he
was obviously worried about failure, in view both of the
financial commitment involved, and also the public commitment entailed by the August public meeting referred to
above.[33]

Towards the middle of 1890, the club did collapse briefly
and had to be reorganized on a new basis, with the women of
the church assuming a larger role in the place of the young
men of limited dedication. The new arrangement was better
and the influence of the ladies helped to subdue the larrikin
element. Writing in the *Sydney Morning Herald*, "The
Spectre" thought the use of the ladies very valuable. On
Monday night there was a lady at every table on the games
floor; attendance had improved; dress was better; swearing
had declined; and the boys were learning not to spit on the
floor. Lady Allen taught singing on Friday night and there

were classes in the three Rs, while on Thursday night the boys themselves gave a concert programme. Half those attending claimed to be Catholics. The only religious instruction was the voluntary service on Sunday evening when about sixty attended, a number which compared well with a week night average of seventy out of a claimed membership of two hundred. "Spectre" thought the work well done and that its good influence on the neighbourhood was visible. His only criticism was that it was run as a mission rather than as a true club. There was no membership fee and control was in the hands of a committee appointed by the CMM rather than one chosen from among the boys themselves. The *Evening News* also praised the club for seeking to make useful citizens of many who would otherwise be only "excrescences and blots on the community".[34]

The work was still strong at the end of 1890, but by August 1891 the club was almost defunct, though one section of it was still functioning. Later that year it collapsed completely due, it was said, "in large part to the action of certain larrikin organisations hostile to the work of the club". Some of its erstwhile members had joined the newly formed Young Men's Club at the mission, which demanded good moral character of those admitted. It was really designed for the young men from the boardinghouses rather than the larrikins from the Clarence Street push. Taylor could only console himself that he would save the rent on the Clarence Street property and that was poor consolation for an evangelical, even one in a financial strait-jacket.[35]

A club "admissions book" survives. Its contents are difficult to interpret, but it is possible to draw some tentative conclusions from them. Only 134 are recorded as enrolling at the initial tea, rather than the 350 Taylor remembered thirty years later. By mid-September the number was 238 and a slow trickle continued for another six weeks until a new enrolment was undertaken on 1 November 1889. At this stage 283 members were listed. There was a further "new enrolment" on 7 April 1891 when 127 registered, though there is a separate list of 56 names at the back of the book which may belong with that registration. (A problem arises from the fact that their registration numbers are not continuous with those of any of the registrations though the type of detail given coincides more closely with the third registration.) If this is correct it would give a total of 183, close enough to the "about 200" being claimed by mid-1891. The first and second enrolments give name, age, address, and sometimes occupation. The third gives only name and, in some but not all cases, address. The average age at admission appears to have been about fifteen years and most fell into the range fourteen to sixteen years, though the extremes were ten and twenty-one years. The occupations listed include newsboy, bootmaker, jockey, confectioner, printer, dealer, watchmaker, carpenter, saddler, powder factoryhand, engine driver, labourer, tobacco twister, signwriter, butcher, storekeeper, plumber, wine store hand, and, of course, unemployed. In the first enrolment no particular occupation stood out for its large numbers, but very few were listed as schoolboys, though some whose occupation was unlisted were young enough to belong to that category. The second enrolment included a higher percentage of schoolboys and less unlisted occupations, while printers seemed to stand out as the largest employed group. Perhaps a "sorting" process was occurring which retained the better educated and disposed of at least some of the others. This would also tie in with the improved deportment being commented upon. Most of the addresses which were listed (and not all were) were inner city: Kent, Sussex, Princes, Hart, and Cumberland Streets and Millers Point. There was a handful from Woolloomooloo, Redfern, and Ultimo, one from the Glebe, and one from the North Shore. The club was contacting boys in its 'home" area as intended. This may also help with the interpretation of the hostility of certain larrikin pushes which Taylor regarded as responsible for the breaking up of the club. These could have been from other parts of the city, or the suburbs, and jealous of the advantage being given to the pushes in the Centenary Hall sphere of influence.

Each enrolment has one boy marked "expelled" or "forcibly expelled". If these were the only boys from such a rough group who had to be ejected then it is a truly remarkable record, but it is impossible to be certain. Similar uncertainty hangs over three people in the second enrolment marked "workers", but it may be reasonable to assume that they became workers through their membership of the club and perhaps they were numbered among the few converts Taylor won in this way. The only other fact which may be gleaned from the "admissions book" is that a badge was required for admission, evidence that some attempt was made to exercise a genuine control and, perhaps, to keep rival pushes apart.[36]

It seems unlikely that his club contributed as much to the decline of larrikinism as Taylor hoped it would. The story of Teenage Cabaret in the 1960s will show that inner-city youth work has remained difficult, even when adequate experience and help is available.

There had always been a fear about the financial viability of the CMM and Taylor vowed to work it without debt. The problem was compounded by the heavy debt on the Centenary Hall. At the opening, the Hon. E. Vickery indicated a need to reduce the debt by £10,000 in the first two years if the burden were to be tolerable. This was not done and the burden remained oppressive. It became fashionable to say that Centenary Hall should not have been built, that it was Conference's delusions of grandeur which had forced this scheme on the CMM when all that was needed was a modest scheme of alteration to and enlargement of the old building as planned by Taylor himself and costing about £2,000. Taylor and his supporters were always anxious to sheet home to the Executive of the Church Sustentation and Extension Society and to the Conference, the blame for the burden which Centenary Hall became, though he once admitted that it was the economic circumstances which had developed so soon afterwards, rather than the decision itself, which caused the problem and that the buildings themselves were a matter of pride.[37]

There were serious problems about the decision to pull down old York Street and to rebuild completely on the same site. The most serious was how to retain the congregation built up in three years of successful effort while operating from a building which would seat only 200. Even that problem was compounded by the removal of Taylor to England for one year and then to William Street, where he was partly in competition with York Street. The other problem which must puzzle the historian, for there is no solution to it, concerns the reasoning behind the decision to create a block of buildings suited to central mission work some three years before the final decision had been taken to pursue the central mission concept. This could lead to either of two conclusions: that the euphoria created by Taylor's early revival of York Street aroused a strong immediate sentiment in favour of the central mission concept which, predictably but illogically, partly evaporated during the time of difficulty which Conference itself foisted upon the church, or that Taylor's opponents never really had more than the power to delay and that the ultimate victory of the central mission concept was always more certain than it appeared to be on the surface. The former explanation appears the more likely. Those problems apart, it is not really difficult to see why the decision to tear down the old and to build the new Centenary Hall was taken. Bollen has made out a strong case for the view that the ethos of nineteenth century Australian Protestant Christianity in general, and Methodism in particular, was numerical expansion and physical building. Wesleyan Methodism provided 10,000 sittings in 63 chapels in 1850 and 71,459 in 460 chapels with an additional 32,860 in 579 preaching places in 1900.[38] That was building with a vengeance, and the Centenary Hall project was a natural and important part of it. Add to that the general community expansion in the 1880s and Centenary Hall becomes almost inevitable. That the N.S.W. Conference was following the example of the Oldham Street, Manchester church is clear from comments made at the time about similarities between the two buildings. In addition, Conference was aware of the unsuitability of parts of the old building for their functions — the schoolrooms were notoriously dungeon-like — and it did have the intention, sensible enough for the times, of using attached warehouses as a means of paying for the whole building and hence virtually supplying the church and rooms for philanthropic purposes without charge to the Connexion. To expect Conference to foresee the forthcoming depression at a time when few others did is unreasonable, and criticism of the Centenary Hall project on financial grounds springs largely from wisdom acquired after the event.

None of this alters the fact that in the economic conditions which developed in the early 1890s the income from hall hire and the warehouses was drastically reduced so that, rather than the trust giving help and support to the mission, it was the other way about, and money had to be diverted each year from the proper work of the mission to the upkeep of the buildings and even to meet the interest burden. Despite Taylor's best efforts, there was usually a small deficit in those early years which could not be removed even by the most determined "self-denial" campaigns, which became a regular annual feature of the mission's life. The CMM was drawing little financial support from outside its own boundaries — in 1891 almost 85 per cent of its income was internal, if the official figures are correct. At least the early fears of its becoming a financial drain on the rest of the Connexion were not being justified, but that was a poor consolation to the hard-pressed superintendent, who had to devote a large proportion of his time and energy to raising money rather than to his real work. Occasionally he might take the Connexion to task, but that altered little.[39] Wesleyans were probably unable and unwilling to change their traditional pattern of giving to the local circuit and also unable to comprehend the representative nature of the CMM.

The overdraft at the end of 1892 was only £668/16/11, small enough to the modern mind, but desperately hard to remove in the conditions of the time. Faced with the certainty that the debt could only increase and the knowledge that the fine buildings associated with the Centenary Hall were a serious and growing embarrassment, the 1893 Conference considered its options: the sale of Centenary Hall; raising money by special services in all circuits; the sale of Hay and Princes Street churches. The first would have left the CMM without a home (thus effectively ending its brief career) without removing the debt entirely, as the property was unlikely to realize its full value in the depressed conditions prevailing. A committee was appointed to report on the future management of the CMM, and other related matters, and Taylor was given authority to visit all circuits in N.S.W. and to visit Great Britain and the U.S.A. to raise funds to reduce the debt. It meant sending a new man to the CMM for some time. The one chosen was the Rev. Rainsford Bavin, a former New Zealander who had already made his mark as an evangelical.[40]

Taylor would be absent from the CMM for five years, first in England and the U.S.A. on his money-raising expedition for two years, then Conference would send him to Bathurst for three years, during one of which he was president of the N.S.W. Wesleyan Methodist Conference. Bavin was his replacement for three years, then the Rev. W. Woolls Rutledge followed for two. Clearly there was a danger at this time that the three-year itinerancy rule was reasserting itself and it is curious to observe the unwillingness of Taylor's colleagues to give up this principle in the face of what was now a well-established English example. Old customs linger on at the periphery long after they yield at the centre and when they have become obstructive rather than constructive.

Taylor was later to describe this interregnum as a period of nonachievement when important agencies went into decline and contributed nothing to the CMM cause. He was careful to explain that the blame for this lay not with Bavin and Rutledge but with the impossible financial burdens they had to endure.[41] This picture was only partly true and Taylor's own frustration at not being at the heart of things may have coloured this view. Both problems and progress must be reviewed in context.

4

The End of the Beginning

Taylor left Sydney on his overseas mission with all the fanfare that Sydney Methodism could muster. There was a luncheon at Centenary Hall on 5 April, chaired by the president, and a lecture on 17 April. He was given letters of commendation and introduction by the lieutenant-governor, the premier, the mayor, the U.S. consul, and an assortment of other people. Some CMM workers hired a launch to follow his ship to the Heads with the CMM brass band blaring its farewell across the Harbour.

Taylor wanted to raise £10,000. An address to the English Conference and articles about the Sydney CMM in the church papers opened the way to a busy schedule of meetings. Yet on his return he had to present a disastrous balance sheet: income £2,184/13/6; expenditure £863/3/7; credit balance £1,321/9/11; additional promises unpaid at that time £1,081/8/2. In the U.S.A. he had met with coldness and sometimes there had been protests against his visiting for such a reason. Yet Taylor could easily comfort himself with the knowledge that he had won almost two thousand converts — "enough to cause one gratitude for the rest of his life".[1]

None of it was surprising. The English and Americans could hardly be expected to give money to a far-off cause of which they knew little. Englishmen who were familiar with Australian affairs generally might well have wondered to what extent the problems of the CMM were self-inflicted. Taylor was so much an evangelist that, no matter how desperately he needed money, he could never put silver before souls. Yet it was as well he had won so many converts, otherwise the two-year absence to raise so little money might

well have seemed a dubious expenditure of time — it
certainly did nothing to ease the financial burdens of the
CMM.

At home, the CMM workers voted themselves a pay cut
just before Taylor left for England and every possible form
of expenditure reduction was practised, but such measures
could not cope with the growing deficit, the actual dimen-
sions of which are not always easy to determine exactly. The
1894 Conference resolved to give the mission an interest-free
loan of £10,000 from its own Rev. William Schofield Loan
Fund, provided that the property debt did not exceed
£32,000 at the end of 1894 and that the overdraft on the
current account had been liquidated. That eased the interest
burden without reducing the principal of the debt. It was
reported to the 1898 Conference that the debt was as
follows: mortgage at 4 per cent, £15,000; owed to Schofield
Fund, £8,625; owed to Bright Estate (another Methodist
loan fund), £9,750; total debt, less cash in hand, £32,946.[2]

The problem was beginning to arouse dissension within
Wesleyan ranks.[3] In a letter to the *Methodist* from Bathurst
(29 January 1898) Taylor referred to a series of "carefully
formulated suggestions" he had made to the Centenary Hall
trustees some months before but to which he had received
no response. Unless something drastic were done, the York
Street property would be lost. The CMM was not fulfilling
its purpose: once-active branches were now scarcely alive
and there was little aggressive spiritual development. By this
time the CMM should have controlled one or two of the
leading city theatres for its Sunday services. "I have long had
the impression that, rightly handled, this mission should be
the feeder of every circuit; a help, both financially and
spiritually, to the whole connexional machinery". The reason
for failure lay neither in the superintendent nor the committee but in the need to pay £800 a year from mission funds
toward trust expenses. The situation had to be improved so
that the mission could work effectively, like those in
Melbourne and England. If Conference would not do this, it
must end the mission, and in so doing cover itself with
shame.

Rutledge, angered at the accusation that some branches of

the mission had been allowed to run down, raised some charges of his own. When he had gone to the CMM he had found that it had only a limited hold on the people of Sydney and the Methodists of N.S.W. and that it had never paid its way. Earlier deficits had been heavier than those in his own time. Taylor argued later that the CMM had always paid its way and still did as far as expenses properly chargeable to the current account were concerned and that the deficit was only the result of making contributions to the interest payments. In the long run, that was a mere quibble.

Taylor's concern was real, but his letter did bear some of the marks of being the first shot in a campaign to get Conference to reinstate him at York Street now that his term at Bathurst was ending and a year before Rutledge would have expected to move. There was just a hint of the view that there was only one man who could run the affairs of the CMM satisfactorily. The tone of the reference to city theatres was surprising, given that he appears not to have raised the subject before, though the concept was well known in England and the U.S.A. and he had probably become acquainted with it in London on one of his two visits.

Conference held a long debate on the CMM. A few conservatives urged that it was of no great value, was not wanted by the people, and should be abolished, but they never appeared likely to succeed. Hay Street and Pyrmont churches were created a separate circuit, the mission's own paper, the *Gazette*, was incorporated in the *Methodist*, while an appeal from the superintendent to the Methodists of N.S.W. for financial assistance was endorsed and debt repayments to the Schofield and Bright funds were rescheduled.[4]

This was all very depressing and might be thought to justify Taylor's charges referred to above. Yet the overall position was less bleak and during the interregnum there had been important positive developments which bear examination.[5]

Evangelical effort had not slackened. Accounts of conversions still abound, and it appears that they occurred at almost every evangelical service. A special mission, under the well-known Australian evangelist, John Watsford, was held in August 1893 but the CMM gained little as most of the converts came from other circuits. Some of the antagonistic attended the meetings to disrupt them. A few of these were converted, but the CMM missions suffered from the same limitations as others: those already at least marginally within the church might be moved to deeper commitment but the true outsider was rarely won. There was great rejoicing a year later when a well-known free-thought lecturer was converted at an ordinary CMM service.

Open-air services increased to twelve per week. CMM evangelists continued to assist in other circuits near and far and the workers' conference was still well attended. A new and significant bright spot in the life of the mission was the Bible class started on Sunday afternoon by Mrs Bavin, originally for young women only, but eventually for adults of all ages and both sexes. With an attendance of fifty-four after eight months it was showing strength and was a genuine replacement for the long defunct class run by W. Davies in the early days of the CMM.

The Seamen's Institute suffered in this period because the missionary of long standing, H. D. Gilbert, left to go to South Africa. There was no satisfactory permanent full-time replacement until Gilbert returned in March 1898. While there was a problem with funds, it is unlikely that this downgrading would have occurred had Gilbert remained. The unrelated work among "bluejackets" continued unabated. Sick visiting and police court work continued, a theology and homiletics class for evangelists, sisters, and local preachers began, and a Christian Endeavour group flourished. Class meetings, bands, the midday businessmen's service on Tuesday and Thursday, and the Workingmen's Club were maintained. Temperance and philanthropic work continued. Young women's and young men's clubs were formed, a tearoom was opened for factory and shop girls at lunchtime but was not as successful as expected. A Converted Gamblers' and Drunkards' Brigade was also formed. The PSA, which seems to have ceased at some unknown date before Taylor left the mission, had a brief and spasmodic revival. More importantly, the numbers and work of the sisters of the people were fully maintained and their efforts increasingly appreciated by the church and the community. Their courageous work filled a gap which could not have been filled in any other way.

There was at least one positive initiative of great significance for the future during this period. Although Taylor's 1889 plan for the CMM contained no reference to a children's home, the sisters undoubtedly contacted many neglected children and it is likely that there was talk about future provision for such children. However, the practical impulse which led to the first Methodist children's home in N.S.W. being established by the CMM actually resulted from the imminent collapse of a Dorcas Society associated with the William Street church. Rev. J. A. Nolan and his wife thought its work for the children of the poor too important to be allowed to disappear and during 1893 asked Mrs Bavin that the Ladies' Sectional Committee of the CMM take it over. This was done and Mrs Bavin thereafter became the driving force and was responsible for acceptance of the home concept. Bavin announced the intention to begin this work in September 1893.

Reaction in the church paper was mixed. The concept of "rescue work" for children won immediate and complete support, but some wondered whether the CMM should expand its operations at a time when it was suffering from financial constraints. It might be better to strengthen existing agencies first. Some thought that this work should be left to the state, since it was already involved with it, while others argued that, as the issue involved connexional policy and finance, the Conference should have been consulted. Bavin and his colleague, James Colwell, arrogantly rejected all advice and criticisms and insisted that they wanted only the prayers and the money of the people. At the opening, on 31 October 1893, Bavin criticized N.S.W. Methodists sharply for being slow to follow Wesley's example and pointed out that each of the denominations in Victoria had a home despite state provision. The children's home did not need Conference approval because it was only an extension of the work of the sisterhood. God had opened a door to the ladies and they must accept His guidance. Other branches of the mission would not suffer.[6]

Although Bavin and Colwell were implicitly claiming for themselves and the mission understanding of the divine will not vouchsafed to others, their expectations of help were fulfilled. Children proved to be a favourite charity. A fourteen-roomed house at 104 Woolloomooloo Street was provided rent free by Ebenezer Vickery and was furnished without cost to the Ladies' Committee. Within four months of opening, the home had a matron, thirteen children (maximum capacity was twenty), and £90 in the bank. Companies supplied some goods and services free, Sunday schools responded to a request to help, and individuals were persuaded to "adopt" a child (six shillings a week kept one fully and 2/6 clothed one). A parent who could contribute something to the upkeep of a child in the home was expected to do so. By 1898 the home had drawn two government grants of £100 each, a mark of official approval. The children were sent to local schools if old enough, trained in domestic duties, and generally fitted to earn their own living at a later stage. Many were adopted out to Christian homes, especially in the country. By 1897 the Ladies' Committee was looking for land in "the country" for extensions to their home.[7]

No less necessary, but more controversial, was the Medical Institute (or Retreat) established under W. W. Rutledge for the treatment of alcoholics. The CMM had always been interested in temperance work and Taylor and others had fulminated against the evils of drink from its platforms. The pledge book was always available at services and the mission had its own Social Reform League which met monthly. Through this body, the CMM joined in the pressure group activities associated with the electoral campaigns of the period. But in late 1896 or very early 1897, Rutledge had the opportunity to do something more positive and constructive. Dr. C. Harrison Dukes of the Oaklands Institute, California, visited N.S.W. to promote the "cure" he had devised for alcoholism. Rutledge investigated his credentials and decided to experiment with the cure which was said to be simple. The patient entered the retreat (at first at Sir John Young Crescent, Lower Domain, later at Stanmore, and

W. Woolls Rutledge, CMM superintendent 1896–98. By courtesy of the Wesley Central Mission.

then Warren Heights), received four hypodermic injections daily of a "vegetable compound" and four daily doses of a tonic and then was allowed to live a normal life, even drinking liquor if he wished. The treatment was claimed to cause aversion to liquor and to restore the patient's will-power by an increase of physical strength. It usually took about three or four weeks.[8]   This description leaves the actual nature of the cure vague, but it may have involved very large doses of certain vitamins.

Publicly, the retreat received a warm welcome. The *Daily Telegraph* thought there could be nothing "more worthy of a Christian Church" than this attempt to release men from degradation. It also praised the church for recognizing that sufferers needed medical help rather than punishment or preaching. The *Evening News* also made a favourable editorial reference. However, the very people who should have helped did not. After thirty months Taylor reported angrily that not one patient had been referred there by any temperance body. Neither they nor most of the Bands of Hope contributed anything towards the scheme for free beds for the poor which he had hoped to maintain. Consequently this scheme broke down entirely and the retreat was often short of patients: it was "almost without patients" in mid-1899 and early 1900, though, curiously, it had been full (its capacity was twenty) in late 1899. In fact, it must rarely have operated near capacity as its average annual number of patients in the eight years 1897–1904 (inclusive) was thirty-nine, with a high of fifty-one in 1898 and a low of twenty-four in 1900 and 1901. Since most of the patients were only short term, the number at any given time must have been low.[9]

The institute had a chequered career. Of the 310 who passed through it in the period 1897–1904 most were men (89 per cent). Women were "difficult", unwilling to admit their problem, and intractable to discipline. Most were from the city. All ranks of society were represented, from ordinary working people to doctors, lawyers, and clergy (no Methodists!) Patients were from all denominations, though the largest group were Catholics, and no religious pressure was exerted. Charges depended on the length of stay, ability to pay, and the actual services provided, though the average charge was in the range £13—20. Both Taylor and Rutledge admitted many failures, Rutledge suggested 25—30 per cent, because no attempt was made to force a person's will. There were many claims of cures. These came not only from the church, which was always guarded in its claims, but from people who had been treated and employers who had sent men there rather than dismiss them. Henry Fowler Cotterell, proprietor of the *Bulli Times,* willingly and publicly attested to his own cure.[10]

A further article in the *Daily Telegraph* of 9 January 1904 disclosed the fact that the CMM Medical Retreat was the only home licensed under the N.S.W. Inebriates Act. It favourably contrasted the advanced thinking at the CMM, which recognized that at times purely moral means were inadequate to defeat alcoholism and that a medical approach was necessary, with the view of the Salvation Army that a cure was only possible through conversion and that medicine must not be substituted for faith in God.

The same enlightened attitude was taken by, and probably required of, the staff of the retreat.[11] Such thinking was far ahead of that common in the Protestant churches of the day and this must account for the complete unwillingness of the temperance organizations to cooperate with a progressive experiment in the treatment of a major social disease. For them, the liberal view that the drunkard was in the grip of a disease, rather than of sin, and that he needed help and medication rather than punishment and preaching was too much, even without the theological implications of accepting that a solution other than personal salvation was necessary. That Taylor was actually prepared to provide patients with alcohol as long as they still sought it was a final, shattering blow. The consequence was the ultimate failure of the retreat. The last reference appears to be a resolution of thanks to its medical superintendent, Dr W. C. McClelland, passed at the 1907 Conference.[12]

It is interesting to contrast the relative failure of the Sydney CMM retreat with the more enduring success of that run by the Melbourne CMM at the same period. The Melbourne institution opened in 1900 when the CMM took over

Dr Wolfenden's Bichloride of Gold Institute at Jolimont. The treatment, which came to be recognized by the Medical Society of Victoria, again sought to end the craving for drink. The institute was still operating as late as 1918 but no attempt has been made to trace it further.[13] The historian of the Melbourne CMM makes no comment on the attitude of the temperance societies there.

It was during Bavin's time that the Sydney CMM first became connected with work among the Chinese. A man named Coffey began this work in a small house in Sackville Street on 4 July 1894 and a month or two later it came under CMM control. There were two aspects to the work. The first was a night school, operating Monday to Thursday evening, primarily to teach English to the Chinese. This started with a dozen students and six teachers. A year later, sixty students were said to have passed through it, though actual attendance at that time is unknown. This fed the evangelical work and may be said to have made the latter possible. Here Coffey was helped by a Chinese Methodist preacher, David Shing, and a Miss L. McWilliams. The work grew and by August 1895 consisted of a singing class Friday evening, a Sunday morning class meeting with six members, followed by a Bible class with ten to fifteen members. There was also a 2.30 p.m. service with an average of twenty-nine attending. After this, Coffey, Shing, and Miss McWilliams visited Chinese business houses and gambling dens to get people out to a 6.30 p.m. street service at which the congregation might range from fifty to a hundred and fifty. At 7.30 p.m. a further service drew forty to eighty and was followed, in true CMM style, by an after-meeting. There had been few conversions and only one baptism, but an influence was being exercised.[14]

When Taylor returned to the mission in 1898, he made his dissatisfaction public. The Evangelists' Training Institute was almost empty, the Medical Retreat was taking too much of the superintendent's time, he had to spend eight to ten hours daily directing the spiritual and other work and preach to the largest congregation in N.S.W. on Sunday, yet he had no ministerial colleague.   He was being asked to bear a burden not imposed upon the missioners in Melbourne, England, or the U.S.A.   The debt on current account was over £1,300. If he could not remove that in a year, he would resign.   He wanted to raise £1,000 outside the CMM and £300 by an internal self-denial effort.   It was a threat he would not carry out.   The debt had been reduced by the next Conference, but it was far from removed.   There was no mention of the resignation.[15]

There was a continuing surge in the evening congregation. By mid-November two thousand were packing into the hall, despite the heat created by the gas-lighting.   Hundreds remained for the after-meeting.   By April 1899, the CMM was at its wits' end to know what to do with the people who were sitting in the gallery aisles, on the rostrum, and even on the steps leading up to it.   At Christmas and the New Year Taylor tried the experiment of a second (8.15 p.m.) service in the Opera House.   The mission band played on the balcony from 7.45 p.m., then the indoor service was made as bright as possible with much hymn singing and a brief message.   On Christmas Day the Opera House was packed with almost one thousand people: "The dregs of the street were there — drunks and n'er do wells, flash girls and larrikins in the pits. In the stalls were many of a slightly higher grade.   But even a casual observer could see that here was a congregation of non-churchgoers.   No church had been depleted to fill this theatre."   The congregation was only a little smaller on New Year's Day.   No mention of conversions was made in connection with the Christmas service, but there were two at the New Year.   Attendance at Centenary Hall was not affected on either occasion.[16]

This was wonderful news for the CMM.   It was able to make first contact successfully with the lowest levels of urban society when it worked on "neutral ground".   This latter concept was not new but had been tried in England and even by Taylor himself in his Queensland days.   However, Taylor could not be expected to take two Sunday evening services on a regular basis.   Nor could the CMM continue to depend on a private individual for the Opera House rent.

The task imposed on Taylor was really beyond the

capacity of one man to bear. The Melbourne CMM had three ministers and an organizing secretary. For this reason, in 1899, he refused an invitation for a further year if conditions remained unchanged. The committee immediately employed a lay assistant and Taylor agreed to stay and began to plan expansion. Minutes of staff meetings held during 1900 suggest that others began to take some of the burden of decision making and direction from his shoulders.[17] Meanwhile the need to turn people away from the CMM continued to attest its success, as did the 1902 decision to create the Newcastle CMM in its image. It was also about this time that the governor of N.S.W. first became a regular attender at special mission services, a clear sign that the mission and its work were now widely recognized within the community. The recipe for success remained unaltered: intense concentration on the spiritual life of the church, especially prayer.[18]

Taylor remained conscious of the need for a permanent neutral venue, a regular theatre service. The twenty-first anniversary, on Sunday 28 May 1905, saw the beginning of the move to the Lyceum. A gathering was held there in the afternoon and a lantern service at night, in addition to the usual service at Centenary Hall. In August–September that year, the old theatre saw a successful evangelical campaign and was filled nightly.[19]

By the 1906 Conference, not only were the Lyceum services a proven success, but CMM membership was up to 633, despite the fact that it was little more than a "clearinghouse" for converts, with most passing on to other churches. Taylor remained convinced that he was working among the "submerged tenth" of the city, the "flotsam and jetsam" of society, and that 75 per cent of his congregation would attend no church if they did not go to the CMM. He was proud of what had been achieved and was determined to continue to advance "until the devil's kingdom was smashed up". His greatest worry remained the indisputable fact that N.S.W. Methodists would not support his work as they should have. It always puzzled him that while his mission was well known and appreciated and was having its effect on the life of the city, his own people would not part with their money to put the work on a really firm footing. Yet, with some justification, his faith remained firm, for by this time the CMM was running not only its ordinary evangelistic and worship services, but a PSA, guilds of service for young men and women, a variety of social and philanthropic agencies which included men's shelters, women's rescue homes, a children's home, factory visitation, luncheon- and tea-rooms, a people's bank, a legal aid system, as well as educational lectures and dressmaking classes. The Sunday evening service often filled the Lyceum with a congregation of 2,500.[20]

The impact of the CMM on the community was again made evident in mid-1909 when the *Sydney Morning Herald* heaped lavish praise on it and concluded that "from the civic point of view is of vast importance and has won golden opinions in the country". It found all the institutions to have value but attached particular merit to those dealing with fallen women and with children and it praised the "boundless horizons" of the Executive Committee and pointed out that every N.S.W. government had taken an interest in the work.[21]

An anniversary tea at this time drew about 2,550 to the Town Hall on a wet night while, at the meeting which followed, hundreds had to be turned away from the overflowing hall. The guest speaker and former prime minister, George Reid, commented, "I had no idea there were so many Christians in Sydney". Of course, he probably had little regular contact with them. Public figures did not always really understand the work of the CMM and, on another occasion, a state treasurer, Mr Cann, described it as "one of the best moral policemen roaming the city".[22]

The major development of this period was the removal from Centenary Hall, York Street to the Lyceum Theatre, Pitt Street, the site of the CMM ever since. According to Taylor, Ebenezer Vickery told him one day that he had long wanted to do something for the CMM and that his plan included the purchase or erection of a large hall to replace Centenary Hall, which had become too small. He also had a long list of suggestions for activities. He took Taylor to inspect a building that morning but it proved too small to be useful. In the afternoon they inspected the Lyceum and Taylor told Vickery to buy it. Vickery demurred because the price was higher than he had intended to pay but Taylor replied, "Never mind, you have got the money and can afford it. This is the chance of a lifetime". So the Lyceum theatre passed into Vickery's hands with its 70,000 square feet of floor space, two halls (the larger seating twenty-five hundred), and 130 rooms.[23]

As Taylor told the story, Vickery always intended that the Lyceum should pass almost immediately into the hands of the CMM for its sole use and as its headquarters. But Vickery's intention was much less clear at the time and it will be as well to look at the acquisition and transfer of the Lyceum in some detail.

On 15 April 1905, the *Methodist* recorded Vickery's purchase of the Lyceum, an adjoining hotel, and land running back from Pitt Street to Castlereagh Street on which stood a notorious two-up school and two cottages used as brothels. An enemy fortress had been captured, and while the *Methodist* did not know what Vickery intended to do with it, the use would be social and moral and a great improvement on the past. On 8 July it indicated that Vickery would not work the theatre in rivalry with any existing Christian organization: the CMM was in charge of Sunday night work and was already gathering a congregation of fifteen hundred, mostly men, without harming its Centenary Hall service. August 1905 saw the CMM sponsor a twenty-day mission there, led by the Rev. Dan O'Donnell. The challenge was unmistakeable: "The Lyceum is situated in the very centre of the gambling, drinking, unclean district of our great metropolis. To reach that dreadful centre and to purify it for Christ, is a call that knocks loudly at the heart of every lover of his country." Battle was being carried right into the enemy heartland and every method characteristic of the CMM would be used.[24]

A change of venue for the CMM had become important by the end of 1905, when a report to the Legislative Council of N.S.W. named Centenary Hall "one of the most dangerous [buildings] in the city" and "unsuitable for the reception of an audience" because of the fire risk. Worse, the CMM Committee had ignored a request to make alterations, apparently choosing to take advantage of a loophole which made the law on public halls unenforceable. The Parliamentary Committee was not much happier about Vickery's failure to make changes to the Lyceum while still allowing "public entertainments" there.[25]   Action was painfully slow and the Methodist Connexional Premises Committee first tried unsuccessfully to have the demands of the Theatres Inspection Committee modified.   In May 1906, it decided to sell Centenary Hall, though it later held over action on this until it had contacted Vickery, absent in England, and asked him to exchange the Lyceum for the Centenary Hall since the only sites in the city regarded as suitable for a new CMM were close to the Lyceum and activities at the two missions might clash.   Vickery was unenthusiastic.   He favoured selling the Centenary Hall site once legislation closed the loophole which allowed its continued use against the recommendation of the Theatres Inspection Committee, though in the meantime he preferred its continued use.   If all else failed he might consider the exchange.   The Connexional Premises Committee continued to look for a site and almost settled on one between Elizabeth and Castlereagh Streets at a cost of £14,500, but that too was sidetracked.   Meanwhile the situation was altered by Vickery's death in Leeds on 20 August 1906.[26]

Before his departure from Sydney, Vickery had settled the Lyceum on four trustees (members of his own family). They were to hold the property until 1915, using it for evangelical and philanthropic work, then, in the centenary year of Methodism, it was to be conveyed to the Methodist church for similar use, or the site sold and the money invested for such work.[27]   Negotiations were immediately begun between the Connexional Premises Committee and the Lyceum Trust over the leasing of the premises for CMM purposes.   A lease was signed on 1 February 1907, though alterations still had to be effected and the property could not be occupied for some time.   The CMM would have a main hall to seat about twenty-five hundred, a second hall for five to six hundred, a block of buildings in Castlereagh Street which included four shops, Home and Foreign Mission offices, a presidential room, classrooms, and other offices.[28]

Taken together, all this leaves little doubt that it was not Vickery's original intention to allow the Lyceum to fall immediately into the hands of the CMM.   Probably he saw it as an extra Christian agency in the city and intended, while in England, to persuade the Rev. H. Biseker, a prominent evangelical, to work there. This view is supported by the remark of the retiring president, Rev. J.G.M. Taylor, at the 1907 Conference, that a solution to the problem of finding a home for the York Street mission had come in an "unexpected way" in that Vickery's death had brought the Lyceum into the hands of the trustees who had been willing to lease the premises to the CMM.

Years later, in 1945, E. Frank Vickery, a grandson of Ebenezer, offered an alternate account which suggests that the purchaser intended the Lyceum mission to be conducted as a separate institution, in cooperation with the York Street mission, but free from Conference control.[29] There is no real contradiction here. Certainly the property was to come as a centennial gift to Methodism in 1915, and in view of the terms imposed, it was likely that it would be used as an adjunct to the CMM, or as a second such institution, but there is no evidence at all to support Taylor's own account of the purchase.

For several months Taylor had been planning the use of the improved facilities offered by the Pitt Street building. Apart from the auditorium and the enlarged office space, he foresaw a boarding home for Methodist visitors from the country, rooms for workingmen, a cheap restaurant, homes for both evangelists and sisters, a roof garden for open-air meetings, and possibly a "great central brotherhood" holding Sunday afternoon meetings and other week-night gatherings.

Alterations were finally completed and the Lyceum opened under CMM auspices in April 1908. The *Sydney Morning Herald* recorded that the capacity was "altogether inadequate" for the opening evening service, that one thousand remained to the after-meeting, and that there were thirty to forty inquirers. A more religious writer recorded the "manifest presence of the Holy Spirit".[30]

General work among men made only limited progress in the period under discussion. Mid-September 1898 saw the formation of a Crusader group among young men (one for young women was formed later), members of which pledged themselves to evangelical service among their contemporaries, but there was no evidence of great success. A new Lyceum Boys' Club was started in 1906, but its work is unrecorded. A 1904 appeal to the young men of Methodism to give money to a property where larrikins might be instructed in farm work came to nothing. One interesting development, which did have impact, was the "Two-up School Mission" (1906), an evangelical work among the gamblers of the Lyceum area and the forerunner of Charlie Woodward's famous Friday night men's meeting (founded about 1914).

The mission had always involved itself with general philanthropic work for the poor, having found that the best way to reach some people was to mend the leaks in their boots. Apart from special Christmas efforts, the work remained ad hoc and was rescue rather than preventative in nature. Acquisition of the Lyceum allowed the establishment of a number of low-priced accommodation centres for working men in Castlereagh and Kent Streets, and later at Woolloomooloo, along with facilities for cheap meals. There were also quarters for the unemployed, a Working Girls' Institute, and a Labour and Registry Department.[31]

Quite separately, a little earlier, the construction of Rawson Hall to replace the old Princes Street building, led to an expansion of the work among sailors, though the real advance came in 1912 when the hall was redeveloped and renamed the Queen Victoria Seamen's Rest. It then had dormitories upstairs, while downstairs were rooms for reading and parlour games. Two free concerts and a religious service were provided each week. Letters were received and money was held for seamen. The CMM had always regarded its work among sailors as important, largely because of the loneliness and temptation to which they were subject when ashore. The instinct was shown to be sound in that 9,676 vessels visited Sydney in 1912 and 11,591 beds were occupied at the Rest in 1913 (an average of almost 32 a night).[32]

The years immediately before World War I saw an attempt by the Commonwealth government to interest the states in assisted immigration. While the states did not respond either quickly or fully, there was some increase, especially after 1910.[33]   State arrangements for the reception of assisted immigrants were never adequate and the church acted to fill the gap. The Presbyterians were the first Sydney Protestants to do so, but the CMM entered the field in the first half of 1907, using its Seamen's Missionary and one of the sisters for the work. The 1911 Conference realized that this work should be connexional and placed it on that basis but still operated it through the CMM. Arrangements were made with the Melbourne Methodists to forward information about Methodist passengers coming to Sydney so that the CMM agents could contact them the more easily.

From the beginning, the Mission provided what shelter it could at Castlereagh Street, since many migrants could not afford Sydney accommodation by the time they arrived, but it was not until the second half of 1912 that it was able to make comprehensive arrangements. By that time it could accommodate 120 persons (young men, young women, families) at Castlereagh Street, 150 men in a three-storeyed woolstore held on long lease at Circular Quay and converted into two- and four-bedded rooms, and 30 women and children at the former Hope Haven (see below) in George Street north. Cheap meals and a labour bureau were also provided. Labor Premier McGowen commended all this as it "relieve(d) the Government of the necessity for action".

The CMM paid dearly for its enthusiasm when the number of migrants declined late in 1913 and it was left with spare capacity at Circular Quay with no chance of ending its lease and no hope of recouping either the rent or the money (£1,500–2,000) spent on alterations. The CMM's aim had, of course, never been purely humanitarian, important as that aspect was. It was anxious to prevent the "leakage" from the church which is a prominent feature of all migration whether between regions of one country or overseas. Thus it not only provided accommodation and food at a cheap price but issued an open invitation to its own services and, when the migrants moved on, wrote to inform the appropriate clergymen of their coming. It always concerned itself first and foremost with the Methodist immigrants, though it would help others if it had the room.[34]

As the end of the century approached, the sisters of the people were an established and accepted group as they performed numerous deeds of mercy in the worst slums of Sydney and assisted with the enormous variety of work associated with Centenary Hall. They worked among especially difficult groups: the caretakers of city offices and warehouses and the factory girls, whom they reached with lunchtime services. Perhaps they should not have been surprised that the managers and proprietors welcomed them warmly in this last enterprise, since they probably hoped that a "little bit of religion" would lead to a more docile and reliable work-force.[35]

In his book *Sydney in Ferment*, Peter Grabosky argues that certain forms of deviant behaviour attract more attention at particular times without necessarily being more prevalent than at other times. Around the turn of the century, deviant sexual behaviour was one such, as a result of the strict standards of sexual morality developed in the 1880s and remaining extant for some time afterwards.[36] Whatever may be the truth of this contention, Methodists were very anxious to introduce fallen women to "Magdalene's Saviour". The mission was not prepared to blame the sinfulness of girls and their partners entirely, but recognized that environmental, including prenatal, and economic factors played a part. In 1899, a sister strongly attacked employers who paid low wages and were responsible for confronting girls with the choice of suffering privation or taking to the street.[37]

On 29 November 1902, the CMM opened its Alexandra Home in Lindsay Street, Burwood to accommodate up to twenty girls. Alexandra, with its beautiful surroundings, exemplified, both physically and spiritually, an environmentalist approach to the problem. The staff mixed and ate with the inmates and visiting clergy acted in a supportive, not censorious, way. A *Daily Telegraph* reporter found it "homelike" and cheerful. There was, she said, "The steady building up of character, the retrieval of lost ground, the conviction brought home to each individual that 'God loves You'". Laundry work, gardening, dressmaking, and housework were taught, as most of the girls were remarkably ignorant when they arrived. In any case, the home had to pay its own way.

Only younger girls, generally from sixteen to twenty-four years, were admitted on the (probably correct) theory that to mix them with hardened prostitutes would greatly reduce the chances of reclaiming those new to the life. There were no bars, and any girl could leave if she wished, though the sister in charge would endeavour to dissuade her. The sisters often experienced discouragement, but girls were sometimes restored to families, or found jobs and remained clear of their old associates, thus making it worthwhile. The occasional genuine conversion brought enormous joy.

On 19 May 1906, the capacity of the home was doubled. The sisters not only went to court each day in the hope that first offenders would be committed to their care, but undertook after-dark patrols through the red light areas at considerable personal risk. The rescue work was greatly aided in mid-1907 when the Hope Haven shelter opened in George Street north as a halfway house to which the sisters could immediately take a girl, or where the girl herself might call. It was a "collection depot" for Alexandra and remained valuable until 1912 when it became an immigrant home and the night shelter was moved to Crown Street. The move was regarded as beneficial, probably because the centres of prostitution were moving out of the city proper; the *CMM Report* for 1913 commented on the improved moral tone of the city streets and attributed it to Premier Wade's new Police Amendment Act. Nevertheless, the problems associated with the work continued to cause the occasional breakdown of a sister involved in it.[38]

By 1898 the children's home had outgrown its original quarters. During the following year, a new property, "Dalmar", whose name the home has borne ever since, was purchased at Croydon for £1,800. The children moved in during January 1900. The work of the home was greatly helped in 1898 when W. Rutledge secured a N.S.W. government subsidy for it. At first this was £100 p.a., but it later rose to £200 p.a. At the 1903 Conference, someone decided that Methodist principles must be upheld fully. The church had long been against state aid for schools, and now a resolution was forced through declaring such aid for religious charities "objectionable" and compelling the church to approach the government to have such grants discontinued. The grant was paid again that year and there was heated debate at the 1904 Conference. The church had approached the government, which had readily agreed to delete all such grants from the estimates. However, when other churches complained that their charities could not cope if the grants were suddenly cut off, they were reinstated, that to Dalmar along with the others. The CMM obviously wanted to retain the government aid, but it was not received again and the Ladies' Committee had to struggle to maintain solvency.

The main source of income was from small direct donations, of which the most interesting example was the £13/16/8 a year collected by a Mrs English in penny-a-week subscriptions from the employees of E. Way and Co. Sunday school donations gradually increased, but the Christmas Day church collection, suggested as a substitute for the government grant, was not significant before the twenties. The home would never have survived had it not been for gifts in kind from individuals and companies and the 'adoption" of individual children for maintenance purposes already commented upon. Despite the difficulties, the CMM and its Ladies' Committee recognized the importance of rescuing children from vicious or careless parents and accepted that the work could be done better by the church than the state, since the latter could provide for physical need alone.[39]

The debt on current account continued to plague Taylor until his retirement in 1913. There were years when the mission's income was higher than its expenditure and the deficit never really got out of hand, but it was a nagging problem which drained the superintendent's energy and reduced the mission's effectiveness. There were two real problems: the amount of interest which remained payable on the Centenary Hall trust debt and the continuing failure of Methodists outside the CMM itself to recognize the connexional nature of the work done there and to assist financially.

Little could be done about the former problem, but the

latter should have been soluble. It was not. There were 40,000 to 50,000 adult Methodist adherents in N.S.W., but only 341 responded to Taylor's 1898 appeal to remove the debt and their gifts totalled slightly under £300. Three years later, Taylor claimed that 93 per cent of the total income was raised in the mission itself. Naturally, the capacity of the CMM to raise funds was limited by the nature of its congregation, many of whom were poor, with a fair number of unemployed. The point is illustrated by the fact that on anniversary Sunday 1898 the treasurer counted the number of coins gathered: 1 sovereign, 1 crown, 21 half-crowns, 22 florins, 240 one-shilling pieces, 479 sixpences, 1,320 threepences, and 135 pennies, or a total of 2,219 coins from congregations totalling over 6,000 persons. Taylor seemed satisfied with an average collection of £15/9/4 per Sunday in the third quarter of 1898, along with an extra £5 from his week-night entertainment. The average peaked at £27/5/3 in 1910 and fell back to £22/3/9 by 1913.

Monies won within the CMM more than paid what could be described as "normal" circuit expenditure. Only those philanthropic activities which were genuinely connexional work were not covered. Accounts usually showed substantial deficits on items like the sisters' home, Evangelists' Training Institute, Seamen's Mission, Alexandra Home, Hope Haven, and the social wing (which included the immigration and accommodation branches).

It worried Taylor that N.S.W. Methodists did not support his mission to the extent that Victorian Methodists did the Melbourne CMM, or British Methodists their forty CMMs and there was undoubtedly some contradiction between his occasional claims that the mission had a strong hold on the hearts of the people and the hard fact that many of those people preferred to give to other charities. There was little to be done except press on with local self-denial campaigns and collections. In 1901, Sister Nellie raised £2/13/9 from twenty-five donors, with two of those donors giving £1 between them. That was doing it the hard way.[40]

Two questions trouble the historian confronted by the above facts. In his autobiography, Taylor indicates that the CMM was often beholden to Ebenezer Vickery for financial help. In the 1908 *Report*, the treasurer, H. M. Hawkins, wrote, "What a prince of givers the late Mr Vickery was. How many scores of times he came to our aid, just when we needed it most". Such evidence cannot reasonably be rejected, yet the surviving, incomplete, financial records do not really support it. Obviously the rent-free use of various houses was important, but the giving of actual cash is implied and it is difficult to see how this could have been concealed, or why it should have been. Annual *Reports*, as in 1904/05, occasionally recorded substantial gifts (£100) from him, which makes it the more surprising that the same was not done on other occasions.

The other problem lies in the lack of any adequate explanation why the Sydney CMM should receive less generous support than its Melbourne counterpart, although it was older and its work should have been better known and understood. Insufficient appropriate research has been done for us to know whether N.S.W. Methodists were more conservative in outlook than Victorian Methodists or whether in N.S.W. a greater predominance of rural interests led to a correspondingly lower concern with the problems of the city. The fact that circuits, both suburban and country, were still expanding and consolidating in N.S.W. — Bollen's view that the Australian church was first and foremost a building church must not be forgotten — may explain the difference with England, but not that with Melbourne.[41]

In mid-1897, his concern about the ability of Methodism to make contact with the urban masses and win them for Christ led Taylor to suggest that a "committee on Methodist aggression" be set up to examine the whole condition of Methodism in Sydney and to prepare a scheme for the adaptation of methods to altered circumstances. After discussion in the *Methodist*, the 1898 Conference appointed such a committee. The subject was extensively discussed at the Sydney Ministers' Meetings during 1898. Taylor and P. J. Stephen came out strongly for the use of specialist ministers in mission-type situations for longer terms than the statutory Methodist three years. They blamed the itinerancy rule heavily for the failure of Methodism in the cities. J. E. Carruthers thought the appeal for specialists "overdone", but had no alternative to offer. Rev. B. J. Meek, a long-time opponent of the CMM, declared that mission a failure and condemned as unscriptural the novel methods used by Taylor. In his view, the problem lay in the lack of consecration among ministers, lay preachers, and Sunday school teachers and in the lack of effective pastoral work done by the ministers.[42]

The committee devised a complex scheme to combine six city circuits for evangelical and philanthropic purposes as one metropolitan mission, while each would retain its circuit identity for administrative, financial, and ordinary circuit work. This was accepted by the Sydney District Synod with little question, though Carruthers later suggested that the dual organization would lead to the collapse of pastoral visitation and religious instruction in the schools.

Taylor regarded the scheme as "inspired". The CMM Committee approved it, provided that the recommendations of the committee for the annual payment of £100 towards the liquidation of the CMM debt and for the passing of all assets to the CMM in the event of the liquidation of the Metropolitan Mission were adopted. Conference accepted the proposal, with the single change that in the event of liquidation both assets and liabilities would pass to the CMM. The CMM regarded this as a "material alteration" and refused to proceed. Taylor had enough liabilities of his own and was not prepared to risk adding more, despite the blame which naturally fell on him for reneging on a scheme which he had once called "inspired". The "city problem" did not mend and continued to gain attention in the *Methodist* from time to time. Another committee on Metropolitan Methodism was set up by the 1911 Conference and, while it did recommend the formulation of plans for the improved working of the city, the only practical suggestion it made was to incorporate the weak William Street circuit into the CMM for a trial period. This was acted upon.[43]

Discussion of this whole question over the years revealed worry at a worsening situation outside the CMM and a search by a few men to find a solution, while others hung back from

dramatic experiment. However, the first attempt at a metropolitan mission was too complex and Carruthers's view was
probably correct. Taylor's timidity over finance was intelli-
gible. Perhaps Conference should have agreed to take all
liabilities on itself, or share them proportionately among the
circuits involved, in the event of the collapse of the proposed
mission. Methodism would never really solve the total
problem of Sydney, and the discussions at the turn of the
century only served to highlight the complexity of the
worsening situation and the general lack of interest in it.

One question, relevant to the whole period from 1884 on,
has been left to this point for discussion: that of socio-
political involvement. There is a natural tendency for anyone
who lived through the period of Alan Walker at the CMM to
assume that there must always have been a socio-political
aspect to its work. The same impression might also be held
by anyone familiar with the early years of the Melbourne
CMM, when it was under the direction of A. R. Edgar, who
had hardly taken up his position before he launched an all-
out attack on "sweating". He later became first chairman of
the White-Workers' Wages Board under the Wages Board Act,
and later again of the Coopers' and Jam Makers' Boards.
On one occasion he was called before the bar of the Victorian
Parliament to answer questions concerning outspoken comments he had made about parliamentary life.[44] Taylor took
a less bold stand.

J. D. Bollen in *Protestantism and Social Reform in NSW,
1890–1910* seems to argue that the Protestant churches
gradually changed their approach during the 1890s from one
of insistence that their only task was to preach the Gospel,
which alone could bring peace and might by individual conversions solve the social question, to one of genuine concern
with social reform and progress and the creation of a world
in which justice and mercy reigned among men. In debate on
political questions they may have been muddled and self-
justificatory in their thinking, but in practical action they
were quick to sense needs and supply them. Christians
showed themselves "staunch allies" of "movements which

protest against social arrangements that tend to force men, women and children into... squalor, disease, and immorality, and which seek to bring about their alteration".[45]

At the mission, as in any Methodist church, "social reform" was likely to mean temperance work, and there is no doubt that Taylor and his co-adjutors took considerable interest in the political campaign to pressure governments into action in this field. There was nothing surprising about this, since it was not only an old Methodist hobby-horse, but of vital concern to people who saw an immediate connection between drink and the poverty and squalor from which they were constantly concerned to rescue men and women. A similar concern was shown about gambling, the decline of family ties, and the loosening of moral constraints generally.[46]

Other social questions were not entirely neglected, but Taylor's approach was limited. In February 1890 he attended a gathering of unemployed at the Protestant Hall. He spoke up strongly against the distress evident in the city and expressed sympathy for those unable to get work. He joined a deputation to the minister for public works but was not present when it reported its failure and he was not on a new deputation to the premier a few days later.

In August 1890, he arranged a conference on early closing and invited several officials of the N.S.W. Shop Employees' Union. This was held in response to a request by the union to the clergy of Sydney to speak on the question that day. He spoke up strongly in favour of reasonable hours (8.30 a.m. to 6.00 p.m., with an hour for lunch) for shop assistants, criticized the churches for paying too little attention to the bodies of men and women, and blamed the whole problem chiefly on the public, especially women, who insisted on being able to shop when they wished. Six months later he declared that "the proper remedies for social misery were agitation for laws which would make sweating impossible, legislation and united effort which would prevent drunkenness", while in the middle of 1891 he took part in the deputation to Premier Parkes referred to earlier. This was an extremely limited approach, given the revelations made around this time by parliamentary committees with respect to hours in general and those worked by children in particular.[47]

A curious incident occurred early in Bavin's tenure. In the evening of 19 November 1893 a large number of men (estimates vary from two hundred and fifty to three hundred) marched through the streets to Centenary Hall carrying a crucifix bearing a man dressed in rags and marked "humanity crucified" and "murdered by the rich". The symbol was seized by the police in York Street but the men entered Centenary Hall where they remained quiet throughout the main service. During the after-meeting, when an invitation was issued to pray or testify, Thomas Dodds rose and asked God to protect the starving and curse the sweater, including such clergy as were hypocrites and shareholders in sweaters' dens. The choir then interrupted him and most of the men left the building.[48]

Whilst it is clear that the unemployed saw the churches in an unfavourable light, or they would hardly have employed the mockery of the crucifix, it is difficult to interpret this incident correctly. Presumably the large evening service at Centenary Hall provided them with the best stage on which to act out their protest. The CMM response would not have seemed especially encouraging. Their behaviour suggests that the men, though seriously disenchanted, were still not ready for a total break with the church.

This event made little impact on the Methodist church at large, and the 1894 Conference heard the retiring president, J. E. Moulton, declare that the church's whole strength should be spent in counteracting the deadly influences of sin. It would be "wrong" to use the resources of the church to solve the problem of the unemployed. True, another former president, George Martin, argued that if the church neglected the great social issues of the day it was no better than the priest and the Levite in the story of the good Samaritan, but when Rev. S. Maddern asked Conference to express sympathy with the unemployed and declare it part of the role of Christianity to promote the spiritual and physical well-being of people and seek the "removal of the preventable ill conditions of life", the church did decide to "pass by on the other side" and confined itself to an expression of sympathy and a willingness to relieve suffering on an individual basis. Protestantism was reasserting its dearly held individualistic heritage. On 10 June, when Bavin said that he saw strikes in the same light as wars and would not accept that some were unavoidable, he was putting the CMM generally in line with the rest of the church and society. The *Sydney Morning Herald* thought that about 100 heard him deliver this masterpiece, but the *Methodist* estimated his hearers at 300 and found the occasion "free from party spirit".[49]

Probably due to the change over between Bavin and Rutledge, the CMM, like Methodism generally, was not represented at the April 1896 public meeting on the need to introduce old-age pensions, but in 1897 it was to take a more forthright stand over the Lucknow strike. In July 1897, D'Arcy Wentworth's goldmine at Lucknow, 250 kilometres west of Sydney, reduced the miners' wages, introduced change-room searches, and even threatened searches of their homes to prevent thieving. When the men struck, the management refused either to meet union delegates or to allow the premier to mediate. On Sunday, 22 August, Rutledge held a PSA on "The Working Man and his Master" at which he and the Rev. P. J. Stephen (then at Parramatta) spoke. Rutledge declared it the duty of the Christian church to raise its voice against tyranny and oppression and damned the searches for branding every man a thief. He also heavily criticized the low level of wages in a variety of trades. Stephen, a fiery, emotional fundamentalist preacher, thundered his support for the strike and hoped for the success of the miners in what he saw as the cause of all the workers of N.S.W. Until a proper system of industrial arbitration was introduced, there would be no better way of adjusting differences than by strike, even though it smacked of civil war. According to the *Daily Telegraph*, Stephen became a "forcible advocate" of trade unionism, said that capital was always the aggressor and that the Lucknow men were asking only for bare justice and that the mining company should be "crushed out of existence". Out at Lucknow, Labor parliamentarian, J.S.T. McGowen, was supported on the platform by Evangelist Walker, of the local Wesleyan church, who had been through the CMM Evangelists' Training Institute. The *Methodist* thought that the Christian church should seek to create a "fraternal spirit" rather than accentuate differences, and while some of its correspondents supported Stephen and Rutledge, a majority thought that ministers should keep clear of political questions, though all these writers made it clear that they were on the side of the employers.[50]

The Lucknow incident was explosive, and, for the CMM, an aberration. It occurred because the superintendent at the time was a man of powerful feelings and strong labour sympathies: as retiring president at the 1903 Conference, Rutledge declared himself a Christian Socialist and urged the church to fight a system in which avaricious employers grasped all the profits and allowed workers to starve.[51] Rutledge was prepared to take a stand regardless of the offence he might give to the wealthy supporters of the church. Having become aware of a piece of oppression and injustice, the superintendent called in the strongest speaker available on what he believed was the correct and Christian side and invited him to denounce the evil in clear terms. There was no attempt to present a "balanced" view or to look at all angles. It is hardly surprising that Rutledge drew fire in 1897, as Alan Walker did later.

With the return of Taylor, the CMM went back to quieter ways. A meeting in October 1898 (with union and political leaders from both sides present) passed some mild resolutions in favour of the early closing of shops and a deputation (of which Taylor was not a part) met the minister for education and labour three days later. He again criticized "sweating" at a Christian Endeavour Convention in September 1901, but blunted the edge of the attack by arguing his familiar line that the real blame lay with the purchasers of the goods, among whom were some union officials. He was glad that the tailoresses had formed a union, but his only answer to the problem of sweating was that Christians should not buy sweated goods.[52] No further socio-political utterances by Taylor have been found.

The experience of the CMM, which might have been expected to be more socially and politically oriented than other churches, does not support Bollen's argument referred to above. Rutledge's action over the Lucknow strike was clearly an aberration and was not repeated. When Taylor departed from traditional Methodist social questions, he kept to "safe" issues like sweating and was careful to avoid blaming the employers; rather, the real sweaters were always seen as the general public who bought cheap goods or shopped late. The stance was weak given the economic and social conditions of the day and surprising considering the geographic location of the CMM.

Much of the explanation is to be found in Taylor's own nature, for evangelicals have often been socially conservative, and he had grown to maturity in the north-country of England. Yet it is impossible not to wonder how far he was influenced by Ebenezer Vickery to whom he was very close. Vickery was a tough-minded conservative who, in 1894, in the Legislative Council, in speaking on the Coalmines Bill, had defended capitalism, attacked union leaders as "socialist agitators", and had opposed the eight-hours clause and the proposed minimum age of fourteen years for boys in mines. According to Richard Broome, the failure to use inexpensive safety lamps and to take other elementary safety precautions, caused the death of ninety-five workers in 1902 in a Port Kembla mine of which Vickery was the principal shareholder. A self-made man and prominent speculator, he treated his workers harshly but was generous in his philanthropies through both church and secular organizations. Broome may be right in suggesting that his last philanthropies (including the Lyceum) could be seen, in part, as an expiation for the above accident.[53]

The contrast between the Sydney CMM and that in Melbourne, or West London, is clear. Under Taylor, it was an excellent illustration of Patrick O'Farrell's remark that "when the conflict between Australian labour and capital came to a head in the early nineties, the sects, once hostile to the status quo, would not countenance any thoroughgoing measure of social radicalism". According to Broome, the few Protestant clergy who did advocate social welfare reforms did so primarily to convince the working classes to return to the Christian fold rather than to support the principle per se. This may well apply to Taylor. For all that, he did show more concern in the pastoral care of the working

P.J. Stephen, CMM superintendent 1913–15. By courtesy of the Wesley Central Mission.

class than any other Protestant clergyman of the times except the Anglicans Boyce and Hammond.[54]

When ill-health forced Taylor's resignation at the 1913 Conference, twenty-nine years after his initial appointment to York Street (twenty-two of which had actually been spent at the CMM), he was replaced by his friend and sometime colleague, P. J. Stephen. Deteriorating health caused Stephen to stand down to a less demanding appointment in 1915 and so ensured that his superintendency would be only an addendum to Taylor's rather than new and significant in its own right. There was no doubt that the CMM had made a mark in Sydney Methodism, and on Sydney at large, and that it was well accepted as a religious and philanthropic institution in the heart of the city.

The basic reason why Taylor had succeeded in reviving a moribund cause and making it the liveliest centre of Methodism in N.S.W. lay in his insistence on the importance of the inner life and fellowship. The CMM stood for "spiritual Christianity", and the class meeting, consecration service, and prayer were the sources of power responsible for the eagerness with which it sought to save the lost.

In a sermon preached at Christmas 1902, he pointed out that at the Incarnation God "put his arms around the neck of humanity's outlaws and let them know how much he loved them". Christians were required to be equally practical in their demonstration of God's love and a revival inspired by the Incarnation should send the best-dressed "elect" ladies of the fashionable suburban churches into Woolloomooloo brothels "with a sister's smile and a sister's offer to show the way out" as it should make temperance societies "vitalized, workable forces of rescue" instead of organizations in which members congratulated themselves on their own virtue. Thus the CMM also stood for "practical Christianity" and sought, following the example of Christ and the Epistle of St James, to relieve the needy, though it did not attempt to "solve the social question" and remove the causes of poverty and crime. For it, "the only answer to the challenge of [the] new paganism is the Gospel of Christ, not only preached, but lived in human lives. It is for this the CMM stands".[55]

Although the CMM had not succeeded in winning the city

for Christ and, indeed, the formal strength of Christianity
had actually declined over the period, it had revived the
Methodist cause in a way not dreamt of in 1884. Formal
membership of York Street was up from seventeen or
eighteen to five to six hundred and attendance at services
from two to three hundred a week to more than five
thousand. A large auditorium was being filled regularly and
sometimes overflowed. Outdoor work had become a vital
part of Methodist activity. There is no real way of measuring
what percentage of this gain at the heart was at the cost of
the peripheral churches, but descriptions in Methodist and
secular sources suggest strongly that much of the congregation was new, that the poor were being reached in a way
that Methodism had not been capable of for a very long time
before 1884. The "good news" for Methodism was not only
that the working class had been penetrated, but that men
were now forming half or more of the CMM congregation.
Methodism was also "news" in the secular press in a way that
it had not been for a long time. It was not that there was a
constant stream of articles about the CMM, but a large
institution like the mission drew the interest of the press as
the scattered suburban churches never could. Thus the
CMM's main service, and its social and philanthropic
activities, were regularly and favourably reported. It was not
just that the CMM provided a focal point for the reporting of
Methodist activity, but its superintendent understood the
value of publicity and made himself available for interviews
willingly and generously. He was articulate and provided the
reporters with "good copy". Yet the fact that the press
turned to the CMM must indicate that it believed that there
was community interest in the mission and that it was
significant in the life of the city.

5

War, Unrest, and Depression

The outbreak of war saw a broad national consensus in favour of total support for Britain. The church was a part of that consensus. For many clergy, the war was a visitation from God, the result of sin, and would have a regenerating effect on Australian society. In thus embracing the war, churchmen saw themselves to be employing Christian doctrine to make sense of the conflict.[1] They also hoped that the war would allow them to acquire a new relevance and a new sense of belonging in the Australian community which they had previously lacked. Unfortunately their shallow response and their failure to confront the great moral problems raised by the war ensured that the church would ultimately be seen as even less significant than it had been in the prewar world. Churchmen participated in recruiting campaigns and organized patriotic demonstrations to coincide with their conferences and synods. Some Protestants urged conscription even before there was political pressure for it, presumably because the regeneration of the nation would be more complete if larger numbers went through the fires of war. Outside of South Australia, Methodists were a little less enthusiastic than other Protestants in recruiting and conscription campaigns, fearing the effects of army life on the salvation of young men. Such fears were inevitably reinforced by the increase in prostitution during the war and the presumed increase in venereal disease among men at home as well as abroad and by occasional drunken brawls involving soldiers in Australian camps. Reports of similar happenings in Egypt filtered back.

In his study of the conscription plebiscites, A.G. Gilbert argues that "the response of Christianity to World War I confirmed what has been obvious many times since Constantine went into battle with the Cross as his emblem. Individuals and small sects might remain basically religious in their attitude to war and conscription, but Christianity as an institution in a temporal world was dominated primarily by temporal considerations." At the very least, there is force in the contention that Protestants were influenced by the opinions of that section of the community from which they drew most of their members and that Catholic divergences were influenced by the greater depth of their penetration of the working class.[2]

If the war provided problems for the churches, so did the interwar years. There was a growing divorce rate, a loosening of sexual morality, a search for pleasure, the growth of sectarian conflict, industrial disputation, economic depression, and, eventually, the burgeoning threat of a new war. An "uncertain, cautious and shabby era" had succeeded the "naive optimism" of the late nineteenth and early twentieth centuries.[3]

Churchmen, H. C. Foreman among them, declared that religious sentiment was at a discount and that organized religion was unable to restrain public evil: "We ought to rid ourselves of delusions. We are not a Christian, churchgoing, God-fearing people. We are a pagan people, with a Christian fringe".[4]

In a perceptive study of the churches in the interwar period, Donald Hansen shows that the community at large did not share this view and that most Australians continued to think of themselves as "practical, if not practising Christians" and as "believers at heart". The problem lay in the differing perceptions of what being a Christian involved. For all clergy it certainly involved an enduring and developing relationship with God expressed through public worship and private devotion as well as good works. For Methodists, especially, that relationship usually began with a definite conversion experience and its end was scriptural holiness. For none was church attendance adequate proof of Christian experience, but the wilful or careless neglect of that duty was proof of its absence. It is hardly possible to know with certainty what was thought by those who claimed to be

Christian but omitted the usually accepted overt acts associated with religious belief. Presumably it included being baptised, married, and buried with the aid of religious ceremonial, keeping the Golden Rule, being a good family man or woman and a good neighbour, and avoiding the grosser evils of life. There was little common ground between such views.

From an analysis of the census figures for N.S.W. in the interwar period, Hansen argues powerfully that they reflect stability rather than religious decline, despite the clerical allegations of growing paganism. However, a polarizing process had taken place in which regular church-goers were likely to become fully aligned communicant and active members, while the more casual "adherents" often fell away altogether. Thus church-going became "less a matter of custom and convention, and more a matter of conviction".[5] Nevertheless, with little real progress being made, the period had to be seen by the clergy as one of stagnation and frustration, a time when the churchman's dream of winning Australia for Christ, was finally given up in favour of something more attainable — the maintenance, or possibly extension, of His Kingdom on earth.[6]

Hansen also detects the growth of new problems within the church with the development of the doctrine of "modernism" and a tendency for sermons to become more scholarly but less assured. Doctrinal issues gave way to topical themes and most interwar sermons were "inadequate" as stimuli to action. New methods of evangelism had to be developed as the conservative message of the old evangelists proved offensive to liberal churchmen. New means were tried to bring in the outsider, but without much enduring success.[7]

The "industrial problem" bubbled unpleasantly throughout the twenties, with substantial unemployment and numerous strikes. It culminated in the Great Depression of 1929. Because the Protestant churches were out of touch with the working classes well before the end of the nineteenth century and exercised little if any influence over the nascent labour movement in Australia, they were badly placed to deal with the growing crisis of the interwar years. The Rev. F. T. Walker tried to come to grips with the industrial problem through his

Men's Own Movement (MOM). Founded in 1916 within N.S.W. Methodism, it eventually embraced most states and cooperated with the Congregational church as well, but it was usually Walker and his successor, Rev. William Coleman, who made the running. Walker and his helpers conducted lunch-hour meetings in the larger factories in the metropolitan area and Sunday afternoon lectures in the Domain. They conducted church services by invitation and spread their message through a paper known successively as *Men's Own*, *New Man*, and *Christian Industry*.

Walker was no red revolutionary, despite the fears of some conservative Methodists. He saw the capitalist system as inadequate, but necessary for some time as it must not be replaced by something worse (communism). Its problem was the selfishness which prevented employers and employees from seeing their common interests. In effect, this argument reduced the economic problem to one of sin and so brought it within the clergyman's purview. In Walker's view, Christianity also provided an answer to the class issue: Christ had come, not as a king or priest, but as a carpenter, a worker at tasks vital to every day existence. No man or woman could now be despised because of the lowly work he or she did, class distinctions had been destroyed, and barriers obliterated by the Incarnation.[8]

Essentially, Walker's message was one of the reconciliation of the social classes by the application of Christian principles to social and industrial life. Once the environment had been restored in this way, the traditional pattern of the conversion and sanctification of the individual would presumably take effect. It was a superficial approach, but it was the best that the churches had to offer and it was unlikely to have much impact at a time when the weakness of parliamentary labour ensured that the unions would turn more and more to direct action to keep up with war-induced inflation.

Of the actual events of the Depression years nothing need be said. Fred Alexander believed that the travail of the period 1929–39 proved to be "a process of purification"[9] and his judgment is very close to that which Phyllis Peter, in her work on the Depression, attributes to the Protestant churches during the period. Once again they saw the hand of

God punishing man for his sins. Man had devoted himself exclusively to the pursuit of material well-being and needed to return to frugal living, and to God. There was more interest by Protestant clergy in drink, gambling, and sabbath desecration, and by Catholics in mixed marriages, than in poverty and unemployment. The most outspoken exceptions were the Anglicans Burgmann and Moyes, while among the Methodists "a few" clergy spoke seriously about poverty and unemployment but found no real support from their church. Peter believes that many Protestant clergy feared becoming involved in the political wrangle, or even being labelled "red", though their real problem was their inadequate training.[10]   While Hansen generally supports this view, he argues for a slightly more complex response in that he sees a growing unwillingness, by the end of 1931, to attribute the crisis to the intervention of God, whatever His motives may have been thought to be. He also argues that, like the rest of the community, the clergy gradually realized that the complacent detachment of the 1920s which had allowed them to view the unemployed as lazy, unenterprising, and work-shy was no longer possible. The inefficient social system was also blameworthy.[11]   In the years that followed the gradual lifting of the Great Depression, as new and complex issues of war and peace confronted the churches, they showed no more preparedness to cope with that crisis than they had with those that had gone before.

The years after World War I were years of disillusionment and nonachievement, sterile and uncreative. If this was so for the community at large, it was also true for the Christian churches. Having failed to gain the place in the sun they had sought during the war, they plodded on uncertainly and with a growing realization of the limitations which would always be placed on their achievement. They were allowed a role in public affairs, but it had to be strictly nonpolitical: they were confined to the enunciation of Christian principles, moral guidance, and the provision of physical assistance to the needy. If they tried to go beyond that they aroused uneasiness: if they stayed within their limits, they were respected but not followed. Their place was a declining one, but they were in no danger of extinction. It is against this

Dr S.J. Hoban, CMM superintendent 1915–21. By courtesy of the Wesley Central Mission.

background that we must view the efforts of the CMM and assess its achievements in this period.

Patriotism at the CMM predated World War I. From its earliest days the mission took an interest in the "bluejackets" in the port of Sydney and held special services for them. Taylor was appointed a naval (port) chaplain and was followed in this in 1913 by P. J. Stephen. On 5 October 1913, the prime minister, Hon. J. Cook, took part in a Sunday afternoon "patriotic service" in the Lyceum and defended compulsory military service, though in his efforts to please his Methodist audience he did so mainly on the grounds that it would remove boys from bad influences and subject them to good. There would be no canteens, cigarettes might not be carried during training, and foul language might not be used. In his mind, defence seemed to run a poor second to the inculcation of a public-school, boy-scout type morality.[12]

Brilliant and sympathetic preacher that he was, Samuel J. Hoban was bound to excel in his use of the war. Few of his sermons from the period survive, but there are enough to illuminate his approach.[13] On 29 August 1915, he attempted to answer the question which must have been troubling many by that time: "The War — Why Does not God Intervene?" He saw a great moral problem in the apparent indifference of God to catastrophe and his seeming unwillingness "to give righteousness an instant and overwhelming victory". But the demand for "a portentous demonstration of supernatural force" really sprang from a loss of faith in God's sovereignty. God had stood by while Christ suffered at Gethsemane and Calvary but had vindicated Him triumphantly in the Resurrection. "God does intervene. But He does not assume the form of a largely magnified Lord Kitchener or Oliver Cromwell. He intervenes in the almighty ministry of His Holy Spirit". There was both good doctrine and convenient sophistry in this approach to the problem which also entirely neglected the question of whether all the "righteousness" lay on one side.

Two weeks later, Hoban took up the text, "My mother

and brethren are those who hear the word of God and do it" (Luke 8:21). After a beginning which suggested a sermon on Christ's attitude to women, and perhaps the place of women in the church and the world, the preacher took a sharp right turn to argue that Christ had broken the chains of family to save the world and that His mother had made a great sacrifice in this. The mothers of 1915 were invited to make the same sacrifice with respect to their sons and so rank beside the mother of Jesus.

At the end of the year he declared that 1916 would see the climax of the struggle and that the strain would be "fearful". He went on to criticize the government for action described as "trifling with the safety of our heritage" and concluded that "we must move heaven and earth to compel attention to the moral well-being of our men". Obviously Hoban shared the one great Methodist doubt about the war, namely its possible effect on the salvation of "our boys". Despite this doubt, members of the CMM and readers of *Our Weekly Greeting* (hereafter, *Greeting*) were requested to offer prayer, regardless of what they were doing or where they were, at noon each day, for the army, the navy, and the speedy coming of true peace. The 1916 *Report* declared at once its hatred of war and its pride that the CMM had shared the Empire's sacrifice and glory when it was "forced to unsheath the sword" in 1914. Years later R. J. Williams, his colleague in 1915–16, said that it had been the war which gave Hoban his chance to build up the biggest congregation in Australia and that "it was [his] fine faith in God, blended with an ardent patriotism and proclaimed with a burning eloquence of voice and gesture, and a fine frenzy of soul, that made Dr Hoban's war-time services such a tonic for the dispirited".

Hoban met returning wounded at the wharf and also held church parades for them. He acted as college chaplain to the naval reserve and to the men camped at Moore Park. Through-out the whole war patriotic PSA programmes were common. The topics included: "German Brute Force Versus Christian-ity"; "Alcohol — the Hun's Ally"; "War Clouds and Silver Linings"; "What Lord Kitchener Teaches Us".

Years later, H. C. Foreman could still describe 4 August 1914 as a "great day" in British history because the nation had entered "the valley of the shadow" for the sake of righteousness. Even as the shadow of a new war loomed close, Empire Day would be celebrated at the Lyceum with a guard of medal-bedecked veterans turning out to welcome the governor, though one speaker perhaps gave the game away when he said that we could only keep Australia white while we stuck to the Empire and kept it together.[14]

It is clear then that the shallow perception of the war which deluded the church at large also held sway at the Sydney CMM. It would be folly to expect anti-imperialism or pacifism to be preached at that time. Despite the brash nationalism of the quarter-century or so before the war, the bonds of Empire were very strong, and stronger in the church than in the community at large. Yet Hoban was a man of superior intelligence and it is disappointing to find him preaching and encouraging glib acceptance of the "God, King and Country" philosophy and apparently incapable of analyzing the deeper issues raised by the war. It is also surprising that a church which sought to contact the urban working class and link it to Christianity should adopt middle-class attitudes quite so wholeheartedly and be so completely oblivious to the problems which at least some of the working class had with the war in increasing measure as it dragged on. It is a measure of Hoban's stature as a popular preacher that, despite these problems, he increased his congregation significantly against the general trend, though it would be interesting to know just whom he drew to his services.

On the industrial front, it is at least arguable that the mission missed a golden opportunity during the war years and after. In 1917, Conference decided that F. T. Walker should be appointed colleague to Hoban and operate MOM from the William Street church, now temporarily attached to the CMM. The move was initially welcomed by the superintendent who, in his 1917 *Report*, found the association "fitting" because of the "unique nature of the Movement, and the splendid facilities afforded by the CMM as a base for its operation". MOM attempted to apply Christian principles to social and industrial problems and "reach[ed] out to the unchurched mass of men with the message of individual salvation". It was an attempt to achieve in the industrial sphere, by specialized means, that which the CMM was already trying to achieve in other areas. Yet one year later Conference discontinued the experiment and Walker was set aside solely for the work of MOM. The *Methodist* (16 March 1918) stated that this was because the outlook for Walker's work was so "inviting", but the *CMM Report* for that year suggests that Walker's work for the mission interfered too much with MOM, which, by now, had undoubtedly become his absorbing passion. Apparently Hoban had insisted that the general mission work take precedence over MOM work and Walker was not prepared to tolerate the situation any longer.

However, that may not be the whole explanation. On 27 September 1917, the *Methodist* carried a substantial article by Walker entitled "Men's Own Movement and the Strike". He pointed out that the church had generally opposed the great railway strike and had regarded the strikers as having rebelled against constitutional government. Yet there were many church leaders, Sunday school teachers and lay preachers involved on conscientious grounds and the church owed a duty to the strikers. Condemnation was easy; to try to win them for Christ was a very different matter.

This was a bold stand and liable to be misunderstood by his clerical brethren. Possibly Hoban's general conservatism and his enthusiastic support of the war led him to object to Walker's stand. Later, the CMM took little special interest in MOM. A great opportunity was missed. MOM never received much support either from the Conference or the church at large, which failed to understand what it was about. Hoban's first instinct, that the CMM was a good base from which to operate such an agency, was right. Both MOM and the CMM might have gained in depth and extent of penetration if they had been permanently interlinked, but this would have required a more careful working out of arrangements and probably an additional unmarried minister to ensure that Walker was not overburdened with everyday circuit work. Interestingly, in 1917, Hoban employed Charlie Woodward to work among men generally, including those in factories, and Foreman allowed the work to continue. Perhaps it was the highly specific nature of Walker's work which troubled Hoban, along with the twin facts that it would have involved him well beyond the bounds of the CMM itself and that it may have appeared to the traditional evangelist to have had nonreligious overtones.

The CMM was concerned about the problems created by the industrial situation of the 1920s and the Depression of the 1930s but, while it recognized a spirit of change in the social order and knew that it should rise to meet this, it really did not manage to readjust and continued to see its role as giving assistance to the victims of unemployment rather than attempting to alter the existing system. In 1916 it opened a "people's hostel" in Princes Street with the object of providing workingmen of very limited means with cheap accommodation (one shilling per night or six shillings per week) and safety from the streets and hotels. At the same time it continued to maintain a rented warehouse in Nicholson Street, Woolloomooloo as a shelter for forty indigent men. There was a nominal charge of sixpence a night but this was often waived as the mission could not turn away even the most degenerate "soaker" if it were to fulfil its purpose.

In 1922, the trustees of the Sydney Night Refuge (hereafter, Refuge) in Francis Street asked the CMM to assume responsibility for it. The Refuge had originated with George Lane in 1864 when he and his wife had first sheltered homeless men. Two years later a large committee of management had been formed and premises bought in Francis Street where the work was carried on until the committee decided that it was not able to raise the funds necessary to repair the dilapidated building. The CMM decided to demolish the old building altogether and to construct in its place one which would carry out the functions of both the Refuge and the Hostel and so consolidate its social work for men in the one spot. Money was slow coming in, but the new building was eventually opened on 2 July 1927, E. Frank Vickery, a grandson of Ebenezer, playing an important part in the work. The ground floor provided a refuge for thirty with stretcher

H.J.C. Foreman, CMM superintendent 1921–31. By courtesy of the Wesley Central Mission.

beds, lavatory, shower (compulsory once a week), and fumi-
gation facilities as well as a dining-room and assembly hall.
The first floor provided a hostel with forty beds at one
shilling a night and the second floor thirty-four cubicles at
nine and six to twelve shillings a week with windows over-
looking the harbour.   Breakfast and an evening meal were
provided; there were religious services two nights a week and
occasional entertainments.[15]

As the economic crisis deepened, the Refuge became a distribution point for clothing and an advisory centre. Residential and other facilities were fully stretched from the opening
in mid-1927 through to the end of the thirties.   The new
building had come at an opportune time.   The CMM had no
difficulty in recognizing that people were not to blame for
their poverty and by mid-1930 was helping 150 a day in
some way.   While the Methodist church developed other
organizations to dispense assistance during the Depression,
the mission, operating through the Refuge, was always the
most important.[16]

The mission did not concentrate unusual attention on the
Depression in its services and the PSA, though the economic
crisis did provide a recurring theme.   The preaching of H.C.
Foreman and A.J. Gould (his colleague for much of the time)
seems to have kept closely to "religious" subjects in the
narrower sense.   Once, in the midst of the Depression, in a
sermon entitled "The Glad Game", he urged his hearers to
find occasion for thanksgiving even in the drab lives they
were leading.   Like other ministers, Foreman was out of his
depth and in the attempt to stand on solid ground preferred
to see the economic crisis as a moral one.[17]   The story of
the 1914-18 war was being repeated.

R.J. Williams proved more thoughtful than his predecessors, though he too could argue that the crisis would
not be all loss if it brought people closer to God and to each
other.   However, he was well aware that wrongs waited to be
righted and tyrannies to be broken and that it was not good
enough simply to blame the "apostles of revolution" for the
woes of a society which itself needed substantial reform.
In February 1935, he went as far as any Methodist minister
was likely to go at the time in declaring it the church's

responsibility to stir men to action to reform the social order. Later that year he returned to the same theme, criticizing Christians for being more concerned with symbols and ritual than "the primary expression of religion in practical affairs". The true Christian was fully committed to activity in the social and political world as a response to the "disturbing influence" of Christ in him. While the church should not meddle in politics, believers might campaign against social evils, should "consecrate themselves to the highest citizenship", and should work to improve living conditions for those who could not help themselves.[18]

Williams wanted more than palliatives. He had abandoned the socialism he had inclined towards in his youth, but still sought fundamental reforms in the cause of social justice and would not be silenced by the comfortable. He was one of that small band of Methodist clergy whom Phyllis Peter saw as honourable exceptions to their church's general policy of remaining silent on the great issues raised by the Depression.

The mission's work for men throughout the period was not confined to relief; some of the spiritual work is of considerable interest. The main agent of this work was the "converted burglar", Charlie Woodward, who began a men's meeting at the CMM late in Taylor's time and joined the full-time staff at Hoban's request on 6 August 1917. Charlie Woodward had spent many years in the gutter. Initially handed to the police by his headmaster for stealing toys from his playmates, he descended through a long list of drunk and disorderly and housebreaking charges, the latter mainly to get money to feed a gambling passion. On 5 January 1905 he entered a small suburban mission hall to plan the theft of the organ. He was converted, returned to give his testimony at an open-air meeting the following week and remained a consistent Christian worker thereafter, never again being involved with drink, gambling, or the police.[19]   It was this man, once totally unpromising material for a Methodist worker, who became the CMM's chief agent among men from 1917 to World War II.

Charlie Woodward's technique was to conduct an open-air

meeting then hold a torchlight procession back to the Lyceum in the hope that the men would follow. Numbers were low to begin with and he adopted a typical CMM approach by having recourse to extensive prayer. Numbers grew. By 1922 the attendance was "sometimes 60 or 70"; in mid-1925 around 100, and by 1930 about 150 and perhaps even more when the venue shifted to the Francis Street hostel in mid-1931. The prospect of a bun and a cup of tea at the close attracted some, especially during the winter, but there was little doubt that many came for other reasons and a significant number responded to Charlie's appeals to turn to Christ and thereafter led consistent Christian lives.

Apart from this, Woodward regularly visited railway work-shops for lunch-hour meetings. He visited the cells at the magistrates courts at Redfern and Newtown to work among drunks and petty criminals. When men were freed from prison he met them, helped them with money or to find a job, and invited them to the Lyceum. Results were limited but worthwhile. He also regularly visited the Chinese quarter with New Testaments and tracts. The special interest in this work was to win back young women who had joined the Chinese before they became hopelessly addicted to opium.[20]

Other churches carried out similar work to that done by Charlie Woodward for more than two decades, but none did it more successfully. The secret of his success was that he had been through the mill himself: it was very difficult to reject the testimony of a man who had sunk to the lowest depths reached by any of his hearers and who could yet demonstrate that the power of Christ had raised him to new life. Charlie instinctively knew the way to reach his hearers, knowledge which was denied to men and women of middle-class origin. He depended heavily on his own personal testimony (and that of similar men) rather than on sermons or other means of instruction. In doing this, Charlie Wood-ward was simply applying an old Methodist technique with greater vigour and success than was usual.

While the period under consideration was one of almost continual disturbance and saw two major crises, the CMM had necessarily to continue its normal work. The war had temporarily suspended the mission's work for immigrants and left it with a debt of £2,250 on the People's Hostel at Circular Quay. This caused some problems. After the war, immigration was reintroduced, and the CMM again met Methodists at the wharf, but while it continued to assist them to find accommodation and a job it no longer provided the former as a matter of course and it no longer bore the costs involved. These now fell upon the Home Mission Society. This work continued throughout the interwar period. Similarly, the use of the Queen Victoria Seamen's Rest declined during the war and never recovered. A partial answer to this was found in the mid-1920s by throwing it open to wharf labourers as well.

The work of the Evangelists' Training Institute declined during the war as many actual and potential evangelists enlisted and left the institute almost empty. However, this branch recovered after the conflict and continued to provide the basic training for raw young men of little education who nevertheless believed that they had a call to the ministry but who could not as yet cope with the candidates' examinations. The syllabus and the demands on the time of the evangelists remained largely unchanged from earlier times. After 1934 the CMM and the Newtown Mission cooperated in this work, jointly providing facilities for the evangelists and sharing their services. By 1937 it was being claimed that of the more than two hundred evangelists who had passed through the institute, well over one hundred had joined the ministry of the Methodist or a sister church.[21] It is very difficult to estimate the net gain to the ministry from this work. Some of these young men must have found their way into the ministry without it: their families or the local minister would have assisted them with the examinations. Yet a substantial number would probably have fallen by the wayside without this more skilled and organized assistance. All must have gained from supervised experience in work more difficult than most were likely to confront later in the circuits to which they were appointed. Above all, the institute must have made the beginning of a dent in the problem so evident in the late nineteenth century of having a largely country-bred ministry unfamiliar with the problems of the industrial city.

It is difficult to make meaningful statements about membership or attendance at the Lyceum over this period. Allowance must be made for the temporary inclusion of William Street (1917–19), and of Bourke Street after 1929. The capacity of the Lyceum was reduced by remodelling in the mid-twenties. Add to this the fact that church membership statistics are notoriously unreliable, not only because of the failure of some ministers to delete the names of dead, removed or lapsed members from the roll, but the equally apparent tendency of some Methodist clergy to cleanse the rolls on their arrival in a circuit and then let the numbers build up as their regime progressed. This was a more significant problem at a mission where long terms of office were the rule. With due allowance for all this, N.S.W. Methodist Conference statistics suggest a decline in membership from about five hundred at the end of Taylor's regime to a little over three hundred at the arrival of Hoban two years later. Despite fluctuations, there was little overall change by his departure in 1921. Figures for "attendants and adherents" showed a similar pattern but the variation was much smaller and numbers suggest that Hoban probably did fill the Lyceum regularly, though there is no evidence that he was able to gain the additional commitment involved in becoming a confirmed member. Foreman's period possibly showed the opposite trend; a restoration of membership numbers to the level of Taylor's day but a substantial decline in attendance below that warranted by the remodelling of the Lyceum. He was a deeper and more scholarly preacher than Hoban and also faced the challenge of the radio service as well as bearing the brunt of the "gay twenties". Under Williams, attendance seems to have remained steady at the relatively low level to which it had sunk at the end of Foreman's time, and membership, after an initial decline, again grew slowly. The figures provide limited corroboration for the tendency noted by Hansen and referred to earlier in this chapter.

It must have been impressive, during Hoban's regime, to see an auditorium which seated twenty-five hundred filled to its limits and with people standing around the walls at a special service. Reports of the congregation always stressed that it included a complete cross-section of the community: professional men, students, policemen, entertainers, business-girls, old ladies, "down-and-outs". The same reports usually stress that, unlike most church congregations, there were as many or more men than women. A related point of interest is the information concerning considerable numbers of men who became "regulars" at the mission's open-air services in the Domain or at the Town Hall corner. These outdoor congregations seem to have been almost totally male and while, by this time, they were serious and silent, with none of the trouble caused by the hostile secularists in the 1880s, the services were very dependent on rapid-fire testimony and homely addresses: the street corner was no place for lengthy or scholarly sermonizing. Such work was often, accordingly, in the hands of the evangelists or Charlie Woodward, though the superintendent sometimes set an example.[22]

The CMM formula for success remained devotion, organization, and ceaseless activity, in that order. Devotion continued to be expressed not only through the ordinary Sunday services, but through the weekly class meetings, the Saturday consecration service, and the Sunday afternoon prayer meeting. The old Methodist institution of the class meeting remained vigorously alive at the CMM though in few other places. It was based on a programme rotating on a four-weekly plan between a special address, Bible study and prayer, hymn singing, and, finally, testimony, praise and prayer. There were also special classes to train personal workers whose job it was to spot and guide those who appeared to be in spiritual trouble at the Sunday evening after-meeting. The Saturday night consecration service, which has already been discussed in detail, continued throughout the period though there would appear to have been some considerable decline before Williams's arrival as a letter from a Bundaberg visitor, published in the *Greeting* of 8 February 1930, while declaring the meeting helpful, suggested it would be of greater value if more of the CMM people attended it.

At least as early as 1919, and possibly during the Great War, a Sunday evening prayer meeting started and was to undergo considerable development under both Williams and Rayward. The PSA was followed by a quick tea for workers and then the prayer meeting, the open-air and Lyceum services. From small beginnings, this meeting had grown to 130 by mid-1932.[23]

Activity in the spiritual sphere was indicated by the regular programme. On Sundays, there were two services and the PSA at Headquarters, along with junior Christian Endeavour, the tea and fellowship, the prayer meeting, and the after-meeting. In addition, there was an outdoor service in the Domain in the afternoon and one at the Town Hall corner in the evening. During the week, Charlie Woodward ran his men's meeting, there was the superintendent's class meeting, young women's Bible class, Methodist Order of Knights, and Girls' Comradeship, an additional outdoor service on Thursday evening, a further Christian Endeavour meeting, and the consecration service on Saturday.[24] All this took no account of philanthropic activities.

The PSA was an important feature of some of the English missions from the beginning and was seen as a link between the man in the street and the worship-life of the church. The Sydney PSA has only been touched on in relation to specific events hitherto and it is appropriate to comment more extensively now as it reached maturity in the 1920s under the direction of the superintendent's colleagues, F. H. Rayward[25] and, later, A. J. Gould.

Taylor, aware of the importance of an "unorthodox", less formally religious service as a means of drawing into the orbit of the church those who would not normally attend, attempted to use the English idea as adapted by Hugh Price Hughes at West London. There was a two-pronged attack, with a Sunday PSA and a midweek free "people's entertainment". The latter developed well, the former did not, despite periods of hope, and gradually disappeared. The explanation is uncertain. Sufficient to say that the PSA (or "Lyceum People's Own", as it was known 1908–18) did not really become a permanent part of the life of the CMM until the move to the Lyceum in mid-1908, a fact which in itself may suggest a reason for earlier failure.

Initially, the *Methodist* expressed some unfriendliness,

which it quickly abandoned, believing that the use of Sunday afternoon for the discussion of political and social questions "is open to grave objections" and that the church should not take the lead in breaking down the barriers which protected the sabbath from secular concerns.[26] Nevertheless, the LPO movement forged ahead rapidly and attendances ran as high as thirteen hundred on occasion. After six months, there were nearly a thousand members (these were people who paid a subscription and had a voice in the election of the organizing committee which ran the programme), while attendances ranged between twelve hundred and two thousand. There was a considerable decline from this early peak, and the average attendance in 1910 was put at "almost 800", still a worthwhile figure. The name changed from LPO to PSA in April 1918.

Although figures were not given regularly throughout the twenties, it is evident that its popularity was growing and that two thousand might sometimes attend, even on a humid February afternoon. On 17 August 1930, fourteen hundred attended to hear the chief railway commissioner discuss the not overexciting topic, "The Problems of a Public Administrator". On a number of occasions, the building was described as being full. It was also an indication of popularity that the PSA was reported with reasonable regularity in the secular press.

It is more difficult to say who went. The fact that the LPO committee early developed plans for a reading-room, gymnasium, social clubs, temporary assistance to the unemployed, as well as educational clubs for winter and outdoor clubs for summer suggests that it was aimed at the city-dweller and that it also had some interest in the young. Some of the topics discussed in 1908 point in the same direction: "God and the City", "The Claims and Credentials of Jesus Christ", "Jesus Christ — the Working Carpenter", "The Story of my Conversion", though there were others of a more exalted nature like "Christ and Social Problems". An attempt in 1910 to make special provision for those in domestic service also points in the same direction. The 1922 *Report* said of the audiences that "we have always the quality and quantity that gladden us, but make us long for more", while that of 1923, by suggesting that the PSA was "the brightest spot in the week for a considerable portion of the large audience" might be thought to be in conflict with it. The *Report* thought it attracted businessmen, professionals, and members of Parliament, as well as those "who live grey and lonely lives". All such found in the PSA "a glowing hour of enjoyment". Thus the comfortable middle classes seem to have mixed with the inner-city working classes. The nature of the subjects discussed throughout the interwar period was more likely to attract the upper levels of the working class and the middle class than the slum dwellers of downtown Sydney.[27]

From the outset, the organizers of the LPO/PSA set out to disarm the criticism that the movement involved the secularization of Sunday by the church itself. Party political questions would be avoided and "leading men of known character" would address the people on subjects designated to assist "the moral uplifting of the man, the community, the nation". Two years later it was claimed that "secular topics are guardedly kept from our platform" and that the most popular topics were those moral and spiritual in character. In the 1922 *Report* it was asserted that "our PSA is not an entertainment. It is a religious service, with a wider range of topics to be discussed than ordinary worship can permit".

During the Great War, PSA topics were heavily slanted towards the war and the duty of loyalty. There was also a fair sprinkling of talks on liquor reform, particularly early closing, which may be viewed both as typical Methodist social reform talks and as further patriotic addresses, since drink was seen as the ally of the "Hun" and the enemy of the Empire. There were many musical, general religious, and missionary programmes to complete the picture. Peace saw a disappearance of the purely "war" addresses, but general patriotic material remained popular: Anzac, Empire, and Armistice days required such addresses annually and they also occurred at other times. Music remained a regular and popular part of the programme and there was a strong upsurge in travel talks, or talks about foreign countries by their consuls. Pseudo-religious talks, like "Communism Versus Christianity", "Mohammedanism and Modern Civilization", or "The Bible and Shakespeare" were also popular, as were missionary addresses.

The claim that the PSA was more than an entertainment was justified. There can be no question of the educational value of many of the topics discussed. This included the travel talks. The claim that the PSA was essentially religious and spiritual could also be justified. Many of the addresses were either religious or pseudo-religious in character and all were encased in a religious service which included hymns and prayers. It was, however, demonstrably nonsense to claim that secular topics were rigidly excluded since the importance of both patriotic and travel talks has been noted.

The claim that party political material was excluded must also be tested. Subjects like "The China Question", "The Balkan Countries", and "Empire Economic Co-operation" could be seen as political but not party political. The same cannot be said for W. M. Hughes on "Australia's Place on the Map", nor for the Rev. James Green's "Labour at the Crossroads", in which he declared that "we want a true blue Australia not a land that is Russian red". Other suspicious titles occur from time to time. What can be said is that when party political material was involved it was always from the conservative point of view.

This last criticism aside, there is not much doubt that the PSA, as it developed under Rayward and Gould, filled a genuine need for both education and recreation. It may also have drawn into the fuller life of the church some not otherwise likely to be contacted. It is quite impossible to test the claims made in the 1921 and 1925 *Reports* that the PSA platform played "no small part in helping to mould public opinion throughout the state on Social and Moral questions", though the interest of the newspapers in it must suggest some influence.[28]

Dalmar continued to be the most popular of the CMM charities during this period and its role was an expanding one. The war, and the more relaxed standards of morality flowing from it, put the limited accommodation at the Croydon home under constant pressure.

The Children's Home, Croydon. From Colwell, *Illustrated History of Methodism* (1904).

The desire for more room, and for a change of format from one large building to a number of cottages, was evinced from as early as 1917, but no active steps were taken until late 1919 when it was decided that it would be better to move to new premises rather than undertake expensive repairs at Croydon. Land was purchased at Dundas with a gift from William Winn, and plans were drawn up for a main administrative building and two cottages as a first stage to accommodate sixty children and staff. Later, other cottages would be partly or wholly donated by individuals. The main building opened on 24 March 1923 and the foundation stone for the first cottage was laid on the same day. The debt on a property which had cost £18,000 was only £3,000.[29] As the cottages were erected, total accommodation gradually expanded, though it never kept pace with demand. A new kindergarten, hospital, and infants' block were also erected during the period and there was a gradual development of less conspicuous facilities for the children such as Guides, Scouts, Christian Endeavour, holidays by the sea, sporting contests, and concerts.[30]   The home became increasingly dependent on the generosity of individuals and groups who clothed one or more of the children or sent donations in kind, though the more than thirty acres of land at Dundas did allow the growing of fruit and vegetables, and eventually, the keeping of a dairy herd.   Money was beginning to come from the United Charities Organization and the State Children's Relief Fund, though Sunday school collections remained very important. Christmas Day collections in the churches became significant from 1926.   The home barely managed to pay its way throughout the Depression and a fall in donations put it in deficit for the first time in 1936.

Throughout his career, Hoban had always taken a keen interest in work for young women and he planned and worked for some provision for young female workers almost from his arrival in Sydney.   Women were taking a larger and more important role in the paid work-force during the war and spent more time in the city.   With a considerable number of young men in uniform, and deprived of normal female company, the women were also more subject to pressure in the streets and parks than before.   By the 1916 Conference, he had determined to establish "cosily furnished rooms" where they might spend their leisure hours.   In this way, young women would be able to avoid morally dangerous environments.   Opened in August 1916, the rooms appear to have been well used.   Shortly afterwards, accommodation was opened at Headquarters for working girls and as time went by provision was also made for the physical, intellectual, and moral development of young women living at or associated with the CMM through clubs of various kinds.

Despite his undoubted concern for the well-being of young women, and the fact that he was always ready to lend an especially sympathetic ear to any woman who wished to pour out her troubles to him, Hoban was even more dominated than most men of his time by the stereotype of woman as "mother":

The day a woman leaves the liberty of maidenhood she gives herself to another.   From that day she is not her own.   The soured and silly critic of such a woman, judging it from tne outside, talks of individuality suppressed — of freedom sold — of drudgeries imposed — of a liberty thrown away. Ask the young wife if she would exchange all the anxieties of motherhood for the lost liberty of maidenhood, and she will tell you she never knew the divinity of womanhood until she was "owned".[31]

It was a view that was already becoming old-fashioned at the time.

Foreman once said that the CMM was "inconceivable" without the sisters of the people, but less has been recorded of their difficult and unglamorous task in this period than was the case in the earlier years. The *Greeting* described the mission's view of their work when it wrote (21 August 1915) that souls had been "dragged back from the mouth of hell" by their arms and that "the path has been made easier for the feet of the poor".

The former task centred around the two homes, Alexandra at Burwood and Hope Haven in Crown Street, the latter acting, in the mission's words, as "a kind of moral dragnet". The sisters called at dubious homes and the haunts of young women, undertook "moonlight scouting" in the streets, and visited prison cells. The object had changed somewhat from earlier days. Originally the work had been truly rescue work, with the sisters aiming to gather in women in their late teens and early twenties who had already turned to prostitution and drunkenness. These they attempted to restore to a purer path. From somewhere about the time of the war, the work became more preventive in nature. Younger girls, inclined to be wayward and hard to discipline, too old and unsuitable for Dalmar, were taken in in the hope that loving discipline, Christian teaching, and care and concern would prevent them from slipping further into moral difficulties. Pregnant girls who lacked acceptance and support at home were also cared for, guided, and often restored to their families after the relationship had been mended and the parental sense of hurt and "betrayal" overcome.[32]

It is not clear why the change of concern from older to younger girls occurred. The 1921 *CMM Report* attributed the "preventive crusade" to "altered times" without further explanation. Perhaps the writer had in mind the general loosening of the moral code so widely commented on at the time and hoped that the CMM's preventive efforts would help combat the problem. However, in view of the perception noted earlier in this chapter, that prostitution and associated problems increased during the war years, it is not clear why the mission felt free to move away from its more traditional "female rescue" role. Possibly the change reflected Hoban's general concern to protect the well-being of those young women who were morally endangered but who had not as yet fallen from grace.

The justification for the decision to end the work entirely in 1929 is equally uncertain. There was certainly a growing need for care for the elderly (Alexandra was to become a home for elderly women) and times made it difficult to purchase an additional site. It is also a fact that the two sisters in charge of Alexandra, Annie and Elizabeth, retired during 1929.[33] What is lacking is any indication that the need for a home for "wayward girls" had declined.

Little will be said of homes for the aged here, since the real expansion of such institutions began in the Rayward era. However, one for women opened on 30 November 1929 and one for men on 7 December 1929 at Narrabeen. A comment in the 1929 *Report* that it had long been intended to start a home for men but that no one had expected to be able to begin one for women simultaneously reinforces the view that the vacation of Alexandra by the wayward girls was a relatively sudden decision — or, at least, one not foreseen but perhaps precipitated by an inability to replace the retiring sisters. The timing of the opening of these homes, just at the onset of the Depression, was impeccable and there was never any trouble filling them. Indeed, the men's home had to be extended in 1935 when the opportunity was taken to rename it the "W. G. Taylor Memorial Home".[34]

All evangelical churches have among their members some excessively narrowminded individuals. The CMM struck trouble with a small number of such people over the fact that its main auditorium, the Lyceum Theatre, was still leased out six days a week for motion pictures. There had been some trouble even before the CMM took over the theatre. During 1906, the Rev. Dan O'Donnell, using it for mission work under the direct patronage of the Trust to which Vickery had left it, complained about the "indecent" posters displayed outside the theatre by Mr C. Spencer, the lessee. This problem blew over, but by early 1909 there were minor complaints reaching Taylor that Spencer was using his office on the premises on Sunday to "manufacture" films and also that he was conducting private viewings of films of prize fights. He was warned against both of these practices.

The 1910 Conference held a "long and searching" discussion in camera of the whole question of picture-shows in mission halls. The good rents available from picture proprietors were often the only way to sustain the financial burdens of the halls and, while it was desirable that the halls be available at all times for mission use, the real alternative to letting them for entertainment was more generous giving to reduce their debts. Proprietors were generally anxious to avoid offence.

The Conference discussions had resulted from sustained allegations made by a supernumerary minister, Rev. S. H. McDade, and Conference passed an innocuous resolution largely concerned with dodging the issue but which did urge strict supervision of films shown in church halls. The CMM appointed its organizing secretary, James Gilmour, as censor (on a £20 honorarium) and left it at that. Less than twelve months later, the Lyceum Trustees wrote to the CMM urging a more vigilant censorship because there were persistent rumours about the quality of the films. It is difficult to believe that the diligent organizing secretary was careless about his work and it is likely that McDade and his supporters were pursuing their campaign relentlessly.[35]

There was sporadic trouble throughout the war with the attention of Spencer Pictures Limited being drawn in 1916 to complaints about their films and to the fact that in future censorship would be "more thorough and drastic in character". Notwithstanding, Conference in 1917, 1918, and 1919 passed resolutions urging the Lyceum Trustees to ensure that only "entirely unobjectionable" films were shown. Meanwhile, Greater Union Theatres, who had bought out Spencer's company and lease, were reminding the Lyceum Trustees that the least objection to material led to its withdrawal.

Mid-1918 provides us with an interesting concrete objection.   M. G. Clarke of Lindfield objected that right alongside the placard advertising Hoban's address entitled "An Unparalleled Utterance" was another showing "the reclining figure of a buxom lady, on which was printed in large letters, 'The woman God forgot' ".   Before dismissing this particular instance as unreasonable narrow-mindedness of a kind almost unintelligible in the present day, it would be as well to pause and note that it was possibly the theological implications of the film title which were offensive to the evangelical mind rather than the doubtless reasonably clad reclining buxom lady.   There was a genuine contradiction involved in displaying such a title in the foyer of a church proclaiming God's abiding concern for His whole creation and the ready availability of salvation for all.[36]

Another major assault occurred in 1923 when, among other things, McDade presented Conference with a forty-five page pamphlet (now mercifully lost) on the subject and pressed for a motion prohibiting the use of the Lyceum for films.   A Lyceum trustee pointed out that not only did Gilmour see every film to be shown in the Lyceum but that at least once a week one of the trustees visited the theatre to check.   They included among their number some of the most prominent clergy and laymen in the Methodist church. He also pointed out that it was useless to argue that an equivalent income could be gained from letting the hall for concerts and the like, as that experiment had failed long since at Centenary Hall: in any case there would be people who would criticize some of the songs.

At the time an estimate was made by the treasurer, P. N. Slade, that if the lease with Greater Union were not renewed the annual loss on the Lyceum would be £2,937/10/-, and this problem was quite insurmountable.   If the revenue from the pictures were lost, then the church would have to give up its central city property.

The lease continued to be renewed and from 1931 the censors were the Rev. R. J. Williams and the new organizing secretary, Miss I. Halbert, who were expected to spend four hours a week on the task. But there is little likelihood that S. H. McDade ever relented before his death at eighty-two in 1934. Perhaps the real trouble was that this fiery Irish Methodist, who had been forced by voice trouble to retire in 1898 at the age of forty-six simply had too much time on his hands in which to cause trouble.[37]

The ghost of the "city church" refused to be laid throughout the entire interwar period, despite the stability of the CMM and the recurring crises of war and depression. It is impossible to estimate accurately the depth or breadth of feeling in favour of a central cathedral church "worthy of Methodism". The impression could be gained that the cause was revived from time to time merely by the editor of the *Methodist*, or a few correspondents to that paper, or a handful of clerical and lay enthusiasts at Conference. Yet the demand did persist and at times worried the CMM authorities. On the other hand, the cause could not triumph despite the best efforts of its adherents. However, this recurring demand must be seen as a criticism of the CMM itself. The reasons for this will unfold below.

In late 1915, when one might have expected the church to be otherwise occupied, the Sydney District Synod recommended to Conference that it acquire a suitable site in the city for a church "to worthily represent [sic] Methodism in the state capital, and . . . form a denominational rallying centre as occasion may require". The *Methodist* supported the argument because recent developments had left Methodism with little but mission halls in the city proper. During the 1915 centenary celebrations it had had to borrow a church from another denomination for the visit of the American Methodist, Bishop Hoss. It also raised the bogey that many Methodists attended the city churches of other denominations, a "fact" which was said to prove the need for such a church. Taylor pointed out that Sydney Methodism had once had a cathedral church and that it had become a total failure. In all the great cities of England and America only mission churches had been able to succeed. The

Anglicans and Congregationalists could only maintain their city churches by the undesirable practice of drawing their congregations from the suburbs, while the argument that many Methodists were attending the city churches of other denominations was spurious. Such a church would kill the CMM which was fulfilling the real needs of the city.[38]

In 1921, the *Methodist* was back on the attack with pathetic arguments: "We have never had so suitable a building for Conference as Old York Street Church". Efficient church offices existed, but "no sanctuary in affiliation therewith". There was no "home" of Methodism in the mother city of the Commonwealth to show to distinguished visitors and if this were not rectified soon the task would become impossible. Two months later it published a front page photograph of the Chicago Methodist church with its 400-foot tower and chimes audible over the roar of the traffic, and with it went the caption, "When will Sydney Methodists have their cathedral? Chicago's example should inspire greater efforts here" So the tedious campaign continued.

At the 1925 Conference, a committee reported recommending the building of a city church and, despite strong CMM objections, was asked to work further on the project for the next Conference. Always the argument was cast in the form, "Our CMM is doing great work, but . . . " Sometimes the "but" referred to the need to impress visitors, sometimes to the provision of a suitable locale for society marriages, and sometimes to the need for a cathedral for the worship of well-to-do suburban Methodists (who should have been content to stay in their home circuits).

Quietly, someone associated with the CMM began to make plans for the possible construction of a chapel on the Castlereagh Street end of the Vickery Settlement Buildings. This would replace the conference hall on the ground floor, though changes elsewhere would allow for a substantial social hall on the first floor while displaced sleeping quarters would move further up. It might also undercut the city church proposal, so potentially dangerous to the functioning of the CMM. As an interim measure "a beautiful little sanctuary for prayer and meditation" was created from one of the first-floor rooms in September 1931, but the periodic bleatings of the *Methodist* ensured that the main project would not be lost to sight. It was decided to open the ground-floor chapel (Wesley chapel) in connection with the Golden Jubilee in 1934. That it was designed with great care, with the panelling, pipe-organ case, and upholstered pews of Queensland silky oak and with the stained glass above the sanctuary illuminated from behind by indirect lighting, tends to emphasize that Wesley chapel was the CMM challenge to the city church concept.[39]

At the 1935 Conference, some thought that Wesley chapel solved the problem, at least for the time, though one man saw church union as the only final answer. But one of the chief protagonists of the city church, Rev. W. N. Lock, successfully moved the appointment of a committee to keep the issue alive. Later, Williams took up the cudgels, pointing out that the archbishop of Sydney was holding a Good Friday night service in the State Theatre because of the advantage that a nonecclesiastical building gave and that many of the CMM converts were people who would never have attended service in an ecclesiastical structure: "To surrender the services now held in the Lyceum, would be to give up a witness which no other church is making". Inconsistently, but delightfully, during 1936, while the CMM was opposing the city church concept with vigour, its Order of Service sheet bore a picture of a large, traditional, gothic structure in the top left-hand corner.

In mid-1936, the Lyceum Trust moved to combat a proposal to demolish at least a part of the existing complex and to replace it with a church to seat 1,200, pointing out the increase of the debt, the loss of revenue, and the interference with the philanthropic work of the mission. The net loss of revenue from the demolition of the Castlereagh Street property would have been £1,254 p.a. or that from the Pitt Street property £7,580 p.a. A long memorandum from E. Frank Vickery rehearsed the history of the Lyceum Trust, and pointed out that the recent expenditure by the Trust of £9,000 on Wesley chapel had been justified on the grounds of increasing the usefulness of the premises and satisfying "if possible, the clamant demand in some quarters for some worthy central place of worship for Methodists". It also argued that to remodel the buildings for the purpose proposed would in spirit, if not in law, be a betrayal of the wishes of the man who had given the property to the church.

Resolutions were submitted to the 1938 Conference to allow the mortgaging and remodelling of the Lyceum property, but these were defeated though, curiously, the City Church Committee was reappointed. Vickery thought the victory significant and believed the new superintendent would now "have a chance to get the CMM to function instead of all the resources going to build another idol of stone". He found it a source of quiet but substantial satisfaction that at the CMM the poor could hear the Gospel without having to contribute to the collection and could "feel quite at home, as you know so many of the poor have" over the years.[40]

The question of the city church may seem only marginally relevant to the life of the CMM, but it was not. It was a variant form of the opposition to the mission which was evident in the 1880s and 1890s. After fifty years, it was impossible to argue that the CMM was unnecessary, inappropriate, or unsuccessful. It was possible to argue that it did not provide for all the religious needs of the city. Nor could its interwar critics accept that the mother church of Methodism consisted of a theatre and a block of offices. Their thinking was still bounded by nineteenth century horizons and relied upon the visual impressiveness of the structure, regardless of its value for reaching the unchurched members of the working class forced by their poverty to live within the bounds of the great industrial city. As one of the critics wrote: "Along with many others, I have always felt that there is a kind of stigma resting upon our church, in that its very centre, its nucleus, is so closely associated with, and located in, a picture show."[41] Such people had missed the whole point of the work of Taylor and his successors and had failed to understand either the traditional evangelical aspect of Methodism or its newer social aspect. Having recognized the challenge, the CMM acted wisely to forestall it by the creation of Wesley chapel.

The question of the succession was never solved easily at the CMM. Samuel Hoban was brought in from Victoria in 1915 to plug an unexpected gap caused by the declining health of P. J. Stephen, a move that was reasonable given his earlier experiences at the Melbourne CMM. It was also successful and Hoban gathered bigger crowds at the Lyceum than ever before to hear his simple but highly articulate preaching. A close warm relationship existed between pastor and people. His organizing capacity and his evangelical purpose contributed further to a successful ministry. Consequently, it came as something of a shock when, late in 1919, Hoban informed the CMM Committee that he would retire from the mission at the 1921 Conference.[42] His reason was that he could not continue to bear the strain beyond a six-year term. No attempt seems to have been made to retain Hoban's services by offering him extended recuperation leave, as had been done with Taylor on several occasions. The committee merely asked him to reconsider and, on his refusal, moved quickly to appoint H. C. Foreman to be his colleague from the 1920 Conference and his successor from 1921.

In early 1920 Hoban accepted an invitation to the Melbourne CMM. Towards the middle of the year, the Sydney CMM Committee unanimously resolved to ask the Melbourne CMM to release him to continue his work in Sydney. Foreman played a leading role in the attempts to retain Hoban but the latter left the matter in the hands of the Melbourne CMM which, not unnaturally, decided that his acceptance of their invitation was "in line with the divine purpose and appointment". Hoban then reaffirmed his acceptance of the invitation.

Sydney bore no ill will to Hoban for his decision to go. It was claimed that almost three thousand crowded into the Lyceum on 20 March for his final service and that almost as many were turned away. Hoban had some difficulty getting into the theatre through the large crowd outside. Some had waited from 3.00 p.m. to be sure of getting in and the service began half an hour early because of the large number standing. Hoban said that those who claimed that he could not wait to get back to Victoria were wrong, and that if he were ever asked to come back he would obey. The various fare-

wells in his honour were all crowded and all pervaded by the
same spirit.   Over the next decade, until his death on 29
August 1931, Hoban returned several times to speak at
anniversaries and was always greeted by overflowing crowds
and expressions of love and goodwill.

There are some curious features to this incident. It was
strange that Hoban could tell eighteen months in advance
that the strain of the mission would have become too much
for him by April 1921 and that the Sydney CMM Committee
should not have offered him leave of absence for six months
or a year to recuperate and rejoin the programme. They
must have had a clear indication that such an arrangement
would not be acceptable to Hoban. It is even stranger that
within a few months of declaring his need to be relieved of
the strain of the Sydney CMM, Hoban should accept the
responsibility of the Melbourne mission, though, admittedly,
the latter was better provided for in personnel and money.
Sydney's appeal to Melbourne to forego its claims on Hoban
clearly implied that divine guidance was not to be taken too
seriously but might be maintained according to the felt needs
of men.   Hoban's remark at the final service could have
carried the same implications.

Why then did Hoban leave? He did suffer a breakdown in
health in mid-1923, but that was after two years of solid
work at Melbourne. This could have been the delayed outcome of a condition of which he had received early warning
in 1919. There were so many denials, by Hoban and others,
that he simply wanted to return to Melbourne, that it is
difficult to accept that as a serious explanation, even if it was
widely believed in Sydney and was a perfectly reasonable
attitude to take. He had returned to Melbourne for a month
for his holidays each January, so it is evident that his links
with that city remained strong. A different explanation has
been given by a later superintendent, F. H. Rayward, who
went to the CMM as colleague to Foreman on Hoban's
departure.   Rayward believes that although Hoban was a
brilliant preacher, he found it difficult to create new material
and felt a continual need to draw upon old sermons to fill
out the new: a sister at the mission claimed that his most
famous sermon, "The Second Mile", was preached in modi-

fied form sixteen times in his six years at the CMM.[43] If this is correct, and his published volume of sermons, *The Great Realities*, lends some colour to the story, there can be little doubt that it would become a haunting problem for a man of some vanity. The well-modulated light baritone voice, the handsome presence, and the winning way with people could not ultimately conceal this important weakness. Yet we must keep in mind that the assessments which preachers make of each other are not always marked by much charity.

Foreman alone emerged from the incident with credit. He was ready to do all in his power to help retain Hoban for Sydney and to subordinate his own interests entirely, even to the point of remaining as colleague, a considerable act of self-denial for a man who was already a senior minister and long past that point in his career when he would expect to take a subordinate role. It appears even more generous if we accept Rayward's view that Foreman and Hoban did not get along very well.

Foreman's own departure was also marked with difficulty. He announced in late 1929 that he would leave at the 1931 Conference and that enquiries would be made throughout Australia, New Zealand, and England for a successor. Foreman himself was asked to go to England after the 1930 Conference and report. Although Australian experience with missions was not in any way inferior to the English, the Methodist church in N.S.W. was slow to abandon the cultural cringe and was repeating its actions of 1889 when there had been thought of by-passing Taylor for a new import, though the 1930 decision was that of the CMM rather than the Conference, which seems to have backed it only reluctantly. Foreman approached Dr Donald Soper of the Islington Mission, one of the great men of British Methodism. Soper was known not only for his work at the mission itself, but for his capacity to gather and hold weekday crowds of two to three thousand men on Tower Hill, as well as for his advanced social thinking. The CMM Quarterly Meeting endorsed Foreman's nomination unanimously and it was understood that Soper would sail from England in September 1931, subject to the approval of the N.S.W. and British Conferences. However, in late August or early September 1930, Soper cabled Sydney

R.J. Williams, CMM superintendent 1932–38. By courtesy of the Wesley Central Mission.

rejecting the invitation because "pressing interests", including the erection of a large and costly hall, made it imperative for him to stay at Islington. In fact, J. E. Carruthers, a former president-general of the Methodist church of Australia and editor of the *Methodist,* had written to Soper telling him that the CMM held its services in a theatre, that it had no regular congregation, and that its officials wanted him for his ability "to capture the crowds". He did this despite the fact that as a member of the CMM Committee he had participated in both the decision to send Foreman to England and in the unanimous acceptance of the latter's nomination of Soper.[44]

The CMM turned to R. J. Williams who, as a young man, had spent four years as colleague to Taylor, Stephen, and Hoban in rapid succession. After that he had spent a period at the Balmain Mission and was known to like a challenge. Though he might lack the flair of a Soper, who might well have turned the CMM into paths like those taken a quarter of a century later under Alan Walker, Williams was a man of proven ability who would guide the mission safely through the Depression.

Very early in 1937, a sense of declining loyalty among some of his senior officers, notably the imperious P. N. Slade, a longtime official who exercised so much power that Williams's successor, Rayward, never felt really in control until Slade died, led Williams to foreshadow his own departure in 1938. This time the mission invited Williams's colleague, C. J. Wells, to become acting superintendent, with the Rev. Henry Hunter as his deputy but with yet another Englishman, Rev. A. E. Witham as preacher at the evening service for most of the first year. When Witham died, the committee asked F. H. Rayward, who had spent several successful years at the Newcastle Mission, to become superintendent with Wells as his deputy. Wells, an able man, had apparently had enough and asked Conference to send him elsewhere. This it did and brought the Rev. W. J. Harper from Narrandera to become Rayward's colleague.[45]

There is just a hint in all this petty manoeuvering that the CMM Committee was losing its sense of direction. Perhaps it was as well that over the next few years death removed two laymen of very long standing, H. M. Hawkins and P. N. Slade.

In any case, in Rayward, who had spent six years as colleague to Foreman and seven as superintendent at Newcastle, it had acquired a man who would make his own mark in new and important ways.

It is worth trying to see what happened to the finances of the mission over a period which encompassed both war and depression. While detailed records are not available, there is an annual balance sheet for the working account for each year from 1915 to 1937 and it is possible to make some calculations of interest.[46]

McKernan has indicated that church receipts were generally well maintained during the Great War, despite heavy giving to patriotic causes. By the end of 1915 the CMM claimed to be hard hit by a serious decline in subscriptions while its responsibilities were increasing. In fact, total income for 1915 fell 17 per cent on 1914 and by 1917 had fallen a total of 40 per cent. Expenditure fell 23 per cent in 1914–15 and a total of 39 per cent over the period 1914–17. It appears that giving by outsiders, but not that by members and adherents, declined significantly since the proportion of total income contributed by offerings held up better than that coming from either subscriptions or the annual Spring Fair. Hoban reinforced his reputation as a man who could eliminate debts as the CMM working account was in credit each year of his superintendency and he turned an overall debit of £704 into a surplus of £224. Later superintendents were not able to maintain the record and the account was in deficit seven times in Foreman's ten years and three times in Williams's seven years, though it is doubtful whether even Hoban could have done better than Williams in this respect.

From 1917, mission income fluctuated from £8,000 to £10,000 until it reached a peak of £10,394 in 1929 only to plunge by 37 per cent to £6,528 by 1933. After that, it staggered slowly and uncertainly upward towards the war. At the same time, expenditure also fluctuated (though the general movement was upward), peaking at £10,548 in 1930, at which point it had risen 29 per cent since 1926. It then plummeted 40 per cent to £6,375 in 1933 after which it also rose unsteadily.

Those figures reflect a determination to meet the rising unemployment of the pre-Depression and early Depression years. Not surprisingly, the worst years for the budget were 1930–31 when income was only about 95 per cent of expenditure. It should not be thought that the savage cuts in expenditure reflect a declining attempt to meet the needs of the time. Apart from the fact that much relief was in kind (cast-off clothing and boots, food) actually contributed in that form by donors, and in shelter, which likewise was not reflected in the accounts to the full extent, some of the most severe cuts were in staff salaries which, after increasing gradually to 1929, fell slightly to 1930, by 15 per cent in 1931 and by a further third in 1932, by which time they were at only 54.4 per cent of the 1929 level. They remained low until 1934 when they began to rise slowly once more. Furthermore, during the Depression years expenditure fell on institutions like Hope Haven, the Seamen's Mission, the Girls' Residential, immigration, the sisters' home, and the tearooms, but rose on the Refuge, the Hostel, and the aged homes. The more relief oriented an institution was, the more likely its expenses were to hold up or expand. This may be illustrated by the fact that in 1929 the income of the Refuge was 78 per cent of expenditure, but by 1931 it was only 27 per cent.

From this it might reasonably be concluded that the impression of the mission staff — that they were struggling to meet increased demands from drastically reduced resources during the Depression — was probably true. It also appears that the brunt of essential cuts in expenditure was taken in organizational areas while reduced numbers of personnel on reduced pay (they took at least one voluntary pay cut), struggled to fulfil the mission's philanthropic purpose to the best of their ability.

Phyllis Peter makes an error in her work on Methodist relief during the Depression by concentrating on the so-called Methodist Relief Fund, which was never significant, and by failing to observe the work of the CMM, which was the basic agency through which the church worked out its philanthropic intent. In terms of money, evidence suggests that it was the actual members and adherents of the CMM itself (who contributed through offerings) who continued to give more generously than did other Methodists from the suburbs or the country (whose giving is reflected in subscriptions or the bazaar). But this impression may be quite unfair, as it was probably the latter group who contributed the most in kind. Apart from this, institutions like the Girls' Residential were used as an important source of income to aid other unprofitable branches and the weekly PSA also made a useful contribution.

During the war and interwar period, the CMM did not stand out from other churches, whether Methodist or not, in the attitudes expressed about the war, the industrial problem in the 1920s, and other social questions. After the arrival of Williams, it did take a sturdier attitude to the Great Depression, but it still saw its main social work as rescue and the pursuit of mild reform rather than as political involvement and the pursuit of radical change. None of its superintendents in the period had the dynamism of Taylor. Hoban was probably the weakest, despite his enormous capacity to draw crowds. Foreman and Williams were sound administrators and capable preachers who kept the place on an even keel in unusually troubled times. There were occasional signs of internal dissension, the will-o'-the-wisp pursuit of an English superintendent and, of course, the perennial attacks of the city church brigade, so well handled by Williams and his co-adjutors, and the unnerving problem of Depression financing. By the time Williams left in 1937, to be replaced by Rayward, although not much further forward than it had been at the outbreak of the Great War, the CMM was at least ready to advance again and had laid the foundation for a future area of major expansion in the founding of its two homes for the aged.

6

War, Reconstruction, and Expansion

Like W. G. Taylor, Rayward had been plucked, not altogether willingly, from a successful ministry elsewhere, to come to the CMM. This was the second such experience for Rayward. In the early 1930s he had been taken, very much against his will, from a brilliantly successful work at Manly to revive the ailing Newcastle Mission. Having done that throughout the Depression and post-Depression years, he was now asked to fill the gap at Sydney CMM caused by the death of Witham. Again like Taylor, he was subject to uncertain health, an unrecognized gallstone problem which had dogged him throughout his Newcastle stay and which would put his Sydney ministry in jeopardy on one later occasion. The difference was that, unlike Taylor, Rayward was being translated to a cause that was basically strong. The spiritual power, the pastoral ministry, the institutions were already there and only required to be maintained and built upon.[1]

Rayward's preaching was that of a man of exceptional natural talent improved by every means which Christianity and art could provide. Careful preparation, the support of the Sunday evening prayer meeting, and twenty-five minutes of massage to relieve tension meant that this trained elocutionist went to the pulpit ready for a flawless performance. He saw the 7.00 p.m. service as the culmination of everything else done during the week, the climactic moment towards which the whole week moved. Nor was Rayward hesitant to use emotion and drama in his services. Sometimes during the evening service the theatre would be darkened completely, save only for a single spotlight focussed on a deep red cross at the front. As the organist played "When I Survey the Wondrous Cross" Rayward spoke of the significance of the cross and called for decisions "for Him who died upon the cross". Similarly, in Wesley chapel, the room might be darkened and even the light shining through the stained glass window of the Last Supper made to illuminate only the central figure of Christ.[2] Such moments of contemplation seem to have become precious to the CMM congregations and their role in worship and evangelism is readily understandable, but the charge of using emotional pressure might be levelled with success.

There is no reference to the Saturday night consecration service after the *Methodist* of 28 May 1938. Why it died remains obscure. It may be that Rayward made a deliberate decision to develop the Sunday-afternoon prayer meeting in its place. Perhaps it was simply more convenient for minister and people to use a time when many had to be on the premises rather than make a special trip in on Saturday evening. Of course, this limited attendance to CMM members and adherents, but they had always been the main participants with just a few from suburban circuits. It also changed the emphasis from preparation for Sunday generally to preparation for Sunday evening in the Lyceum, thus increasing the attention directed to that service.

After his appointment, Rayward moved quickly to build up the workers' tea between the PSA and the Lyceum service. In part this was a matter of convenience, in part it also sprang from a desire to avoid the necessity of buying in shops which it was later said, somewhat sanctimoniously, "most Christian folk dislike". But most of all it was because the new superintendent, a master of the personal touch, found the meal "an invaluable opportunity for happy social contacts and personal appeals". Sunday afternoon became "a time of unbroken fellowship in the Spirit, a real commune of joy and prayer". It was also an excellent way to make newcomers feel at home and part of the great mission rather than simply lost within its vastness. By the middle of 1940, attendance at the tea was never less than two hundred, often nearer three hundred, and people had at times to be turned away.[3]

The prayer meeting followed immediately after tea and, until about the beginning of 1939, was held in the boardroom, but had then to be transferred to Wesley chapel to cope with growing numbers. There is no indication how many attended before Rayward's time, but during his first few months there seem to have been 40 or 50 present. Over the next year, the average was 130 with a peak of 190. It grew consistently thereafter. In mid-1945 the average was 276; on 11 April 1948 an all-time peak of 356 was reached while in late 1954 it was claimed that the attendance was rarely less than 300.

There is no clear explanation why, at a time when most churches could accommodate their prayer meetings comfortably in the vestry, that at the CMM should be flourishing. The personality and vigour of the superintendent, the general sense of purpose about the mission, the belief that a massive prayer input was necessary for success, and the clever timing of the meeting probably all had something to do with it. The meeting itself was led by the CMM local preachers. While other themes were taken up, the main emphasis was on the Lyceum service. CMM authorities were confident that this was the source of the mission's undoubted power. The superintendent was "the most favoured of all his brethren" because few preachers anywhere in the world were upheld each week by so many people met together for just that purpose. D. T. W. Riddle, editor of *The Christian World* (London), thought that no British church had so large a prayer meeting and stressed the value of it. He also claimed that extensive prayer cleared the vision and led to improved understanding of the world's need.[4] Work without prayer was unavailing.

The class meeting, about seventy strong at Rayward's appointment, soon began to expand and more than doubled in six months. It was not just an occasion for praise and testimony, but also for inspiration, and Rayward's favourite dramatic device of the illuminated cross was often employed to this end. As of old, new converts were led into this meeting and expected to find there an opportunity for self-expression and the means for growth. A supernumerary, who attended specifically to see what made the CMM class meeting work when others did not, suggested that it was the informality, the sense of a happy family fellowship, with those present being made to feel that they shared with the superintendent the responsibility for making the CMM accomplish its purpose.[5]

Clearly, a class meeting which often approached two hundred in size should not have worked as it flew in the face of everything ever taught about group dynamics. The superintendent's capacity for developing personal relationships with his members was a major factor in this success.

Rayward placed more emphasis on the sacrament of Holy Communion than any of his predecessors seems to have done. Not only were regular staff communions held, but the service was also a regular quarterly part of the Lyceum meetings, despite the logistic problems associated with this. The number attending rose steadily from a modest 340 on 2 October 1938 to 770 on 8 July 1945 and a record 960 on 1 May 1949. To overcome the problem of the distribution of the elements to so many and still retain that calm atmosphere of holiness, meditative self-examination, and rededication, which Methodists always saw as a fundamental attribute of the communion, required very careful planning. The growing appreciation of this sacrament was an excellent answer to those who, in the past, had not found the CMM service suitable for intelligent people and who had sought a city cathedral church. To those who shared this service, the Lyceum was a cathedral, a "sanctuary of the soul".[6]

By Rayward's time the CMM no longer had the use of bands to assist in its open-air work, but it did have a well-tried formula: begin on time, avoid prayers, sing only one verse of each hymn except the first, recite Scripture passages from memory, make "snappy epigrammatic statements" backed by solid arguments but avoid too many stories, keep to the Gospels rather than the Old Testament, and never speak from notes. A woman soloist was better than a man, provided she had a big voice and clear enunciation. "Buttonholing" in the crowd was useful, but there must be no talking by the workers while the preacher was speaking. Outdoor converts were now few, though some were led to the indoor services and converted there. The noise of passing traffic often made the speaker's task nearly impossible until the purchase of a loud speaker. Even so, it sometimes required considerable faith to accept the scriptural assurance that bread is not cast upon the waters in vain.[7]

There is no doubt from the record that Rayward frequently preached to a theatre between two-thirds and completely filled, but membership was a better test of development. Rayward began with the ritual cleansing of the rolls in 1938, which caused a drop from 437 to 180, though a rise of 350 in the number of adherents suggests that at least a fair proportion of this "loss" of members may have been more formal than real. Thereafter the number rose steadily to a peak of 1,130 in 1954–55–56 and fell slightly to 1,101 in 1957.[8] This more than fivefold increase brought the number of members to a point where it approached the total attendance much more closely than was usual in the Methodist church. (This assumes that the rolls were kept as "clean" later as they were in 1938.) Such a change supports what has already been said about the deepening spiritual tone of the mission since it indicates that those who attached themselves to it were usually prepared to make a full commitment. It also suggests that a much larger percentage of mission converts remained within its confines than had been the case earlier and that it had lost the "depot" function which had been so important in Taylor's time. Of course, this might mean that it was attracting a larger proportion of its congregation from the suburbs and that it was dealing less effectively with the transients. Unfortunately we know nothing at all about the composition of the congregation in this period apart from a casual remark by Alan Walker that on his arrival in 1958 he found that elderly women formed a significant proportion of it. If correct, this would tend to support the preceding remarks. In any case, it is impossible to know how long this had been so or what the situation had been in the war and immediate postwar years.

As recently as Rayward's first period at the CMM, it had been possible to claim it "[had] not within its own membership a constituency of children and that its responsibility to these in the neighbouring districts was sufficiently fulfilled by a grand annual Christmas picnic". Indeed, there is little evidence of much effort in youth work before the end of World War II. Sister Elsie continued her court work for young people and

Dr F.H. Rayward, OBE, CMM superintendent 1938–58. By courtesy of the Wesley Central Mission.

she also continued a monthly meeting called the "Overseas Girls' Club" for migrant women. This had operated at least in Williams's time and probably in the 1920s when the main migration occurred. Rayward held a public speakers' class, directed mainly at local preachers and candidates for the ministry. Christian Endeavour continued to exist at Headquarters (as it had long done) and so did the Methodist Girls' Comradeship. There was a network of clubs at both Flinders Street and Millers Point, at least during the war years, and which (with the exception of Rays at Millers Point) may have been new in Rayward's time. This was very limited in scope compared with the broad range of youth services offered by any large modern church. However, such services have been of gradual growth, with the main development occurring after World War II. Church interest in youth runs parallel to general community interest and springs from the same causes. Thus the fifties marked the "discovery" of youth, the sixties provided a flowering of concern, and the seventies the beginning of disillusionment. No doubt a changing age structure towards the end of the century will see a substantial decline in effort in this area, just as governments already, at the beginning of the eighties, have sharply reduced their interest in education at all levels. In any case, the mission, since the failure of Taylor's early Boys' Club for the larrikins, had always concerned itself primarily with work among adults.

Real development in youth work began about 1947 under the leadership of the Rev. R. J. Noble. The first ever CMM youth camp was held at Woodford over the October long weekend in 1948, with sixty-three attending (fifty from CMM, thirteen friends). Progress was more rapid under the Rev. R. C. Coleman who became Rayward's colleague in 1949. He brought all the youth groups together under an over-arching federal structure called "Couriers for Christ". At the young people's request, a Bible study group was formed after Christian Endeavour and this rapidly transformed itself into a local preachers' class and added theology to its syllabus. By mid-1950, activities included this class, three Sunday schools (all run by Couriers), the annual weekend camp, open-air witness, tennis and football clubs, and a fellowship hour after the Lyceum service with a question box, open forum, films, testimonies, quizzes, and visiting speakers. The last was either a continuation, or more probably a revival, of a monthly meeting which had started in Williams's time. As well, the Couriers conducted the Sunday-evening service at Flinders Street, and, in late 1950, visited more than four hundred homes in the Darlinghurst area in the attempt to win new members, young and old.[9]

In mid-1951 the Couriers decided to open a Christian Community Centre in the Flinders Street hall to cater for all elements of a community known for its high migrant and Catholic populations, and its low level of church attendance. This programme included the transformation of the dingy old hall to provide a range of facilities for the whole family and occurred in two phases over six years, being finally completed in mid-1957. Yet from 1951 on an increased range of activities was built up in the hall. There was an annual "Courier Carnival" to raise funds for the CMM, a teenage study group, known as "Courier Younger Set", for high-school girls, a drama group, the "Courier Cadet Corps" for boys, ten to fourteen years, and its equivalent for girls known as the "Courier Companions' Club", a "Forum Club" for older young people, and a television club to counter the introduction of television into hotels by the United Licensed Victuallers Association. In addition, in 1957, they held a Courier Commando Campaign, visiting more than two thousand Darlinghurst homes in an attempt, later described as having "shown some fruits", to win the area for Christ. Throughout, the primary objective was never merely to provide amenities for themselves but always involved outreach into the Darlinghurst community. There was wisdom in the attempt to provide Christian fellowship for every member of the family and the attempt to create a link with the community through a genuine community centre rather than through traditional church activities which would have had little appeal in Darlinghurst: traditional Methodist youth groups, Knights, Comrades, and Christian Endeavour presumed some Christian knowledge and were hardly practicable in circumstances where this did not exist. Another contributing factor was the genuine insight of Ronald C. Coleman and Sister Hazel, who supervised the Darlinghurst activities.[10]

Not all activities were successful, but it was perhaps not surprising that television was not at first recognized as a desocializing influence, rather than the reverse. At least Coleman saw its importance to the church and sought to use it. No one ever claimed great results for the work, but there was some impact, especially among the young. Probably the deepest impact was on the Couriers themselves, but it is impossible to tell how extensively or permanently their lives may have been transformed by what was a powerful mixture of personal commitment to an overarching spiritual cause and a rich dose of occupational therapy. Furthermore, Alan Walker's innovative youth programme of the sixties may not have been so effective if Coleman had not created a tradition of youth involvement with the Couriers in the fifties.

Neither the war nor postwar prosperity eliminated the need to assist the destitute, deserted wives, or girls thrown out of home as a result of pregnancy. During the war, there was claimed to be a draining away of funds from relief work to patriotic causes, though the evidence for this in the accounts is not clear. There was a minor new venture taken up in 1938–1942 when the City Children's Country Holiday Scheme handed its work over the CMM, the idea being to send slum children to country properties for all or part of the holidays with the hosts bearing the cost of board and the church raising the cost of the fares and of the medical examination which all underwent before departure. Improved financial conditions and transport difficulties were given as reasons for abandoning the scheme in 1942 (except in special cases), though it is notable that the CMM had lost money on the project in 1941 instead of making the modest profit of former years. In 1943 it turned to providing a fortnight's holiday in the Blue Mountains for thirty to forty women pensioners. The CMM provided bus transport, staff, and pocket money, and accommodation in a boys' grammar school at Springwood, and the local circuit helped with hospitality. It was a pleasant, if fairly insignificant, gesture and was still operating at least as late as 1950.[11]

Life at Dalmar proceeded more or less uneventfully through

the war years, though there were periodic pressures on accommodation. Change was in the air in 1947. In large part this was the result of serious budgetary difficulties which hit the institution in 1946 and lasted through 1949. The period between 1943 and 1948 saw income fall about 16 per cent and expenditure rise almost 55 per cent. Special appeals in 1949 raised income much faster than expenditure (42.5 per cent compared with 25.1 per cent) but still left the home in deficit. Dalmar was marginally in credit in 1950 and thereafter income and expenditure rose more or less in balance allowing a precarious credit to be maintained. These problems, the result of a postwar inflation, were a severe blow to the amour propre of an institution which was justifiably proud of a long record of balanced budgets.[12]

Apparently for these budgetary reasons, the CMM Executive Committee became thoroughly dissatisfied with the administration of the home by the Ladies' Committee which had run it, with an entirely free hand, since its inception. After discussions in 1947–48, a new constitution was forced upon the Ladies' Committee by the Executive. Dalmar was now linked much more tightly into the central structure of the CMM and overall control was placed in the hands of a Dalmar Executive consisting of three representatives from each of the Ladies' Committee, CMM Executive, and Lyceum Trustees, along with the superintendent of the Eastwood circuit. A new superintendent of the home, Donald Stewart, was appointed to control the "domestic" affairs and to be responsible directly to the Dalmar Executive. The Ladies' Committee was left powerless but was required to raise funds and administer admission.

Publicly the CMM offered two linked explanations. Because the Ladies' Committee had undertaken to accept thirty British migrant children, Dalmar had to comply with a requirement of the British government to have a resident married superintendent able to exercise constant supervision. His appointment would further burden the budget which the Ladies' Committee had proved unable to balance despite its best efforts. Yet this does not really explain adequately the demotion of the Ladies' Committee after its long and successful regime. The Dalmar Executive would remain dependent on the women to raise money, as churches mostly do. Nor would they or Stewart show any particular ability to rein in expenses. Income and expenditure both continued to rise rapidly throughout the 1950s, the former by 366 per cent and the latter by 274 per cent in the period 1948-58 inclusive, and the budgetary position always remained precarious. One interviewee, who was in a position to know, reported a case of misappropriation of funds by a member of the Ladies' Committee, an incident which was dealt with quietly and effectively by the CMM superintendent and which had led to a decision to take financial control from the Ladies' Committee and locate it at Headquarters. The interviewee placed the incident in the 1950s and attributed its uncovering to Donald Stewart. However, no known event in the 1950s fits the incident described and, indeed, greater centralization of financial control was hardly possible at that time. Possibly the passing of many years led to a confusion concerning the date of an event which would account for the sudden ending of the autonomy of the Ladies' Committee.[13] The mission, itself innocent of any wrongdoing, except perhaps some sloppiness in administration, kept the incident quiet fearing that it would lead to a decline in donations just at the very time when an increase was absolutely essential.

Postwar conditions of full employment and high wages affected Dalmar by making it difficult to get adequate staff and at times the number of children had to be restricted. Dalmar could not compete with wages available outside. Inability to recruit young women devoted to Christ and the care of young children in the prevailing strongly materialistic atmosphere led to a change of policy and Dalmar began to seek married couples as "cottage parents". The rationale was that this would provide a more "normal" environment for the children: "father" would go out to work during the day, but would assist his wife during the evenings and at weekends, while "mother" would be employed on the same terms as the other sisters there. Both would receive free board and adequate time off for leisure. Obviously there were important benefits in this policy. There was probably also a hope that if a married couple received free board, at a time when the housing situation was still tight, and the wife's income became a second one, the material allurements of the world would seem less attractive even in a time of high inflation. This hope was largely disappointed and staffing difficulties continued.   Other factors counterbalanced idealism: the location of the husband's work, interference with one's own family life, and the strain of being constantly responsible for a sizeable "family".[14]   So Dalmar struggled on, performing its valuable work, but finding that prosperous times created more serious problems for it than the darker prewar days.

Work among the elderly was relatively new in 1938 and was to undergo both change and development in Rayward's time. Sunset Lodge, which had never had enough space for applicants, was extended for an additional twelve women in 1939 and again in 1956 by the purchase of a neighbouring cottage which was turned into two flats for the more independent women.   The Taylor home for men gained a multipurpose hall (which served as chapel and social hall for the home and as church for the Dee Why circuit) in 1939 and

Alexandra Rescue Home, successively Sunset Lodge and Pinaroo. By courtesy of the Wesley Central Mission.

it was extended slightly to a capacity of thirty-nine in 1950. In 1958 work began on expensive additions to turn the home into one for women and couples as well as men. In this, Sydney CMM was following its sister institutions in other states and providing the elderly with a more "natural" environment in their last days.[15]

Meanwhile, in 1941, the CMM Executive had agreed, on the motion of P.N. Slade, to the creation of a settlement for aged couples at Sylvania. Plans and drainage of the site were completed, but the worsening of the war, with the entry of Japan in late 1941, meant that all building projects were suspended, Sylvania among them. Money was gradually collected in a reserve account so that progress would be rapid when building was again permitted. The first eight units were not opened until 21 August 1948 but they did provide private and self-contained living for couples. Each unit had a bedroom, lounge, kitchenette, bathroom, and lavatory along with a slow-combustion stove and off-peak hot water service. Ultimately, it was intended that there would be forty units, a large administrative block, staff quarters, community dining- and lounge-rooms, and an amenities room. It would prevent the separation of couples no longer able to cope in the general community. The impetus for all this work for the aged came from a realization of the inadequacy of the pension to provide a reasonable standard of living in the open community and of the very bad conditions in which many lived. It was also desired to provide Christian surroundings for the elderly. The expansion was made possible by the fact that Rayward, in company with the Revs. Irving Benson and Samuel Forsyth (of the Melbourne and Adelaide CMMs respectively) had in 1950 been able to persuade the Menzies government to subsidize homes for the aged on a pound-for-pound basis. By late 1957 this had become a two pounds for one pound subsidy. By this means the mission's capacity to expand its homes was greatly increased and the government was able to ensure a more devoted form of care, at a lower cost, than if it provided and ran the homes itself.[16]

As a spectacular gesture for the CMM's Diamond Jubilee in 1944, Rayward decided to found a hospital for those elderly church people who were invalids. Apart from Rayward's own considerable sympathy for the elderly sick, the two existing CMM homes were unable to handle those who were bedridden or in need of medical care.

The *Sydney Morning Herald* informed its readers that at the evening service Rayward had announced that Sir Frederick Stewart had just informed him that he would give his Dundas home, farm buildings, implements, and eighteen acres of adjoining land free of encumbrances for the hospital in memory of his late wife. He would also give £1,000 towards establishing the hospital and his children would give a similar amount. It would be known as the Lady Stewart Hospital. What the paper could not tell, because it was not revealed until years later, was that Rayward had written to Stewart saying that he believed Methodism should have a hospital for physically hopeless people. He added, "I have not the foggiest notion as to whether such a scheme would be within your reach, but I was wondering if you were thinking of some way of perpetuating the memory of your beloved wife, whether such an institution, to bear her name, would appeal to you."

Stewart had indeed been looking for a way involving the family house to commemorate his wife and willingly and generously became the means by which Rayward's jubilee dream was fulfilled. Rayward's letter to Stewart was a fine example of what the mission calls "consecrated audacity" and perhaps makes the point as well as can be that a CMM superintendent needs to be a toughminded individual if he is to succeed.

Plans to have the hospital open within a year went badly astray and it was not until early 1948 that the first patients entered. The second half of 1944 and 1945 saw a lengthy correspondence with the N.S.W. Hospitals' Commission over registration of the hospital as a "schedule three" hospital, for chronic and incurable patients only. The mission was unwilling to accept the restriction as it might make it difficult to fulfil what was seen as an obligation to accept cases from the W. G. Taylor and Sunset homes. Promised grants towards the buildings and equipment swayed the CMM and agreement was reached on the basis of thirty-three beds being available to the Hospitals' Commission on its terms (although first consideration would be given to requests from the CMM) while the remainder were entirely at the disposal of the CMM. Sir Frederick's political influence was invaluable in the negotiation of the agreement.

Written evidence does not allow judgment on a later hospital officer's statement that the CMM's share of beds had often been allocated not on the basis of need but to wealthy "retired choir girls", whose only observable "need" was release from the trouble of looking after themselves. The same officer also raised the question whether Stewart's use of his political influence over the registration had been improper, but again that is a matter which cannot be settled satisfactorily.

When the hospital opened it was free of debt, could take forty-five patients, and was said to be staffed only by Christian nurses. The new wards had been erected at the back of the old home which was itself to be the administration block, the two being attached by an annexe. The whole property was said to be worth £60,000. It was also now to be known as the "Lottie Stewart Hospital" as Sir Frederick had long since remarried and the name originally proposed would have been unclear.[17]

The Lottie Stewart Hospital experienced few problems in its early years. In the second half of 1955, the Hospitals' Commission approached the CMM asking it to build extensions on behalf of the commission to increase the capacity from 45 beds to 110 to help meet the enormous and growing backlog of patients in need of this type of accommodation. The cost, ultimately more than £300,000, was to be borne entirely by the commission, but the management and staffing were to be the responsibility of the mission. All the additional beds were to be reserved for aged terminal and/or aged chronic cases and half were to be available for cases referred from the Hospitals' Admission Depot (no infectious or refractory cases were to be sent). Outwardly, the CMM shared the view expressed by the N.S.W. minister for health (W. J. Sheahan) when he opened the extension on 11 October 1958 that this was "a fine example of church and state working together", but in private some of the Executive had reservations. E. Frank Vickery saw that the Hospital

Board could really do nothing that was not approved by the commission which was now by far the larger partner in the provision of capital costs and also paid running expenses. Despite the board's power to appoint the secretary and matron, there was a real possibility that it could lose control and Lottie Stewart would become "just another public hospital with purely secular management" and so unable to fulfil its Christian functions which were an important part of its raison d'etre. The location of the board in Sydney made it difficult for it to control the management of the hospital in detail. He suggested the strengthening of the board by the addition of three Christian doctors and the establishing of a Ladies' Committee (with representatives from all the neighbouring circuits) responsible for visiting the hospital each week.[18]

Vickery's worry was understandable in the light of the concern which has always existed at the CMM to ensure that every part of the institution should be seen to minister to the needy in an identifiably Christian way and should not be secularized by its environment. Vickery was simply sharing that concern. However, it must be realized that the defence mechanism he proposed could only succeed if the Christian doctors added to the board were also competent hospital administrators and so able to deal with the commission on its own terms. In actual fact, there appears to be little evidence that the commission has ever sought to exercise any improper influence over the policy of the Lottie Stewart Hospital. Yet, in any partnership between church and state, the former must see itself as effectively the junior partner and tend to stand in some fear of the influence which accrues from holding the purse strings. The only answer to this dilemma is to return to the full purity of the nineteenth century Methodist position on state aid to religious bodies, and that would destroy most of the church homes, hospitals, and schools which have been built up over the years.

Nineteen fifty-seven saw another problem associated with Lottie Stewart, though not affecting its operation. Stewart still owned land adjoining the hospital property and wished to subdivide this for sale to profit from the booming real-estate market. As he wished to provide pedestrian access from the subdivision to the Stewart Street buses, he first approached the minister for the army with a request to purchase twelve feet on the eastern boundary of some army land for a right-of-way. Sir John Cramer agreed but drew attention to a potentially costly problem. To avoid this, Sir Frederick approached the CMM to try to buy twelve feet of the western side of the hospital land, and he also sought to reacquire another piece of land then in the possession of the hospital by exchanging it for a smaller block (said to be more valuable) immediately behind the nurses' quarters but which was still in his possession. He also drew attention to the fact that he had tried to obtain the land from the army for his right-of-way before approaching the church.

The Executive Committee at first approved both Stewart's requests but then rescinded its decision on the motion of W. H. McClelland, secretary of the CMM, arguing that it had been requested to do so by the Hospitals' Commission. McClelland simply informed Stewart that the commission opposed "certain features" of the proposal because it was impossible to foresee what land might be necessary for extensions or new institutions.

Stewart, who had been attacked personally by one member of the commission who had called his proposal "a shocking attempt to recover property which I had given in memory of my wife", demanded to be told clearly the grounds on which the commission objected to his proposal. He also expressed annoyance that Rayward had not shown his correspondence with Cramer to the Executive when they were considering this matter. Eventually McClelland sent Stewart a copy of the commission's letter, a mild document which objected to the right-of-way proposal on the sensible grounds that the hospital was already very close to the western boundary and which also raised a few minor points about the rates, sewering, fencing, and legal costs which the CMM should consider before agreeing to the exchange of the other blocks of land. Stewart, angered by what he regarded as deception, accused McClelland and Rayward of keeping the commission's letter from him without the permission of the Executive, again chastised Rayward for not showing the Executive all the correspondence and virtually accused both men of deliberately misinterpreting the commission's letter because of their own opposition to his requests. He gave up his request for the right-of-way in view of the commission's opposition to it, and agreed to indemnify the hospital against any rates, fencing, sewering, or legal costs associated with the exchange. He sought the implementation of the original resolution and, to ensure that all members of the Executive were fully informed, sent them copies of the whole correspondence. The Executive agreed without demur.[19]

No one emerged from what should have been an insignificant incident with much credit, least of all McClelland and Rayward. Stewart clearly wanted to maximize his profit from the planned subdivision and his action was taken solely with that end in view. However, he did act openly at all times and nothing was ever hidden from the CMM. The Hospitals' Commission member who criticized him so sharply had only very limited justification for his attack and was guilty of gross exaggeration of the position. Rayward and McClelland were less than open with both Stewart and the CMM Executive, though the reasons for their opposition to Stewart's planned exchange was never publicly stated. The only failure of the Executive at large was that it allowed itself to be denied the full evidence which should have been before it and to be persuaded to accept an unreasonable interpretation of the commission's letter.

Waddell House provides another form of philanthropic outreach and a less complex story. Towards mid-1946, the family of the late Hon. Thomas Waddell offered their twenty-five room family home at Ashfield to the CMM as a place for the treatment of women suffering from epilepsy in its milder forms on condition that a comfortable home was provided for the rest of her life for a sister, Ethel, herself an epileptic. The home opened in July 1946 with twenty beds. The hope was expressed from the outset that it would eventually be possible to use Waddell House as a clinic for research into epilepsy but there was no move in that direction until mid-1953 when plans were announced to extend both building and work. There was ample justification for the move as little was being done for epileptics anywhere in the country. The extensions, which cost about £36,000, of which £18,600 was given by the Commonwealth government and £2,000 by the state government, were completed in 1954 and immediately created a minor problem. The Commonwealth Department of Health was prepared to regard Waddell House as a private hospital and pay benefits for forty-five patients, but the state department insisted that if registered as a hospital the number of beds should not exceed thirty. If it remained a convalescent and rest home no treatment at all could be carried out there. After some months of dithering, the mission registered as a hospital, despite the need to discharge fifteen patients into mental hospitals, and carried on treatment and research through the efforts of a group of prominent and Christian psychiatrists. By this time, it was also accepting a wider range of cases and was taking men as well as women.[20]

There has as yet been no study of the reaction of the Australian churches to World War II which can be compared with McKernan's study of World War I, but a reader of the *Methodist* must gain the impression that patriotism was still strong among church people, though the form of its expression was generally less extreme and rabid than had been the case in the Great War. This, of course, reflected a general community change. A significant minority of the clergy was now openly pacifist and though an individual minister might find himself under considerable pressure, he would not be isolated as the Rev. Linden Webb had been at Hay a generation earlier. However, patriotism certainly held sway at the CMM. No one should be surprised that Rayward was a loyalist. His country background, his growth to maturity in the last great days of the Empire, and the experiences of the Great War, as well as his personal conservatism, all combined to ensure that he would take an approach supportive of the national war effort.[21]

Perhaps the best remaining evidence of this patriotism is in the titles of the PSAs for the war period. While there continued to be many "ordinary" programmes of a musical or travel nature, or concerning social evils, there was a heavy concentration on war topics like "The Present Situation",

"Australia's War Aims", and so on. Other speakers tackled "The Triumph and Tragedy of Malaya", "The Battle of Britain", "Comfort Fund Work Abroad", and Rabbi Schenk spoke on "The Nazis and Religion". Even musical afternoons often made great use of patriotic songs and the "national afternoons" for which the PSA was famous in Rayward's time became a celebration of Australia's allies, and when the commissioner of railways came to speak his topic was "The Work of the Railways and the War Effort". Gradually, in 1944–45, the titles took on both a more reminiscent note ("I Was a Prisoner of War") and a more hopeful note ("The Dynamics of Democracy"). None of this is surprising. As the major topic of interest for six years, the war naturally claimed a large share of attention at a gathering which was able to exercise some educative function for the population. The boast made during 1941 was not altogether vain: "The PSA has proved an invaluable means of informing large audiences of the issues involved in the present conflict, the ideals and responsibilities of Democracy, and the necessity for unity, and devotion to the cause".

Other than this, the CMM joined in national days of prayer. At the conclusion of the responses, the congregation would stand with closed eyes and sing "in little above a whisper our great national prayer". This was another dramatic moment somewhat akin to Rayward's contemplation of the cross and doubtless helped to account for the increased attendances which the CMM in particular, and Methodism in general, seem to have been conscious of, at least in the early war years. Today it seems strange, even improper, to implore the Prince of Peace to give victory to one group of His erring servants over another in an essentially political cause. In the 1940s that strangeness existed for few, whether regular church-goers or nominal Christians. Certainly the CMM had no doubts at all about the propriety of seeking divine intervention. Beyond this, the mission was well aware that among those who turned to it were "an increasing number of bereaved men and women who seek balm for their grief in the fellowship of the Christian Church" and wondered whether it was not in "this ministry of courage and comfort" that the church best fulfilled its divine mission to a community "beset by danger, wounded by loss, and needing above all else that reinforcement of spirit that comes from fellowship with God". There could be little doubt about the validity of that ministry then or now.

The ministry of "courage and comfort" was not the only practical way in which the CMM sought to serve in the war. Services personnel were another group of men and women in need who came within its ambit. A group was formed at Headquarters to knit and sew for the troops and the women at Sunset Lodge undertook similar duties; the secretary formed a savings group among members of the staff to buy war savings certificates; the mission helped in the camp and hostel work undertaken by Conference and the Bourke and Flinders Street properties were made available to the National Emergency Services as posts for wardens; a first-aid class was organized and the Christian Endeavour group made a substantial donation towards the purchase of an ambulance by the N.S.W. Endeavourers as a whole. Potentially, the most important project undertaken by the CMM was the provision of a fully equipped mobile canteen to serve hot food and drinks to volunteers, especially in the wake of a bombing or other attack on Sydney. First proposed in February 1942, in the wake of Pearl Harbour, the vehicle was handed over to the city of Sydney National Emergency Services in October of that year at a cost of £500, the maintenance to be a continuing charge on the CMM. Rather belatedly, in August 1943, the proposal was mooted for the conversion of half of Hoban's girls' rest-rooms into accommodation for servicewomen. The facility opened only in April 1944 and at prices which always allowed it to show a reasonable profit. More puzzling is the inability of the CMM to begin a social hour, after the Lyceum service, for service personnel until March 1945, despite its claim that it had long wanted to do this.

V.E. Day saw ten consecutive services held in Wesley chapel, with a total of three thousand attending, and the Sunday following V.P. Day saw Wesley chapel full in the morning and the Lyceum evening congregation was one of the biggest for many years, with an overflow congregation filling Wesley chapel as the people of Sydney expressed their relief at the end of the nation's time of testing and the lifting of their own personal burdens of fear and worry.

The war aside, Rayward and his colleagues built the PSA around the same successful formula he had used in his first period at the CMM. The mission undoubtedly saw the programme as a contribution to the evangelical, musical, educational, and social life of the community and was proud that it had become "an integral part of the Sunday life of the City of Sydney", and felt that it both enlightened the minds and extended the horizons of those who attended. Rayward was deeply offended in 1951 when it was brought to the attention of Parliament that the CMM was in contravention of the Theatres and Public Halls Act in holding a public "entertainment" on Sunday afternoon without permission. It was not that he was concerned about the breach of the law of which he had been ignorant, but the implication that his programmes were no more than an entertainment was repugnant since the "service" invariably included at least one hymn, a prayer, a doxology, and a benediction and the addresses were "always thought provoking, and [were] climaxed by an appeal for the cultivation of Christian virtues".

That there was often a thought-provoking quality is undoubtedly true and readily provable from a selection of titles, like the following from early 1946: "Food from the Sun", "Moral Disintegration and its Cure", Mass Movements in West Africa", "Personal Experiences on D-Day", and "Will UNO Survive and Succeed?" But there were occasions which were mainly or even purely entertainment: "How We Won the Ashes", "British Women's Cricket Tour of Australia", "Great Personalities of the War", and "Mirth and the Microphone". Some of the travelogue and lighter musical afternoons, while not being devoid of educational value, were obviously intended primarily to divert. There was nothing improper in the inclusion of such topics, but it was a pity that the CMM authorities were not prepared to admit what they were doing and let it stand or fall on its merits rather than try to insist on a high seriousness which did not always exist. Regular attendances of more than 1,000 indicated widespread approval of the programmes provided by Rayward and his colleagues.[22]

The attitude of the CMM to political and social questions shows some change from the earlier period. True, Rayward almost never preached on such issues in his evening services, except for an occasional diatribe against the prostitution of high office by men of all parties. This should not cause much surprise and need not be considered significant except on odd occasions as in January 1954 when Methodist spokesmen around the country launched an assault on a plan to cut wheat production by one-third, saying that the surplus should go to Asia. The CMM was silent on the subject, Rayward preaching that night on Christ as the remedy for sin. Appropriate attention was given to a proposal to extend the hours for the sale of alcohol and the introduction of Sunday sport, but it could not be argued that the attitude of the CMM was in any way distinguishable from that of the generality of Methodist churches. There was some anger over the failure of the community to do anything about slums and of the government to deal adequately with the postwar housing situation. The attempted reduction of the old age pension in late 1943 by the Commonwealth Labor government attracted even greater anger, as did the strikes of the late 1940s and the introduction of compulsory unionism in 1954. Special pre-election prayer meetings were held in both 1943 and 1954 while in 1949 Prime Minister Chifley was sharply criticized for broadcasting his "reports to the nation" to clash with the Sunday evening service.[23]

More generally, it may be said that the PSA took on a conservative tone. There was a regular parade of retired army officers and former wartime chaplains across its platform presenting their view on the state of the Empire or the war. Politicians carried their higher profile from the war years into the postwar era and were almost invariably from the conservative side. Sir Bertram Stevens, a former premier of N.S.W. and a Methodist lay preacher was a regular visitor, but so was Billy Hughes (without the same justification), while Howard Beale, E. D. Darley, E. J. Harrison, and Sir Percy Spender also appeared. ALP members were occasionally invited, usually "safe" right-wing Catholics like Premiers McKell and McGirr or a Methodist lay preacher like Norman Makin. Once or twice the dreaded H. V. Evatt spoke, probably because it was unavoidable if it were to be maintained that the speakers were asked because of their ability to contribute on a given subject. There were others no less conservative in their outlook than the UAP/Liberal politicians. One such was a certain Palmer Kent, organizing secretary of the People's Union, who spoke on 20 October 1946, the main objective of whose organization seemed to be to take the "bite" out of Australian unionism as it then existed.[24]

Something of a furore blew up over the PSA on 14 March 1948 addressed by E. J. Harrison, MHR, deputy leader of the Opposition, on the subject "Will Communism Engulf Australia?" At that time the newspapers were full of reports of Communist activity in unions and there was a considerable, if irrational, fear in the community of a Communist takeover, more the result of the situation in Europe and China than of that in Australia. The Opposition was anxious to exploit these fears to the full in the approach to the 1949 federal election (and in the wake of a wave of strikes in Australia) and Harrison was one of its most determined Communist baiters. On this occasion Harrison described the Communists as "vermin in freedom's battledress" and by other equally colourful and uncomplimentary epithets. The Communists asked Rayward for a right of reply the following week and, when he refused, began to publicize his lack of justice and to contrast this unfavourably with the attitude of other "progressive" Methodists, like the Rev. G. Van Erde of Redfern, who had told them that the rules of fair play demanded a right of reply for the Communists. Well-known radical clergy, Revs. E. E. V. Collocott and Dudley Hyde, took up the cudgels for the Communists in the *Methodist*, with the latter arguing that the only view that was ever heard from the PSA platform was that of extreme right-wing reaction, while Collocott pointed out, accurately enough, that the only real threat to democracy in the history of N.S.W. had come from the right, not the left, in the form of the New Guard. Rayward and his officers were unrepentant and argued that they were intent only to represent the "Christian point of view", not all possible points of view, from the Lyceum platform, though Rayward did, a little inconsistently, also try to argue that when the PSA had discussed Indonesia, both the Dutch and Indonesian points of view had been put. From this it might have been concluded that on some questions more than one point of view was allowable to Christians, but on others this was not so. In the second case, the Christian point of view would be decided by the superintendent of the CMM.

The Communists persuaded the president of the N.S.W. Conference, Rev. R.H. Doust, to approach Rayward on their behalf, but he too was turned down and could do nothing because Rayward had the right to determine policy on such questions in his own circuit. So the Communists had to content themselves with rumbling away in the *Tribune*, since neither of the dailies was interested in advertising their cause, and by expressing their pleasure in May–June 1948 when a group of "progressive" Methodists, along with a handful of like-minded people from other denominations, formed a new Christian Socialist Movement, which the *Tribune* hoped would help combat the war-mongering, racialism, and oppression of the working class in the churches and help to usher in the age of communism.[25]

Rayward would have insisted that the CMM, in common with other branches of the Christian church in Australia, had no specific political attachment and that it kept out of the realm of party politics, though it did necessarily deal from time to time with significant social issues. What he failed to realize, then or later, was that the nature of his approach to such issues induced a generally conservative attitude at the CMM. Looking back a generation after his retirement, it is impossible not to feel that there was a degree of politicization about the PSA in his day which had not existed before and that there is no wonder that he enraged the small number of radicals in the church almost as much as his successor enraged the much larger number of conservatives.

There is little to be said about the finances of the mission during the Rayward period. Minor deficits were shown on current account in the years 1939–41, 1943, 1945, 1948–50, and 1953, otherwise there were equally slight margins on the credit side. During the period total income and expenditure multiplied several times over without affecting the tendency to a balanced budget on average. The annual anniversary declined relatively in importance as a money winner, but general collections expanded at roughly the same rate as overall expenditure and income. Income from the PSA grew at a slower rate, but that from the annual Spring Fair out- stripped all other sources in its rate of growth with the main leap forward occurring in 1944. Perhaps this was a sign of a community looking for new ways of entertaining itself and spending its money; the church could make a superficial contact with that community, enough to win some financial support, but not enough to bring members of the community firmly within its walls. The Girls' Rest Rooms continued to make a modest profit and the W. G. Taylor home could always balance its books. Sunset Lodge was in a similar position until 1957–58 when it made substantial profits. The Men's Hostel made a modest profit, but the Refuge lost heavily. Once Waddell House became established it made substantial profits, but Lottie Stewart Hospital had mixed fortunes. The costs which were really frightening were those for salaries, which rose much more rapidly than anything else, though council rates also escalated rapidly. Of course, the rent-earning capacity of the Pitt and Castlereagh Street build- ings also grew substantially; an example of this was the 1953 increase in rents obtained from Greater Union Theatres to £10,073 p.a. against the previous figure of £7,800 p.a. According to Rayward, the only really big donors during his period were Sir Frederick Stewart and Sir Edward Hallstrom. None of the big city business institutions was of assistance.[26]

The twenty years, 1938–58, during which Rayward was superintendent of the CMM, were a period of remarkable expansion. The Lottie Stewart Hospital, Waddell House, Sylvania Settlement for aged couples, Wesley Hostel, and the foot clinic were all new developments, and the first three were of major significance. Above this, there had been additions at Sunset Lodge, W. G. Taylor Home, Dalmar and the Men's Hostel, while the Lyceum had undergone recon- struction. All these additions were free of debt, despite the problems imposed by war and inflation. Rayward had had a hand in persuading the Commonwealth government to assist with the building of homes for the elderly. He himself had been awarded an honorary DD for his work by the Southern Methodist University at Dallas, Texas (1949) and an OBE (1951). When he told his Quarterly Meeting on 16 October 1957 that he would be retiring in 1958, the decision was a fairly sudden one based on the fact that at sixty-six he believed he had no further ideas to contribute and that he would leave, as he said, "with all guns blazing", rather than just fade out. In the circumstances, there was no surprise that he enjoyed massive farewell services and no question that the tributes to his vision and ability as an evangelist and executive were well merited. A key feature of his work seems to have been his ability to get close to people of all types, bring the best out of them, and weld them into a hard-working team. In this respect he was more like the founder, W. G. Taylor than any other superintendent has been. He himself seems to have attributed his success to the primary place he gave to evangelism and his determination "to con-duct the King's business as skilfully as any businessman conducts his commercial enterprise".[27]

He was right to go in 1958, for, in a sense, he belonged to an age that was passing. Country-bred, a loyalist and Empire man in the Menzies sense of the term, he handled the war years and the postwar reconstruction and consolidation with considerable skill. The 1960s would demand a new approach to which it was unlikely that he could have adapted. It was a part of his wisdom that he went when he realized that the time was appropriate.

The CMM itself was to have some difficulty adjusting to the need for change and it fumbled its attempt to choose a successor. The Quarterly Meeting of 16 October empowered the Executive Committee to act over the appointment of a new superintendent, but when that body met on 25 October and A. E. Symons, a treasurer, outlined a conversation he had had with the president of the Conference on the subject and moved that the Rev. Alan Walker be appointed, it proved unable to reach a decision and deferred the question to allow the submission of further names for consideration. At the next meeting, Symons said that he had no new proposal to bring forward and the Executive, unwilling to appoint Walker, decided to hide behind a technicality, resolving that since no invitation had been issued at the September Quarterly Meeting (the normal procedure under Methodist law), it was now "constitutionally impossible" to issue one and the appointment should be left to Conference. Rayward was to arrange with the chairman of the district to have Symons appointed as a lay representative on an enlarged Stationing Committee. The problem was that the Executive Committee included a small number of hardline conservatives (including the Hon. Richard Thompson, MLC, and a Mr Booth) who were not willing to call as superintendent a man who was known as a pacifist and internationalist, who was prepared to let Communists speak at church forums and was (ludicrously) regarded by some as a "fellow-traveller". He was also known to be outspoken and prepared to experiment. In other words, Walker stood for the new world into which the CMM would have to move and he was therefore frightening to those on the Executive who wished to remain in the world they knew. Fortunately, the Conference was more prepared than the Executive to step forward and duly appointed Walker who was already the best-known Methodist minister in Australia, and who was about to become much better known.[28]

7

A New Beginning

By 1958 Australians had all but forgotten the days of Labor reformism at the end of World War II and were more than half way through the long, stable Menzies era. The Korean war and the Labor split were behind them, though the effects of each were still felt on the domestic political scene. The Vietnam war, with its unprecedented capacity to divide the Australian community, was still in the future. Loyalty to the British tradition existed alongside what were by then well-tried ties of common interest with the U.S.A. With the passing of Menzies in the middle sixties, the latter would predominate, though there would remain a significant group, especially among the young and the intellectuals, uneasy about the too-ready identity of interest which leaders like Holt, Gorton, and McMahon would make with the U.S. especially over Vietnam, but also over the whole question of communism and of relationships with Asia.

As the sixties wore on, more and more Australians would be troubled about racial issues: the White Australia policy which continued to hamper attempts to foster better relations with Asia, and the treatment of the Aborigines at home. The latter would not really become a major issue until the early seventies, with the advent of the land rights movement and a higher degree of activism among the Aborigines themselves. In the meantime, Australians would largely be able to salve their consciences by pointing the finger at the South African policy of apartheid, which everyone could abhor from a safe distance and which would allow the honest enjoyment of a "holier than thou" attitude.

Economically, as Menzies often told them, Australians had "never had it so good". In retrospect, once the inflation caused by the Korean war had subsided, the period through to the oil price surge in 1973 looks like a long continuous period of growth and expansion marred only by relatively minor wrinkles in 1961 and 1966. Population increased dramatically under the stimulus of immigration, but it did so without significant unemployment. Full employment was central to the policy of both parties and was sought almost as earnestly by employers as by unions. Failure in this area simply would not be tolerated by the electorate.

Real GNP was increasing rapidly, though the nation was not in the forefront so far as development was concerned. Secondary industrial production increased rapidly and primary production more slowly. There were almost as many savings bank accounts as people and life assurance polices were common. Almost every home owned the major electrical gadgets though they had often been acquired on hire purchase.

This is not to suggest that all was well with the economy. Economic power was highly concentrated in a few hands and by the end of the sixties the level of foreign, mainly U.K. or U.S.A., ownership was high enough to be worrying, especially in the mining, pharmaceutical, motor vehicle, and telecommunications industries, since it meant that policy could be determined without regard to Australian interests.[1] While private enterprise was expanding, the provision of public utilities, like schools, hospitals, and sewage schemes was falling further behind demand.

A price had to be paid for affluence. Increasing mechanization in the factory meant that work was even less meaningful than in the late nineteenth century. By this time, technology had also invaded the big office blocks and the mass processing of people and information was under way. There was also the widely noticed growth of materialism. "The good life" tended to consist of getting and spending. Australians became deeply enmeshed in consumerism. The consequence of this emphasis on material gain, and the subsequent aggressive economic competititon, was some breakdown in interpersonal relations which may have been reflected in rising crime and suicide rates, an increase in violence, in wife and child bashing, and in pack rape, worsening alcoholism, and drug abuse.[2]

Eventually, as Russell Ward argues, many young people from the comfortable middle classes began to question the point of affluence and full employment in a world where warfare, greed, and injustice still seemed to be accepted by constituted authority as part of the natural order of things. Some merely "dropped out" of the conventional pattern of living, but others, members of the "new left", sought to hasten the day of revolution by confronting the government and society physically, with their rejection of war, racial discrimination, and authoritarianism.[3]

The spirit of confrontation largely died away as the 1970s progressed and some of the radical causes, like the Vietnam war, which had the greatest power to draw protest, disappeared. As the economic situation worsened, unemployment became a major preoccupation of youth. Most now saw only two real alternatives: to join the pleasure-seeking materialistic majority or drop out into some inexpensive, group-oriented lifestyle which, in reality, was probably little less self-centred than the materialism of the majority but was cheap enough to support on the dole and, at the same time, gave something of a "warm inner glow".

Long before either protest movement or subsequent reaction occurred, an increased level of pleasure seeking was noted and a corresponding decline in what many called "puritanism". In his widely read book, *The Lucky Country*, Donald Horne argued that "wowsers" were in "slow and disorderly retreat" throughout the 1950s. This was exemplified for him by the gradual extension of hotel trading hours, of betting facilities, the modification of censorship laws, and the relaxation of sexual restraints. In *Profile of Australia*, Craig McGregor argued that for many the "pub" was the centre of "the good life", though it was coming under challenge from the clubs supported by poker machines which were rival centres for "dispensing beer, entertainment and good fellowship" and that "the club has replaced the church as the main centre of Sunday activities". Drinking provided a release from, and a defence against, the pressures engendered by the urbanized, competitive community.[4]

Among the youth there grew up a distinctive lifestyle which separated them from the older generation. This often revolved around surfboards, motor cycles, cars, and pop music. Pop music will feature largely in the investigation later. McGregor's view (in *People, Politics and Pop*) that the pop of the late fifties and the sixties was "optimistic, affirmative, blatantly sexual" seems unexceptionable. It represented the triumph of the "hot" music of the negro over the predominantly "cool" tradition of European music. This "hot" tradition "creates a fierce physical reaction in the listener", seeks to promote excitement and emotion and "invites us to take part in the sexual ritual of the dance".[5]

Sydney itself in the sixties covered over 1,500 square kilometres and, along with other state capitals, was the frequent target of attack for its suburban sprawl. Pseudo-intellectual critics, such as Allan Ashbolt, poked fun at the supposed inanity of suburban life, but failed to notice that most found the suburban situation better for bringing up a family and for working out their own lifestyles in relative freedom than any of the alternatives available. If they could not enjoy the inner-urban socializing that occurred in some European cities, at least they were relieved of the pressures which inevitably go with living in high-rise human filing cabinets. Mercifully, the latter remained reasonably rare until the seventies and although in 1971 one-quarter of the population of Sydney was living in flats, most were in blocks of less than sixteen units.[6]

This is not to suggest that Sydney lacked its full share of urban problems. As in all large cities, people met each other in highly segmented roles and their contacts, although face to face, were "impersonal, superficial, transitory, and segmented". Each acquaintance was perceived as a means of achieving an end of one's own and "the morale, and sense of participation which come from living in an integrated society" was lacking.[7]

Both Horne and McGregor believed that the influence of the church was waning in the fifties and sixties and saw it as fighting a rearguard action against the onward march of rationality and liberalism in moral and social matters. Jonathon King, in his study of materialism in Australia, wondered whether the low church attendance — probably less than one-third of all Australians went regularly during the sixties and one-half never went at all — was connected with the lack of appeal of a religion which preached that there was no real worth in possessions to a society which was busy building itself a material paradise. Manning Clark also sensed that "material well-being for all was stripping away even the need for the great comforters of the past" including the promise of happiness in the hereafter.[8]

The religious situation was particularly bad from a Protestant Christian viewpoint. The 30 per cent of regular attenders shown up by the Gallup polls masked a considerable decline among Methodists and Presbyterians which was partly compensated for by an increase among Catholics. Hans Mol, in an important study of religion in Australia published in 1971, opined that Catholics often went from a sense of duty whereas Protestants only went if religion integrated well with their lifestyle. The Protestant concept of the priesthood of all believers required them to represent holiness in their own lives whereas the Catholic layman could pass this responsibility on to the professional, the priest, as long as he attended and gave money. This explanation ties in well with the decline among Methodists for whom the pursuit of "scriptural holiness" has always been a primary objective.

A "Religion in Australia" survey in 1964 showed that Bible knowledge was very low, even among church-goers, and that there no longer appeared to be any integrated, interdependent belief system. This spelt danger for the future. The survey showed some justification for the popular linking of religiosity and the maintenance of strict standards, though apparently the close link was between morality and prayer habits rather than with church-going as such, presumably because regular prayer habits indicated that religion was taken very seriously, whereas church-going did not necessarily do so. Church-goers were likely to be conservative on the question of patriotism, but Christians generally, and especially really active Methodists and Presbyterians, were likely to be far more liberal than the general community in relation to humanitarian and social justice causes. On the question of the White Australia policy they were the spearhead of progress.

It was still true that in all denominations the manual

workers were the least likely to attend church, closely followed by the higher professionals. The strength of religion lay among the rural occupations, the lower professionals (teachers), and clerical workers.[9]

Churchmen were concerned about the situation. Indicative of the rising concern was the National Christian Strategy Consultation held in February 1965. Speakers showed considerable understanding of and concern about the role the church might play in the debates relating to international affairs, economic development, the growth of cities, social welfare, and youth problems. While the church was a fringe institution for most, it would be listened to, though not necessarily followed, on moral issues and it should speak up. It was recognized that new methods of working, both in the social service field and among youth would be needed. In the latter area, it was beginning to be realized that work should be extended to provide programmes not only for youth whose families were associated with the church, but for those totally unrelated as well.[10]

Against this background, the Rev. Alan Walker, M.A., O.B.E., came to the CMM in 1958. He was the son of the Rev. A. E. Walker, a former graduate of Taylor's Evangelists' Training Institute and a missioner at Newtown in the thirties as well as a past-president of the N.S.W. Conference. He was also the nephew of F. T. Walker, founder of MOM. Alan Walker himself had spent some time as associate-director of the Young People's Department (1936–38), had briefly worked in English missions (1938–39), and had ministered at Cessnock during the war (1939–44). From 1944 he had been superintendent of the Waverley Mission in Sydney's eastern suburbs and, overlapping with this, director of the Mission to the Nation (1953–56). It was this latter appointment which had made him the best-known Methodist in Australia and which had taught him much about communication with the nonchurch-goer and the press. He had been a delegate to the Amsterdam assembly of the World Council of Churches (1948) and an official adviser to the Australian UN delegation (1949). He had conducted missions in New Zealand

(1950), several American universities (1951), had attended a convocation of Muslim and Christian leaders in the Lebanon (1954), given the launching address for the Canadian Mission to the Nation, and spent six months (1957) as visiting professor of evangelism at the Boston School of Theology. This was a range and depth of experience probably not enjoyed by any previous Australian Methodist minister.

The kind of message which this preacher would bring to the mission may be gauged best from a book written just before his appointment, *The Whole Gospel for the Whole World*.[11] Walker was disturbed by the fact that for several decades before World War II the churches had worshipped but not witnessed, evangelism had been dead, with the result that masses of the population, and especially the working-class groups and trade unions were largely outside the influence of the church. Now, in the wake of the loss of the great secular certainties of the inevitability of progress, the ability of science to save the world, and of secular education to deal with evil, mankind was open to the persuasion of religion, but the church was turning only to the old nine-teenth century kind of evangelism which was entirely personal, lacking any social dynamic and not intellectually adequate for the times. Such an evangelism could never answer in a world in the midst of economic and political upheaval, riven by injustice and racialism and whose most desperate collective need was to outlaw war. The church needed to rediscover the concept of the Kingdom of God which brought evangelism and social witness together where they belonged, inseparably. The preacher must be prepared to make bold prophetic utterances on the great issues of his time, despite the inevitable misunderstanding and tension this would bring. But he must make clear the theological bases for his social criticism: "A preacher whose total life inter-pretations spring from theological insights, and who shows clearly from whence they come, is in the end, respected if not followed." This Gospel of the Kingdom was to be preached in the language of the ordinary man, through the modern mass media, while the local church must become a true fellowship, so providing God's answer to some of man's greatest needs in the mass society of the modern world.

The various elements in Walker's message may be traced back to their origins in his reading: the emphasis on the Kingdom of God and on prophetic utterance to Reinhold Niebuhr; that on social justice to Emil Brunner and William Temple, while the influence of Huxley on his internationalism and pacifism is clear.[12] But the synthesis was very much Walker's own, tempered by his experience in the Mission to the Nation. This interpretation of the Gospel would guide him in the Lyceum pulpit for the next twenty years.

Walker had learned the value of the mass media from the Mission to the Nation experience and he knew that media interest could be caught at the beginning of a new enterprise in a way which was impossible later. He therefore set out to achieve maximum impact on his arrival at the mission.[13] His first PSA address, "The Amazing Challenge of Sydney", was an important aspect of this. In it Walker outlined his policy for the CMM. He intended to base his ministry on five principles: the CMM would endeavour to be the conscience of the city; it would seek to provide a warm fellowship to help overcome the loneliness of the mass society; it would continue its policy of meeting human need according to the concept of the servant church; it would take its place in the struggle for peace and progress; above all, it would be a centre for evangelism, believing that men need the transforming power of Christ more than anything else. This was very much the "whole Gospel" approach and, though he did not then use the words, it could reasonably be said that he was enunciating what he later called the "mantle of Christ" concept. He saw a fierce battle ahead for the soul of Sydney and he launched into it at once by attacking the gambling and liquor interests and the government which pampered them.

The following Tuesday evening an impressive "Welcome to Sydney" was staged in the Town Hall. The attendance was recorded as twenty-five hundred by the *Sydney Morning Herald*, three thousand by the *Daily Telegraph*, and thirty-five hundred by the *Methodist*. The crowd began to assemble two hours before the meeting and there was spontaneous hymn singing on the Town Hall steps. ABC television recorded the meeting for later broadcast. The official welcoming party included the president-general of the Methodist church of Australia, Rev. Dr. A. H. Wood, representatives of other churches and of the government. Wood, who shared Walker's "whole Gospel" approach, spoke out boldly in favour of many of the social and political ideas which Walker would espouse over the years.

Walker has been criticized for this spectacular opening to his ministry on the ground that it was mere self-advertisement. The person who intends to offer real leadership has to tread a fine line, especially as he must believe in the leadership he is offering or, in religious language, he must believe that God wishes to use him for great deeds. In view of this, there was a lot to be said for reaching out boldly to catch the public attention for his programme at the outset. The fact that when he left the mission the farewells were generally low-key lends strong support to the belief that it was the programme and not himself which he wished to promote.

The next two decades would be difficult times when it would not always be easy to maintain faith and enthusiasm, when there would be constant and concentrated work, moments both of success and failure, and much criticism. By and large, the work at the CMM in Walker's period may be subsumed under four main headings: worship and evangelism, including Christian education; institutional care; "in place" caring or the "mantle of Christ" concept; and social witness. Some activities overlapped two or more categories and the situation was never as neat and tidy as this classification makes it seem, but discussion under these headings will do no real violence to the work. The first two categories will be dealt with in this chapter and the last two in chapter 8.

Like his predecessors, Walker realized that mission churches always face the danger of allowing philanthropic activity to become a substitute for the proclamation of the Gospel and dependence on supernatural grace, two absolutely essential elements within Christianity. The problem of maintaining the spiritual character of the CMM in the face of powerful secularizing forces was peculiarly acute in the sixties and seventies, but he was determined that there should be no such failure in his time and that morning worship would remain as nurture for Christians while the Lyceum evening service would be "a great evangelical act of witness and worship". Apart from this there were many small ways in which worship could be fostered. The most important of these was the attempt to expand the Sunday evening prayer meeting by creating around it a "Yokefellow Prayer Movement". The object was to link various small prayer cells in CMM institutions and in private homes in the suburbs and country with the large group meeting in Wesley chapel. There was even a printed prayer for the Lyceum service which all were supposed to use at 5.30 p.m.

Sunday-by-Sunday evangelism within the confines of the "neutral ground" of the Lyceum, with a regular call for commitment to Christ, was always Walker's first priority, but it was not all. Special efforts were needed to bring Christ to the city. The annual Easter Mission quickly became the most important of these. Inaugurated in 1959, the Easter Mission began modestly in scope but grew until it became the major Christian thrust into Sydney. The choice of Easter for the mission sprang from the twin facts that it is the pre-eminent Christian festival and that Walker was appalled at its desecration in Sydney where the annual Royal Easter Show was open throughout Holy Week and even on Good Friday, something which he described as "Australia's worst act of spiritual vandalism".[14] The Easter Mission was designed as a deliberate challenge to the creeping paganism which he believed was gradually engulfing Sydney. A purely negative protest would achieve little, but a Christian alternative might succeed.

The programme ran from Palm Sunday through Easter Sunday. In 1959–60 it was surprisingly modest in scope. Apart from Good Friday, it consisted of the regular services on Palm Sunday, but with a special mission emphasis, a series of lunch-hour meetings throughout Holy Week and the regular services on Easter Day with the addition of a 9.00 a.m. "sunrise breakfast" at Fellowship House followed by a pageant in the auditorium there. Friday was the great day with a 10.00 a.m. service in Wesley chapel, lunch at Fellowship House, a film in the Lyceum at 2.00 p.m. followed by a service at 4.00 p.m., tea at Fellowship House at 5.00 p.m., another film in the Lyceum at 6.30 p.m., and an evangelical rally at 7.30 p.m.   The nature of the programme vividly reflects the origin of the scheme. Numbers attending are not available for 1959, but there was a claimed attendance of 12,000 overall in 1960.[15]

After two years experience, the CMM decided to expand the outreach.   The great event of 1961 was the first Easter Day Sunrise Service at 7.00 a.m. at the North Ryde Drive-In theatre with a fifty-voice choir and a leading Shakespearean actor, John Alden, to recite the scripture lesson. This service attracted 3,000 to the theatre, but it was also televised live with a repeat in the evening, thus giving the mission the probability of the widest impact it had ever achieved with a single service.   This was only the most important change. Morning communions for city workers at 8.00 a.m. and daily lunch-time services were also introduced while the Sunday evening drama was upgraded in quality and a new Wednesday evening "Teen Night", with a number of pop singers and bands was introduced at Fellowship House. Several pages of clippings among Sir Alan Walker's press-cutting collection indicate the considerable interest of the secular press in these events.[16]

Other innovations were introduced over the years. In 1964 the youth event moved to the Town Hall and attracted more than two thousand teenagers with a programme which included many well-known pop singers and sportsmen. This "teenage evangelism with a difference" was a clear attempt to capitalize on the continuing success of the by then well-established Teenage Cabaret.   The cautious might wonder whether the 120 decisions recorded at the end were the result of a thoughtful response to Alan Walker's forthright but appropriate message or an emotional response to the stirring effect of so much "hot" music. It is a question which the historian must raise but cannot answer. Successive years saw the introduction of an Easter Family Festival, the lighting of a cross in Hyde Park on the evening of Palm Sunday, and the first Men's Easter Breakfast on the Wednesday of Holy Week. The object of this last meeting was to influence community leaders. Among the hundred who attended were three state ministers, the leader of the federal Opposition, and the N.S.W. commissioner of police as well as representative business, trade and professional, and union leaders and it was chaired by Sir Leslie Herron, the Christian chief justice of the Supreme Court of N.S.W.[17]

By the time Walker left the CMM, he had conducted twenty Easter Missions. This mission was to be one of his most important contributions because it contained within itself all the elements of worship and evangelism which the CMM was striving to express, along with a strong note of social witness as well. It allowed the CMM to challenge the whole process of secularization vigorously, positively, and appropriately. Various aspects of the programme could be directed to each section of the community. It was an occasion which made use of all the CMM's acquired organizing skills, its devotion to prayer as a form of preparation for great events, and its superintendent's unusual ability to exploit the media. While Sydney was listening a little more closely than usual, the message about the Christian attitude to such subjects as racism, war, sexual exploitation, and community corruption could be conveyed as well as the all-important Easter message of the saviourhood of Christ. It was a near perfect answer to the "presence heresy" within the church and the "down-drag" of the community which always threatened to make the CMM no more than a social service agency, a humanist church.

Success is impossible to measure, or even define, but the mission services were often attended overall by a claimed twenty thousand people and there were always converts. Community leaders were anxious to attend the breakfast. All major meetings were fully reported in the media. For a number of years, the *Sydney Morning Herald* and the Melbourn *Age* both published Walker's opening address in full and Channel 7 (Sydney) showed the Sunrise Service live while, in time, a network of country and interstate channels also carried it. This widespread media interest in the missions led to interviews on Willesee's "A Current Affair" as well as articles in several papers. Walker continued to write the Good Friday editorial for the *Sydney Morning Herald* as he had done since the 1940s. It is difficult to imagine how a single church could have gained more attention and made more impact on its host community than the Sydney CMM did through its Easter missions.

Throughout each year, the CMM continued the policy of reaching out to those who would not come to it. Since there were few alternatives open to him, Taylor had pursued this policy by means of the street meeting each Sunday evening at Bebarfald's (Town Hall) Corner. Times had changed, and Walker could pursue new methods, but chose to do so without abandoning the old. Street meetings continued but, in reality, Walker saw the electronic media as the modern equivalent of the open-air service of Taylor's day. For that reason he paid great attention to these media and sought maximum outreach through them.

Within a month of his arrival at the CMM, a new half-hour television series, "I Challenge the Minister", was announced for a trial period of two months on Channel 9 at 4.30 p.m. on Sundays. The programme lasted seven years and for at least a part of that time had the highest ratings of any religious programme in the country. Shown in Sydney and Melbourne, it was accepted as having a weekly audience of more than one hundred and fifty thousand after one year and by 1963, when it was being shown more widely still, a secular newspaper mentioned a weekly figure of half a million. The format was simple: a five-minute address on a subject followed by an unrehearsed question-and-answer period in which the speaker guaranteed not to dodge any question. Difficult enough even in a studio, where the audience could be controlled to a point, this became testing indeed when the programme was filmed on location at Bondi Beach, Sydney University, the Railway Workshops, the Riverstone Meatworks, The Domain or a waterside workers' pick-up centre. The programme led to further publicity in the printed media and to numerous telephone contacts from people who sought help. This would eventually have further repercussions in the form of Life Line. That the programme was allowed to run so long and continued to draw so large an audience would

Sir Alan Walker, CMM superintendent 1958–78. By courtesy of the Wesley Central Mission.

suggest that it had a significant impact on the community.

Ultimately a special multimedia division (under the leadership of Harold Henderson) was established at the CMM to ensure the propagation of the message by cassette, booklet, and press report as well as radio and TV, but when this came in the mid-seventies it was at least partly because the mission was finding it harder to get time and space in the media. There were several problems: the issues had changed and causes like Vietnam and conscription, on which the CMM had taken a newsworthy radical line, had been replaced by the permissive society, where its approach was seen as conservative, wowserish, and uninteresting. After so many years, Alan Walker lacked the novelty he had held for reporters earlier and the CMM thought reporters only interested in events which showed the church in a poor light. Some of its own organizational changes had also unintentionally reduced the emphasis on media publicity.[18]

In mid-1962 the CMM and St Stephen's Presbyterian church (Rev. Gordon Powell) were invited by Rupert Murdoch to join his application for the third commercial television licence to be allocated to Sydney. The two churches were to take up 5 per cent of the capital in a company to be chaired by Country Party man, Sir William Gunn, with the rest of the capital shared between the *Mirror*, the unions and business interests with, it was hoped, both Walker and Powell being given directorships as a reward. This proposal was accepted by the CMM, with Walker arguing that, if the application were successful, he hoped to persuade the company to pledge 5 per cent of time to public service programmes and to minimize, if not entirely exclude, liquor and tobacoo advertisements. Business interests were trying to make use of the character and credentials of two well-known clergymen for their own ends and it is unlikely that Walker's expectation of influence on the advertising and programming policies of the channel would have materialized. It was probably fortunate that the application failed.[19]

Youth work had gradually increased in importance in the post-World War II era. The valuable work done in the 1950s by the Crusader group under R. C. Coleman has already been discussed, but the CMM, like most Methodist churches, provided no youth outreach programme aimed directly at the unchurched youth whose families had often been separated from the church for several generations. In a period when the emphasis was on youth, both as a group with legitimate needs and interests different from those of their parents, and also as a group which might be exploited relentlessly for commercial ends, it is hardly surprising that the CMM should feel the need to exert itself to an extent never attempted before. It introduced many programmes over the years, to cover both the churched and the unchurched, but easily the most eye-catching was Teenage Cabaret.

From mid-1959, the CMM experimented with a monthly outreach programme named "Call to Youth". This used popular artists and, by the end of its run, was drawing 150 to 160, including some from the streets. When the *Methodist* (25 June 1960) published an account by the Rev. Arthur Preston of the Brisbane West End CMM of a cabaret-style programme he had established there in an attempt to reach the street youth, the Sydney CMM was ready to take notice. The concept appealed to Walker since it fitted in with his own view that pop music and dancing provided the best access to modern youth. The new programme, Teenage Cabaret, was launched on 6 August 1960 in a blaze of publicity.

For weeks, a large group of Christian youth had met to train for their responsibilities in keeping order and in seeking to interest the outsiders in the fuller life of the CMM. On 6 August, in a manner reminiscent of Taylor's day, they met early for prayer and the preparation of the hall and then at 6.30 p.m. went out into the milk bars and the streets with handbills to persuade their unchurched peers to come to Fellowship House for the programme. Fifty were involved on any given Saturday night.

The facilities of Fellowship House could be used as a club until 8.00 p.m. when the first of four or five floorshows would begin and the programme run through until 10.45 p.m. Opening night saw five hundred present and large numbers turned away. Over the next ten years, five to six hundred would remain a common attendance, though numbers might fall as low as three hundred and fifty on a bad night and sometimes exceeded eight hundred in later years when the better facilities of Wesley Centre were available. The restrained lighting, with candles on the tables, the variety of facilities available throughout Fellowship House, and the presence of top artists all combined to make the programme attractive.

The first Cabaret was covered by all three TV channels, Cinesound News, all Sydney newspapers, and the *Australian Women's Weekly.* This was probably unprecedented for an event run by a single church and headlines like "Courageous Lead by Methodists in Sydney" indicated widespread community support for a bold attempt to help youth, even if it is doubtful whether the community appreciated the real motive behind Cabaret.[20]

Continuing appeal is evidenced by the fact that as late as 1967 the ABC News Division thought it worthwhile to shoot a whole evening of Cabaret, including the prayer and briefing sessions, and to interview participants. Wesley Centre and 1967 also brought a major change to the format with the establishment of a discotheque in the basement allowing the organizers to cater for two different tastes in music at the same time. Nineteen sixty-eight saw an all-time high in numbers, but the beginning of the end was foreshadowed as trouble occasionally occurred with gangs. This became worse during 1969, partly through lack of adult supervision, but the coming of the "skinheads" in 1970 provided the most dangerous challenge Cabaret had ever experienced. On one occasion the youthful compere was bashed and ended up in hospital with a broken jaw and other damage. By the end of that year, Cabaret seemed to have run its course and 1971 opened with a new programme called "Wesley's Disco", with heavy emphasis on "God-pop". That failed rapidly and "New Teenage Cabaret" was introduced on 1 May, but the magic had gone.[21]

The story of Teenage Cabaret is clear enough, but answers must be attempted to several questions. In terms of numbers, Cabaret was an outstanding success as a youth outreach programme. It drew enormous crowds and lasted longer than any other church or commercial programme of a similar kind.

The basic crowd was drawn from the inner-city areas: Newtown, St Peters, Leichhardt, and Balmain. Groups from suburban churches visited at times, but that was desirable since too great a concentration of toughs would have endangered the purpose of the programme. A strong Christian presence was necessary. The presence of gangs, and the consequent violence, proves beyond doubt that Cabaret was drawing in the kind of youth that was sought, those with no history of church contact at all, and sometimes a criminal element. What proportion fell into this category is impossible to say, since CMM estimates vary from 30 to 90 per cent. Even if the lowest figure is taken, is must be regarded as a significant achievement and one which fulfilled the first aim of the programme.

The quality of contact is another matter. The programme was basically a dance, but it had a Christian message and several numbers of Christian music. Everyone attending was required to be present for the Christian floorshow and spoken message. There were problems about what they "heard" and the ministers quickly realized that some words just could not be used because of their different associations in the teenage subculture: "love" was heard as "sex", and "spirit" as "whisky". Occasionally visiting reporters asked the young people why they came or what they thought of Alan Walker. Many admitted coming simply to hear and see their favourite stars; others said it was a good place to "pick up birds". The CMM believed that a small but significant number of young people from Cabaret attended the Lyceum service and that over the years a number of conversions occurred, but there was no dramatic breakthrough and some disappointment was felt. One other aspect of success should not be forgotten: the effect of this work, with its emphasis on prayerful preparation and on caring concern for one's fellows, on the young people of the CMM who were involved. This must have been considerable.[22]

There was much criticism of the programme in the church when it was introduced. It was only a short time since all dancing had been forbidden on Methodist church property, because of the sexual nature of the activity, and the change was only intended to allow ballroom dancing as part of a general social programme. Most Methodists would have agreed with McGregor that the dancing of the sixties was the most blatantly sexual of all and that its "hot" sexuality far exceeded that of the "cool" ballroom dancing of the older tradition, regardless of the space between the bodies of the partners. It was this "hot" dancing which Cabaret made such a feature of its programme. Yet Walker always felt that the manner in which Cabaret was organized, along with the space between bodies, prevented sexual overtones developing and that this was evidenced by the almost complete lack of cuddling in the corners. He was unlikely to convince his critics.

Traditionalists were bound to consider the cabaret-style programme "dangerous" since it necessarily conflicted with their view of the church as a club for decent middle-class citizens. Cabaret was an outreach programme. It had to depart from safe traditions if it were to make contact effectively with the street youth and slum dwellers, with those who might have been described by the traditionalists as "the unchurched, the unruly and the unlovely". There may be bounds beyond which risk-taking should not go, but those limits are necessarily a matter of judgment.

Comparison will inevitably be made between Teenage Cabaret and Taylor's Boys' Club of the 1890s. Both were outreach programmes of a vital kind, concerned to reach the least respectable elements among youth and to build a bridge into the church for them. Both depended on support from church youth: Walker got it, Taylor did not. Perhaps the difference here lay in the foundation of service which Coleman had built up among CMM youth in the 1950s, even though the people involved were different. The problem of violence was ever present as a threat to both. The great difference was that one enjoyed a measure of success for a decade while the other failed quickly. This is not easy to explain. What is certain is that each superintendent would have appreciated to the full the other's aims, methods, and problems.

With other aspects of CMM youth work in the 1960s and 1970s the overall impression is one of constant change, even chaos, as the mission struggled to find a programme which would work. It never really succeeded in its quest.

The CMM set out to provide both Christian education and entertainment which provided relaxation for the committed and a halfway house for those contacted through Cabaret, further bridging for those drawn to the Lyceum service but not yet fully committed, and opportunities for active Christian service for the dedicated. This was a demanding programme, going far beyond the aims of any ordinary suburban church and requiring a high development of skill and an equally high commitment of resources.

In the sixties a variety of Friday-night and weekend programmes was used to achieve these ends but the most interesting was a student coffee shop at 4.30 p.m. every Sunday afternoon. This began in 1962. In this relaxed atmosphere, with members of the Christian "core" of students mingling with the others at each table, there were musical presentations and a speaker to introduce discussion on a controversial subject. Students seem to have appreciated the quality of the talks (on subjects like the problems of atomic energy, bomb testing, and radiation) but they were critical of the failure of the programme to start promptly and of the inadequate time given for questions and discussion in view of the need to finish sufficiently early for people to attend the Lyceum service. These problems were never remedied and a potentially good programme lingered on for several years without ever really fulfilling its promise. It was a tribute to the CMM that it rated a substantial and not unappreciative comment in *Honi Soit*.[23]

Sunday 11 May 1969 saw the launching by Chief Justice Sir Leslie Herron of a project planned over six months by a group of thirty CMM youth. This was a "Call to Youth" and a linked "Call to Youth Movement". Fundamentally, the 350-word "Call" was a reassertion of traditional Methodist morality and a summons to youth to support the social protest movement which was such an important part of the CMM programme. A cynic might feel that the group had thought along lines remarkably similar to those favoured by the superintendent. The so-called "movement" was little more than a new name to overarch all existing youth organizations. The only really new item was a Youth Parliament to meet twice yearly and promote radical thinking on social and political issues. The key to the considerable fuss made over something which obviously did not justify it is to be found in an associated statement relating to an intention to develop a country property at Arcadia, forty kilometres from Sydney, for the benefit of culturally deprived inner-city youth who would be able to experience the bush there and would also come under the influence of the CMM for a longer and more concentrated period than was usually possible. An appeal was to be launched for this and other associated youth projects.[24] If it could be launched as part of a large-scale new youth movement its fund drawing capacity would be greatly enhanced.

The 1970s saw a kaleidoscope of changing names for the youth work. First came the "Drop-In Coffee Shops" and "SNACS", then a "Drift-In Folk Cellar" followed by a "J.C. Fellowship" and "J.C. Coffee Shop" as the so-called "Jesus Revolution" took hold in the U.S.A. and the CMM tried to follow. After that came "Jesus Meets" and then the ultimate horror, "Jesus Family Gatherings" which had three sections: a "Jesus Blitz", a "Jesus Happening" in the "Jesus Family Room" (once the auditorium), and "J.C.'s Coffee House". Youth work had become disoriented and would remain so for some time.[25]

Teenage Cabaret apart, this description of youth work has been critical. However, times were difficult for such activities. Traditional youth groups were largely outdated even for committed youth and, in any case, had little application to the CMM situation where outreach had to be a main objective. Rev. Alan Jackson, colleague to Walker for much of the seventies, commented, "Let's face it, a city church isn't really aiming to get the 'straight' kids, the church kids. We were always aiming to get the kids who were on the street, out of touch, just the lost you know — really the lost." Jackson admitted that, to the outsider, CMM youth work in the 1970s could appear to be a desperate and largely unsuccessful attempt to keep up with the latest fads, but argued that it was really a case of continued experimentation, of trying whatever means might appeal to the mission's unusual constituency. To maintain a youth programme at all was a continual struggle.[26]

The CMM class meeting, the last in Australia, had remained surprisingly popular over the years, given its strong links with the past and the declining enthusiasm of church-goers for personal testimony. Walker maintained this format only for the remainder of 1958, then launched out on what might best be described as a programme of adult Christian education which was given the grandiose title of "College for Christians". It began with an act of worship and a lecture by the superintendent before the members divided into six groups for discussion and report. Since it is claimed that three hundred attended for much of 1959, these groups must have been unwieldy and relatively ineffective as teaching media. Towards the end of his ministry, Walker wrote of discussion groups of ten or twelve. These were much more likely to achieve their ends. However, the change was probably at least as much the result of falling numbers (attendance was barely a hundred in early 1977, the worst since Rayward's early days) as of any realization of the need for change. The pattern of meeting also seems to have changed with a devotional assembly, followed by either Bible study or an initial training course for Life Line telephone counselling, and then the possibility of an advanced Life Line course. For a period from mid-1973, College for Christians had expanded to a second night each week under the leadership of Dr Vic Hayes. Discussions were to be related to topical subjects, of interest to the individual and the community.[27]

Clearly, College for Christians was designed to service a different need from that serviced by the old class meeting. It could still bring new and experienced Christians together, but the emphasis was on the study and understanding of their faith rather than the sharing of highly personal religious experiences.

In the early Walker years, the Evangelists' Training Institute continued to undertake its traditional function of preparing men for ministerial training, though it did it by means of an upgraded syllabus with more emphasis on personal counselling, pastoral care, and public relations, as well as introducing the students to modern audio-visual techniques. They were also heavily involved in the youth programme at

Fellowship House and were to assist in crusades into the sub-suburbs. Over the years, numbers were never more than a handful and this prompted a change of emphasis to part-time study in 1969. In part, the problem with numbers reflected the difficulty experienced by all denominations in finding men for the ministry, in part it indicated that the increased availability of secular education throughout the state had reduced the need for such a preparatory institution. Young people were now to be trained for leadership in their own churches and this accounted both for taking in external students and women. A new name, Christian Training Centre, also reflected this. In 1972 it became the "Jesus Commune" as an attempt was made under its new principal, Rev. Fred Nile, to link it to the "Jesus Revolution" and to expose students to "radical concepts and methods of evangelism" so that they would become "peer group leaders of the Jesus Movement in Australia and so bridge the widening gap between modern youth and the mainline churches". Students from Asian and Pacific countries were particularly welcome so that they might carry the revolution back with them in due course. Walker, at least, recognized the need to provide a training course which would add depth to the "Jesus Revolution", which was notable only for its enthusiasm, shallowness, and lack of direction. As the "Jesus Revolution" faltered, the Christian Training College also faltered. This was another dimension of the disorientation of youth work in the seventies. It was discovered in mid-1975 that the college was losing $12,000 p.a. for the sake of five students involved. It had to close for the rest of the year, though it did reopen in 1976 in the former Margaret Hallstrom Home at Leichhardt with a new and more elaborate programme. Unfortunately it only ran into more difficulty as its new principal, the Rev. Neil Gough, resigned almost as soon as he joined the mission staff. By the time Walker left the CMM, the college really existed to train young people from Asia and the Pacific for leadership in their own churches. It was a change which in no way departed from Taylor's original ideal.[28]

The second major area of CMM activity, and again it was not new, was institutional work. When Walker went to the CMM he was aware of the valuable contribution being made through its institutions, but recognized that the CMM was doing next to nothing for those who needed "in place" caring. He was worried both that the institutional work might distract him from that and from preaching; thus he tried to concern himself only with overall policy and not to become involved with the detailed execution of that policy as his predecessor had done. Over the years, it proved difficult to maintain that position as institutional work mushroomed and new problems emerged in a period of ever-accelerating inflation and one of his reasons for leaving the CMM was that the move to head the world evangelism programme of the World Methodist Council allowed him to do unhindered the two things that he did best: preaching and writing.[29]

Accommodation at Dalmar had not increased for twenty years when Walker went to the CMM. Population increase, coupled with a changing morality and the more frequent breakdown of marriage, ensured that the home had to turn away in excess of fifty children a week, a situation which the mission could not contemplate with any equanimity. While plans for the extension of Dalmar were being drawn up and executed, the sudden offer of a family home at West Pymble, at a reduced price, and the willingness of a city businessman to pay the costs, enabled the new Bernard-Smith Home for twenty-five handicapped and normal children to open. Overall, an extra forty children could now be taken. This made only a slight dint in the problem and did not touch at all the near-desperate situation of children confronted by sudden emergency and in need of immediate short-term care. The answer to this problem, the Gateway Home, opened in Lewisham in late 1964 to take fourteen to seventeen children until a long-term solution could be found to their problem. Much later, another home, the Wesley James Hostel at Burwood, was opened for teenage children who had been in the homes and had reached the point of starting work. Inevitably, this expansion led to a vastly increased expenditure and hence the need to raise large additional sums of money.[30]

The CMM was determined to keep up with new trends in child care. This was first seen in 1962 with the greater participation of officers in conferences and courses of assistance to them and in the allocation of a CMM social worker to children's home work for two days a week in the attempt to solve the real problems and keep families together. This difficult and time-consuming work increased substantially over the years. The whole concept of child care had gradually changed. Once, children had been rescued from their unsatisfactory environment and put in the home until their adoption or until they left school. Gradually, the aim came to be to avoid putting children in an institution at all. It was hoped that careful screening and subsequent counselling by the social worker would lead to the rectification or easing of family problems and that the child might be able to stay at home or return quickly. Foster care and adoption were also used more frequently in the belief that it was better for children to be in a normal family environment. By 1972 it was claimed that 50 per cent of the children assessed returned to their natural home within twelve months, 25 per cent in one to two years, 10 per cent within two to five years, and 5 per cent never, while 10 per cent were fostered or adopted. It was a natural consequence of this policy that most of the children admitted on a long-term basis were suffering from acute emotional disturbances and in need of special care. A social worker undertook a planned and extensive rehabilitation programme with the help of cottage parents and other members of staff. Smaller groups within the homes, as well as more skilled workers, were necessary. The financial implications were enormous. The cost of keeping a child in a CMM home rose from $10 a week in 1960 to $37 in late 1975, though inflation accounted for some of this increase. Overall costs rose from $68,000 in 1964 to an estimated $200,000 in 1975. The homes had always struggled for money but found themselves with a deficit of $20,000 in 1968 and $40,000 in 1972. For a time these deficits could be covered by using capital funds (legacies), but the Dalmar babies' home had to be closed for a period in 1973. The government contribution to child care was never high (it was lower in N.S.W. than elsewhere in Australia) and, indeed, there were no child welfare payments unless a child stayed in a home for eight weeks. Even then, payments were retrospective for only four weeks.[31]

Enormous development in care for the aged took place in Rayward's time. This continued and expanded under Walker, though his role was to seize opportunities presented by others, especially by the Commonwealth government, rather than to plan new initiatives himself. The detailed response to the initiatives probably came from men like the general-manager, S. H. Manning, and the officer in charge of aged care at any time, while Walker supplied the drive, enthusiasm, and backing.

Late in 1959, the CMM began to develop a new policy in the Sylvania settlement for aged couples. The new plan was to create a self-contained village community with a chapel, shop, small hall, TV lounge, small restaurant, craft centre, and accommodation for both couples and single people as well as sporting facilities. The provision of a range of facilities would eliminate the need for a person to leave the community if his or her partner died. The idea, which was developed over several years with considerable success and the growth of a genuine community spirit, was taken from the Adelaide CMM where such a scheme was already well advanced.

The offer of a private hotel, with motel-type accommodation, in Pagewood in 1961 at a good price allowed the CMM to provide the first home (Hoban House) for the more active elderly in the southeastern suburbs, though it also led to the airing of the mission's "wowser" image when Walker decided not to accept a donation of £100 from the South Sydney Junior Leagues Club because it was from the income of poker machines and thus breached the church's principles.[32]

Late in 1972, the Commonwealth minister for social services, Mr Wentworth, visited Walker to inform him that under a new subsidy scheme for hostels for the aged the CMM would be able to claim about $3,000,000 to build five or six new hostels over the next three years. This was the first major step forward in government thinking in relation to accommodation for the aged since Menzies had introduced the subsidy concept in the 1950s. It was bound to impose a strain on CMM leadership and organization, but there was never any thought that the mission should not play its part in "the great leap forward".

The general manager, S. H. Manning, drew up a philosophy of aged care to underpin the expansion and give it direction. Care must be total, both in the sense that it provided for independent living, custodial care, or intensive care as needed, and in the sense that it catered for all the needs of body, mind, and spirit by providing meaningful activity for residents and also by attempting to integrate them into the community as a whole and especially the worshipping community of the CMM and the churches near the homes. Selection must be on the basis of need alone and there must be a further move away from the "founder–donor" concept (on which the CMM had never greatly relied) so that full advantage could be taken of the government's new generosity. Where accommodation could not be provided, ancillary services, meals on wheels, home nursing, and the like, might be. A chaplain must be appointed to minister to residents and every aspect of the care must be rooted in Christian doctrine and must be unspoiled by paternalism or patronage.

Plans were easier to devise than execute, and two years later Manning was still unhappy with what was being achieved. Nothing was being done to help the inmates of the homes. The staff of the homes were unwilling to co-operate in motivating their charges to meaningful activity. Admission procedures were poor and building and plant were in need of major renovation. The Lottie Stewart Hospital, which had "not progressed very far in its programme for aged persons", had never been integrated into the overall scheme, had no activity programme, employed only part-time physiotherapy and occupational therapy staff, and had never realized its potential as a day hospital for the Parramatta and Dundas Valley regions. He outlined detailed plans to overcome some of the deficiencies and to co-ordinate the work of aged care much more fully than hitherto.[33]

In due course, new hostel accommodation was provided at the Frank Vickery Village (Sylvania), the R. H. Tebbutt Lodge (near the Lottie Stewart Hospital), the R. J. Williams Lodge (the Glebe), and at Narrabeen. There were new nursing homes in the shape of the H. C. Foreman Lodge and the F. H. Rayward Lodge. The latter allowed the removal of all the nursing beds from the W. G. Taylor Home thus increasing its capacity for less intensive cases. During the same period, Sunset Lodge ceased to be a home for aged women and, under the name of Pinaroo, began its third life as a hostel for the intellectually handicapped. Lottie Stewart also underwent major development with the opening of a new Rehabilitation and Training Centre which supplied the therapeutic functions so necessary to the aged yet which had hitherto been missing. Admission practices were also improved.[34]

Lottie Stewart experienced difficulties at this time. Early in 1977, the CMM management was worried about the leadership given by both the matron, Mrs Whitaker, and the chief executive officer, Arthur Jobson. More staff had been appointed than allowed for by the N.S.W. Hospitals' Commission and it was feared that the mission would have to meet the costs involved without aid. When the surplus staff were dismissed, industrial action was taken. Under pressure, Jobson resigned and was replaced by Ken Jenkins, formerly accountant at Lottie Stewart. The matron's resignation was also sought. Whitaker was made of sterner stuff and had to be dismissed (30 May). Following a case before the Industrial Commission she was reinstated. Walker was unhappy about this because, he claimed, Commissioner Dey had not concerned himself with the reasons for dismissal but only with the claims she had brought of improper dismissal. The commissioner had acted as required by law. Whitaker's particular complaint was that she had been harassed by "an officer of the Board" (actually Ken Jenkins, the new chief executive officer). Things settled down for a few months, but at the end of 1977 Whitaker was back before Commissioner Dey with another case of harassment on the grounds that Jenkins was writing and keeping detailed memoranda of every discussion between himself and Whitaker, however trivial. The CMM was also trying to insist that she attend regular staff meetings of the Aged Care Division, a difficult thing when the real lines of authority ran from the Lottie Stewart Hospital to the funding authority, the Hospitals' Commission, not to the CMM, and that she resign in or before February 1979 (she was not due to retire normally until 1984). This time Dey instructed Whitaker to attend the meetings and the chief executive officer to issue detailed memoranda of important discussions only. He would not consider the retirement question until later.[35]

From the mission's point of view the incident was a perfect illustration of the constant battle against secularization. Because Whitaker (unlike the heads of all other CMM institutions) refused to be linked occasionally with the Lyceum service and to attend the Aged Care Division staff meetings, she was seen as giving an inadequate spiritual lead and as weakening the hospital's links with the mission. This was the problem E. Frank Vickery had foreseen in 1958 and it had to be rectified. The means used by Jenkins to achieve the Hospital Board's end were such that they not only largely failed but brought the CMM some public discredit. Unfortunately, Matron Whitaker has not been prepared to put her point of view.

Among the more important areas of advance in CMM institutional work during the period under discussion was the work among homeless men. The responsibility for that work lay squarely with Deaconess Noreen Towers who, at the time of writing, has spent almost two decades in the work. It would be impossible not to link her name with that of Laura Francis. Together they are the outstanding women of 100 years of CMM history, just as Taylor, Rayward, and Walker are the outstanding men. Yet, whereas each man would recognize the outstanding quality of his contribution, each of the women would be surprised at the assertion.

The CMM had been involved with homeless men ever since it moved to the Lyceum in 1908 and had greatly deepened that involvement through the 1920s and 1930s. Later the work continued with the Francis Street Refuge doing what it could for some of the four to five thousand homeless men who were a permanent feature of Sydney life, most of them in the thirty-five- to forty-eight-year age group and many of them seriously affected by alcohol, whether as cause or effect.

The opening of Life Line in 1963 saw the inauguration of what was then known as the Life Line church (later the "church of homeless men" or the "church on skid row") in Flinders Street, but in association with the Sydney Night Refuge in Francis Street. It made little progress until Walker put Deaconess Towers in charge in 1966 with orders to build up the attendance from twenty to eighty. Towers was puzzled how to achieve this until the flash of inspiration came one Sunday morning and she crossed the street to invite two drunks sleeping in the sun to come to church. Amazed by the invitation, they came. After a year the congregation was two hundred. Her action was strictly in accord with the Taylor tradition of going out to get the congregation which would not come to you. Some were probably attracted by the cup of tea and very light snack provided after the service, but this was certainly not true of all as not all stayed for it. She also began a Thursday session at Francis Street for the men, with soup at noon, the opportunity to watch TV or join in discussion, and afternoon tea.

This work led to the 1971 decision to operate a day centre at Francis Street six days a week, to develop a newly acquired house at Galston as a "halfway house" for alcoholics, and to seek government co-operation and assistance to develop a detoxification centre in connection with a major Sydney hospital. These plans were influenced by successful work in Adelaide. When the day centre opened in mid-1971 it was the first in N.S.W., though all groups working with homeless men have since copied it. It provided a meal and the opportunity to shower, shave, clean one's boots, and seek Christian counselling. More recently, government subsidies have allowed improvements in the meals and the better facilities in the new Bourke Street premises (see below) allow medical and dental consultations and haircutting (by a nun) as well. The friendship and acceptance which the men found from others like themselves, and from the staff of Christian volunteers, had an important effect on them.[36]

The very success of the day centre work drove the CMM to plan for improved accommodation facilities as well as the proposed detoxification unit and the Galston halfway house.

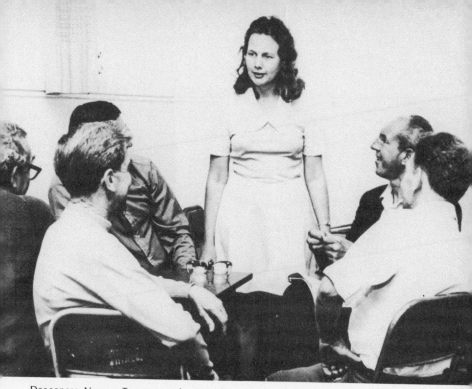

Deaconess Noreen Towers conducts a discussion group. By courtesy of the Wesley Central Mission.

Much was left to Deaconess Towers because it was gradually being realized that groups working among the homeless and alcoholics had too often made the error of leaving the planning and running of institutions for men to men. The CMM was beginning to understand the importance to these men of contact with and acceptance by women of the right type: down-to-earth, firm, accepting, and loving. However, some members had their doubts after an attack on Towers by a man she had excluded from the centre the previous day had left her with a broken nose. It might have been worse had not others of her flock come to her aid.

Plans were greatly aided in mid-1974 by a bequest of $100,000 and early discussions were held with the Department of Social Security seeking further capital subsidies. Ultimately, the department agreed to recommend large grants so that the work could be moved from Francis Street, no longer regarded as suitable, to the Methodist "white elephant" in Bourke Street. The historic old church was to provide room for the day centre, the church services, and for offices on the ground floor while the balcony would become a mezzanine for medical and dental services, library, and counselling rooms.   A new six-storey accommodation block behind the church would provide accommodation for at least eighty-five people.   One floor would be given over to women thus creating the first joint residential facility in Sydney.   Much of the accommodation would be in single rooms to give more privacy and encourage the development of self-respect.   However, the department did not agree to proceed with the Galston project as it thought that city-based men would not adapt to work on a country property. Galston was eventually sold to lessen the CMM's debt burden.[37]

The Bourke Street property opened in 1979, as the Edward Eagar Lodge, under the management of Deaconess Towers and the work has proceeded along her well-tried lines, based above all on the need to offer acceptance to individuals who, in most cases, had been brought low by rejection. Since that time a successful attempt has been made to give residents some responsibility for their centre. More recently, Towers has attained her aim of getting a country property for rehabilitation work.

The mission has never made spiritual demands on the people to whom it has given help, though it has always tried to bring them a spiritual challenge. It is readily admitted that there have been no great spiritual breakthroughs with the alcoholics and homeless. Some attend the Lyceum as well as their own church at Bourke Street and a very few make decisions and live up to them, even becoming church members. The level at which that commitment is demonstrated is elementary and childlike, but it is thought to be real. One of the interesting features of this whole work is the way in which the spiritual work, in association with the church of homeless men, can clearly be seen to have provided the basis for the other aspects of Towers's work.[38]

The CMM had taken no particular interest in work among the intellectually handicapped until the end of the sixties. In

1969 the gift of an acre of land near Rydalmere station caused Walker to ask his Life Line manager for suggestions for its use. Access was also given to some additional government land between the gift and the nearby Rydalmere Psychiatric Hospital and it was decided to develop a rehabilitation centre for the emotionally and psychologically disturbed and also the physically handicapped and intellectually retarded. The institution was to be named the David Morgan Centre after the donor of the land.

Inexperience led the CMM into an impossibly complex operation, the mixing of too many different types of disability on the one site, and to inevitable disappointment. The activity caused immediate concern and initial losses were larger than expected and continued longer than anticipated. The gradual decline in the Australian economy made it increasingly difficult to get contracts from industry. The board of management also failed to make use of its "big name" members to assist the manager with this problem. The mix of handicaps and the range of attempted work (including printing, which proved a highly inefficient and expensive operation) made supervision and the maintenance of standards and schedules impossible. Perhaps no other CMM institution began as inauspiciously, though it later overcame its problems under careful management. The centre also provided continuing education for its employees, linked with Pinaroo Lodge in an accommodation-work arrangement and endeavoured to provide opportunities for worship and Christian growth for all members.[39]

Pinaroo Lodge for the intellectually handicapped also caused some serious problems in its brief history after its opening in 1975. Initially it was intended that all residents should work at the David Morgan Centre, but this was unfair to those already employed elsewhere and had to be abandoned. An apparently serious error was made in the appointment as manager and manageress of a couple whose paper qualifications were impeccable and who were both active Catholics. It was expected that the level of their work would be high. Within a month, both had been assaulted by three people over the treatment of the daughter of one of the attackers. The police were not prepared to lay charges and the CMM was left with the possibility of having to back its employees if they took civil action. This appears not to have eventuated. Within another month, on 26 August 1975, the homes manager, Rev. Mr Aldred, had dismissed the Pinaroo manager for appearing before him under the influence of alcohol while on duty. Thereupon, the manager's thirteen-year-old son organized a protest meeting among the residents and a fire was lit early the next morning. Damage was not severe, but residents had to be shifted to other, strange locations in the middle of the night, a disturbing experience for the retarded. Investigation showed that a substantial sum of money, supposedly held for residents, appeared to be missing and that records relating to such matters were inadequate.[40]

The CMM moved into work for the retarded with good intentions but little understanding. This is not surprising since the general community grasp of the problem was remarkably low at that time. More surprising was the fact that preparation appears to have been less thorough than was normal when a new field was entered. At Pinaroo, problems were compounded by poor selection of top staff, though again it must be noted that paper qualifications and references of the persons concerned were excellent. The manager of the Homes Division should have ensured that proper recording of transactions involving the money of retarded residents was carried out. The impression gained is that the CMM was stretching its human resources beyond their effective limits and was paying the penalty for this. As a result of the experience, work for the retarded was gradually established on a more satisfactory basis.

8

"Mantle of Christ"

Alan Walker, always a Sydney man, save for his brief period in Cessnock and his various overseas visits, held the problems of the city constantly in mind. Throughout his two decades at the CMM he sounded regular warnings against the destructive capacity of the loneliness to which the city dweller is so prone and the phrase, "the lonely crowd", became a prominent part of his vocabulary. Physical need, he believed, had been greatly reduced by prosperity and improved social services. Psychological need was the great problem of the day: "It is an age that is hungry for fellowship. On it are being built the evening beer-gardens, the secular youth societies and the clubs which are the amazing new feature of post-war New South Wales society. Loneliness has become a modern sickness of soul." This kind of worry led him (unsuccessfully) to urge the state government to establish a royal commission on city development to investigate the problems of Sydney and methods of overcoming them and creating a healthier society.[1] It also led him to respond through the CMM itself. Having accepted the responsibility of the church to defeat the isolation of the city, Walker proposed to achieve this by, as it were, throwing the "mantle of Christ" over the city to bring it healing and redemption.

At the end of 1958, Walker argued that the mission's institutional development was strong and valuable, but the mission was weak in its efforts to meet the needs of those who must, and should, remain in their homes and environment. To meet the new psychological suffering and associated community problems, it needed a central service agency to which all in need could turn in the certainty that they would find help. This organization should be able to provide a nursing service, psychiatric help, marriage guidance, personal counselling, social service, pastoral ministry, a telephone service, and a mobile "rescue squad". The load on the CMM would involve additional staff, telephone facilities and rooms at Headquarters, transport and accommodation for the duty team comprising the mobile unit. It could not all be done at once, but he wanted an immediate start with the home-nursing service.[2]

The concept was a towering one, for it involved no less than the attempt to meet the total requirement for care "in place" of the vast and expanding city of Sydney. Small wonder that Walker's treasurers wanted to pause and think before they fell into line with their new superintendent minister. However, they did agree to buy the property next to the Lyceum to ensure the possibility of future expansion. The struggle to translate this new concept into reality would occupy the mission's attention in the ensuing decades.

A church must be concerned with its own as well as those outside of it. In June 1958, Walker had appointed the Rev. W. L. Jago as "minister of membership", the first in the Australian Methodist church. In the great American churches, the ministry tended to be specialized and sectionalized and Jago was to be freed from preaching and organizational demands so that he could concentrate solely on pastoral work. This work included oversight of the membership, visitation of the sick, the fostering of converts, and the training and organization of the laity to participate in pastoral work as a practical expression of the doctrine of the priesthood of all believers. He also followed up new converts, trying to attach them to the church of their choice or the CMM. New lay workers were trained to handle enquirers at services.

This new programme recognized that Christians could only grow in fellowship with others. At one stage, the attempt was made to divide the metropolitan area into fifty-two zones, each containing twenty members or adherents and under an "area visitor" who would visit the area members, arrange group activities for them, advise the pastoral staff of any special needs, act as the accredited agent of the CMM for the area, and arrange for the shepherding of new converts. Later (1967) the operation of small "churchlets" or "house-churches" in the various districts was also contemplated and in the mid-1970s the attempt was made to link the local scheme in with the Methodist World Mission '75 "Share Your Faith Movement".

There were valiant efforts to ensure that none of the widely scattered CMM members or adherents went uncared for, but this pastoral effort was only truly effective in the homes and agencies of the mission and the "pastoral partners" concept could not really be described as a success. Geographical problems and frequent changes of "ministers of membership" did not help. Lay people were unwilling to commit time and effort to this work, reflecting a lack of previous experience and an understandable preference for pastoral visits made by a minister.

The scheme was not a total failure; it simply never lived up to its full promise. Undoubtedly the ministerial staff were kept better informed of special needs and the links were closer than they might otherwise have been. Membership rolls were probably kept more accurately than they would otherwise have been, a fact which helps to explain the lack of real growth of membership, despite constant effort.[3]

The pastoral ministry probably helped to awaken the ministerial staff to what they eventually recognized as distinctive subcultures within both church and society. Several of these will be referred to below because of the special form in which the responsibility to them was exercised, but the ministry to the Pacific Islanders was essentially pastoral and may be discussed here. It should be recalled that in its very early days the CMM had exercised special ministries to the Chinese and, very briefly and without much success, to the Pacific Islanders. This was an important revival.

It is not clear exactly when the work was revived, but by 1968 it was developing strongly under the leadership of Deaconess Noreen Towers who created a Pacific Island Council to organize the various national groups, relate them firmly to the CMM, and give them a real sense of controlling their own affairs. In 1972 the first Tongan clergyman was appointed to minister to the community, the cost being shared by the Department of Overseas Mission, the CMM, and the Tongan–Australian Association. Special services appropriate in language and style to Fijians, Rotumans, Samoans, and Tongans were organized on the four Sundays of the month, with a combined service when there was a fifth Sunday. On 15 May 1977, Walker attacked the immigration policies of the Fraser government with respect to Pacific Islanders, alleging racial discrimination. A further charge of exploitation by some members of the Australian community was confirmed by the minister for immigration. Ultimately, about a thousand Islanders were claimed to be in some sort of relationship with the CMM and in late 1977 the Tongans, at a thanksgiving service, contributed $14,000 to its funds, a very significant donation.[4]

When Walker moved to the CMM, he stated that he wished to transform it into a "seven-day-a-week church". On the surface this seems a strange remark, since through its homes and services for members it was apparently already that. In fact, he was concerned that the mission was too much of a preaching centre with an outcropping of social service agencies and his desire was to transform it so that its ministrations were available to the "lonely crowd" of nonmembers all day, every day. The development of Fellowship House and, later, Wesley Centre, was enormously significant in the attempt to achieve that objective, for it was through them that the facilities for a seven-day-a-week church would be provided.

A month after Walker assumed the superintendency, the Epworth Press building at 218 Castlereagh Street became available. He urged his Executive Committee to buy the building and provide a hall, club premises, and eating facilities for the CMM and "a haven of fellowship" for country Methodists visiting the city. It would provide an opportunity to gather into the church those, old as well as young, on the fringe of Christianity. The meeting was not going well until Sir Frederick Stewart indicated his support and offered the first £1,000. That clinched the matter.[5] Walker quickly assembled a citizens' committee comprising some of the leading business and political figures of Sydney to head an appeal for £70,000 officially launched on 16 September 1958.

It was natural that Walker should stress the importance of his concept to youth, the "blind spot" of the community, the group for whom governments did little. Everyone could be expected to support a scheme which would assist in the battle against delinquency. Yet Fellowship House would incorporate the Sydney Christian Community Centre which had a number of very broad objectives: to win for Christ the thousands of "leaderless and causeless youth" in Sydney; to provide fellowship for the lonely; to provide a place where business people could be confronted with the challenge of the spiritual; to care for foreign students. To achieve this, Fellowship House needed a substantial hall, stage facilities, a dining-room and kitchen, a lounge, a games and recreation area, a conference room and office space. Its programmes should include community centre activities, youth meetings, luncheons and/or meetings for businessmen and women, a married couples' club, groups for university students, an Asian students' fellowship, women's meetings and study groups, a city Sunday school. The opening on 18 July 1959 attracted considerable interest in the press. That interest would continue to surface from time to time.[6]

Many clubs and groups developed at Fellowship House over the years: Couples' Club, Senior Fellowship, Teenage Club, Twixt and Tween, Youth Club, Compass Club (to bring immigrants and "old" Australians together), Crossways (a club which sought to bring together businessmen, unionists, and professionals), Business Women's Club, Christian Action (a meeting of churchmen to discuss social and political problems), and College for Christians. Their success and duration varied and there is no point in discussing them all in detail. Equipment also improved with the provision of a chapel, TV, and better eating facilities. Every endeavour was made to use Fellowship House effectively as a halfway house to bring the unchurched into vital contact with the CMM's practical Christianity and to promote the kind of group dynamics which would give people the sense of belonging to a fellowship.

The struggle was always hard; the tribulations associated with Teenage Cabaret show how hard. Yet if Walker's plan were to be fulfilled, there was no other way. There were serious difficulties in having Fellowship House separated by some distance from Headquarters: it was at 218 Castlereagh Street whereas that end of the main CMM block was at 139. People brought into contact with the church through Fellowship House groups tended to look there for help at other times and they found no one to give it.[7]   That problem would only permanently be overcome as a result of fire.

At 6.00 a.m. on 25 February 1964, the phone rang in the Roseville parsonage to inform the Rev. Alan Walker that the Lyceum was on fire.   The whole theatre was gutted but the Castlereagh Street end of the property was unharmed except for some water damage.   At breakfast that morning, Walker received a telephone call from Sir Norman Rydge, chairman of Greater Union Theatres, the lessees of the Lyceum, offering him the use of the State Theatre for Sunday and Good Friday services, without charge, until the Lyceum was rebuilt.   At 9.30 a.m. an emergency Executive meeting was held to authorize damage assessment and arrange necessary clearing.   At 12.30 p.m. on 26 February, Walker presented the Executive with a tentative report on redevelopment.   Six days later it had been decided to recommend to the Lyceum Trust to build a new theatre within the existing shell and to invite five firms of architects to provide sketch plans within fourteen days for the redevelopment of the whole property. On 18 March an architect was appointed.   The speed of the response was remarkable and amply justified Rayward's later comment that "Alan Walker was brilliant over the fire. I was amazed that an evangelist could be such a brilliant businessman".[8]

The physical details of the rebuilding are of little significance to the historian trying to understand the life and work of the mission.   For two years the CMM was without a "home" and its superintendent and staff were greatly burdened with extra work and worry.   The debt associated with the building project made that burden a continuing one. Yet it is equally true that this disaster gave the CMM its "finest hour".   There is simply no evidence available which suggests that it ever faltered in its task as a result of the fire. Change there had to be, and some dislocation, but the real work went on almost as if nothing had happened.   The opportunity was taken to ensure that a more appropriate structure, better adapted to the needs of the time, would rise from the ashes. In part, this impression is possibly a trick of the kind of records which survive: there are mostly minutes which record positive decisions rather than the doubts which may have preceded them. In part, it is certainly due to the faith, vision, and drive of the superintendent who, conscious of the task he believed himself called to perform, regarded the fire as no more than an aspect of the strange providence of God and therefore as necessarily a stepping-stone, or even a spur, to better things. This aspect of the incident is far more noteworthy and revealing than any difficulties over money.

Within three months plans were announced for a seven-storey building facing Pitt Street and a new arcade between Pitt and Castlereagh Streets. At a later stage it was planned to rebuild Wesley chapel and a new headquarters and office building facing Castlereagh Street but the immediate interest was in the Pitt Street end, to become known as Wesley Centre. Walker had a rapid survey done by a leading firm of consultants to determine the likely direction of Sydney's society to the end of the twentieth century. They foresaw a society increasingly affluent and leisured, working probably only twenty-five to thirty hours per week. They also foresaw an intensifying problem of loneliness in the ever-expanding metropolis which might reach a population of five million and might extend from Newcastle to Wollongong. Social problems were likely to intensify greatly, especially alcoholism, compulsive gambling, sensualism, and suicidal despair.

Walker took another step even more unusual for a Methodist minister. Scandalized that so many church buildings stood empty for all but a few hours each week, while the teeming population around them remained in desperate need of fellowship, he took some of his officials and the CMM architects on a tour of five institutions he believed were meeting that need in Sydney better than the churches — five licensed clubs. He commented "I believe the poker machines and liquor bars of N.S.W. are a judgement on the church. There was a vacuum, people wanted somewhere to meet outside their homes, wanted fellowship, and the clubs came into that vacuum because the church was closed." He wanted his church to be able to provide the good facilities of the clubs, both organized activity and the casual "drop-in" style, but without the evils of drink and gambling which spoiled the clubs from a Methodist point of view. Walker's attitude in this respect was very different from that of Methodists who merely criticized the clubs, for he realized that the concept expressed something wholesome and good and that clubs helped to provide for social and personal relationships.[9]

Wesley Centre was Methodism's largest-ever building project in Sydney and an appeal was launched, at first among Methodists but later in the community at large, for £100,000. The chance had come to centralize all the mission's activities at Wesley Centre. For this purpose, halls large and small, club rooms, office space, and a restaurant were needed so that an enlarged Sydney Christian Community Centre could come into being and help fulfil Walker's "mantle of Christ" vision. The very size and boldness of the project ensured its support from the premier, the chief justice, and many prominent members of the business community as well as the secular press. The reopening of the Lyceum on 5 June 1966 indicated general public support for the mission. The Salvation Army band led a procession of 1,000 people from the State Theatre to the Lyceum. Pitt Street was completely blocked by a crowd estimated by the *Daily Telegraph* at more than 3,500, then 1,270 crowded into the Lyceum (capacity 1,222), with another 400 in Wesley chapel, for a ceremony attended by a number of community leaders.[10]

A Christian club, Wesley Club, was started. Open to all who paid a fee of $3 and who could obtain two satisfactory references, it provided a range of Christian, recreational, and informational services. But, despite the excellent facilities available in Wesley Centre, the expresso coffee, restrained lighting, the organized and unorganized activities, and the "soft-sell" religion, the club concept did not really work. Many joined initially but the renewal rate was low. The problem was twofold. In the ordinary club, the facilities and privileges are restricted to members alone. They can therefore get something for their money which is not available to others. Since the CMM wanted to use Wesley Centre as a means of drawing the outsider into Christian fellowship, it could not restrict in this way and even the imposition of a small fee on nonmembers for some services did not give the member any sense of advantage. A later attempt to sub-stitute the idea of people becoming "Friends of Wesley Centre" and supporting it by a donation instead of seeking privileges for themselves was more Christian in concept but also failed to work. Nor was anything ever found to replace the drawing power of the two things which the CMM could not provide: a liquor bar and poker machines. The organized activities, groups and clubs, at Wesley Centre worked reason-ably well, but the unorganized, "drop-in", activities were not a success. Wesley Centre had never been expected to pay its way, but the limited success of the "drop-in" activities, high lighting, and cleaning costs, and a heavier-than-expected interest burden, the result of the escalation of building costs, meant that the property was a financial burden throughout the 1970s. Nor was the position improved in 1978 when the tenancy of a large area of the building by Grain Elevators, originally arranged by a senior official of that body who was also closely connected with the CMM, came to an end and the space proved to be very difficult to let in the then rapidly deepening Australian economic recession.[11]

Despite the serious problems encountered with Wesley Centre, there were important successes involving hitherto neglected groups within the Sydney community.

The first was School for Seniors. From the beginning of Fellowship House there had been a programme for senior citizens, but it had been limited and traditional in scope. During 1968 the mission developed the idea of providing an educational and activity programme one day a week for retired people. Men and women were living and remaining active longer and were sometimes confronted with many years between retirement and death. They were often capable of using these years in creative and meaningful ways. Society had not then caught up with these changes and the CMM should lead the way forward. It did. School for Seniors was opened on 6 March 1969 and for $1 a term anyone over fifty-five years could go to Wesley Centre from 10.00 a.m. to 4.00 p.m. and join in the variety of classes and the devotions or merely chat socially in the restaurant.

Numbers started at more than three hundred but they expanded considerably over the years until space became cramped and in 1974 classes had to be held on two days a week. Over the years, the school also introduced summer schools, held exhibitions of paintings, and had published some of the stories written by its students. Success was indicated by the idea being copied in many places and by the attempts of some to advance their age so they could qualify for membership. It is probably reasonable to predict that in a society where free time is increasing and the life span lengthening such activities will continue to thrive and grow.[12]

An article in *Time* in the early 1970s dealing with America's new "single's society" sparked Walker's interest in yet another Sydney subculture. Research showed him that at the 1971 census there had been 560,965 single persons of twenty years of age and over in Sydney. Of these, the largest proportion (313,981) were young adults who had never been married, but there were also 47,571 permanently separated, 42,111 divorced, and 157,302 whose partner had died. Little if anything was being done to meet their needs, despite the fact that the last three groups might have very special needs and problems not easily met in groups intended for all sections of the community. Singles' Society was launched on 15 March 1974 to provide creative activities, fellowship, social life, intellectual life, and a link with the Christian church for single people of all ages. It was on Friday evening and consisted of a (fruit) cocktail session, a dinner with a speaker on current affairs, a devotional period, then a variety of group activities and a coffee shop. Additional social gatherings and conference weekends were arranged as well. The society remained successful throughout the period primarily because it provided most of its members with their best opportunity for friendship and, in particular, it provided a supportive atmosphere for newly bereaved or divorced persons. It lost a number of its members through marriage. A number also linked with the church as a result of membership of the society.[13]

The most important new element in Walker's "mantle of

Christ" proposal was the suggested twenty-four hour telephone counselling service. Despite his setback in 1958,
Walker remained determined to implement this proposal and
called a group of thirty people to his home during 1961 to
discuss it. The concept involved the manning of telephones
twenty-four hours a day by volunteers so that there would
always be someone to whom a person in desperate need
could turn for help.

The proposal needed careful development. The concept of
a Christian counselling service was perfectly reasonable in
itself, but it was not possible to employ just any volunteer.
Neither Christian experience nor professional expertise alone
could be considered adequate for the work by the mission,
despite its awareness that some Christians could see no need
for the latter and some professionals no relevance for the
former. In addition to constructing the necessary facilities,
the CMM would carefully design and implement a training
programme before it opened the service early in 1963.

Planning for the Christian Service Centre to be built by the
reconstruction of the old Flinders Street church began early
in 1961 and was expected to cost £30,000. As well as the
telephone service, it was expected that a home-nursing
service, marriage guidance clinic, centre for the distribution
of clothing and general relief, foot clinic, and trouble team
would be located there. A citizens' committee was established to raise funds. From the start, the project drew considerable media attention.

From 8 July 1962 the Life Line Movement (the counselling service was given the title "Life Line" after a *Sydney
Morning Herald* subeditor had used it for a headline on the
work) got under way. The object was to recruit the laity on
the basis of spiritual commitment and to equip them for
effective service and witness. The six-month training course
included theology, biblical studies, and specialized courses in
counselling and witnessing. Eventually, though not for about
two years, the Life Line Movement became the general
service agency within the mission wherein the laity were
trained not only as telephone counsellors, but as volunteer
workers in Wesley Centre or in the homes. The actual area of
service was decided on grounds of suitability as well as

inclination.   At the end of the training period, all workers were dedicated to their task.[14]

The Life Line Centre opened on Saturday, 16 March 1963 and immediately filled a real need in the city. Each telephone counsellor worked a four-hour shift once a fortnight and summarized the details of every conversation. At 9.00 a.m. each day, a small committee examined the reports and determined any action to be taken. Callers might be interviewed by a full-time worker or directed to specialized personnel (social workers, psychiatrists, and the like) for further counselling, or, as time passed and the scheme developed, to groups like Gamblers' Liberation, which operated on lines similar to Alcoholics Anonymous. More important was the establishment of the Caring Division of Life Line which provided, where necessary, a "shepherd" to offer friendship to callers for a minimum period of three months. Life Line could always call on CMM homes and hospitals to help urgent cases. A "trouble team" was sent out to potential suicides and other desperate cases and was in regular use. It should be recalled that worship remained at the heart of Life Line Work since the church of homeless men originally began as the Life Line church.[15]

Many factors demonstrate the success of Life Line. In the first year there were 11,664 first contact calls, a figure which had risen fourteen years later to more than 25,000. Some analysis of calls appears in Appendix A. Press publicity was considerable and continuing. The Life Line ministry first drew the CMM's attention to the need for a children's emergency home and a night refuge for women. Life Line was also an organizational success in at least two ways: it helped to concentrate and organize the relief work of the mission in a way that had not previously happened, and it led to a better-trained and more-involved laity. Success was also evident in that Life Line became a world-wide movement with a common charter based on that used in Sydney, and led by Alan Walker.[16]

Life Line did not have an untroubled existence. On 8 August 1967 a fire destroyed a large part of the premises housing the welfare, child care, clothing store, therapy room, main auditorium, kitchen, and two flats occupied by "trouble team" personnel. Phones were out of operation briefly. An appeal through the media ensured that clothing stocks would be replaced over time and help was given with collection and storage, but it was seven months before the centre became fully operational again. The opportunity was taken to update and improve facilities. Publicity created by the fire led to an enormous increase in calls for help.

Apart from this, there was one serious case of misappropriation of funds from a Life Line store in Parramatta. However, this was dealt with expeditiously and the matter placed in police hands. As at Pinaroo, the real problem lay in procedures for the selection of staff. These had allowed the appointment of a person with a criminal record, and who was under the supervision of an adult parole officer, to a position of trust.

November 1972 saw Alan Walker report that, for a year, Life Line had been suffering from internal divisions, the result of leadership difficulties. Two months later, the director, the Rev. Ian Miles, resigned because the Executive Committee would not meet a series of demands he had placed before them.

Apparently Miles and a group associated with him had desired to eliminate the specifically Christian element in Life Line and to separate the movement from the mission so that it would become just another secular counselling service based solely on skilled counselling and not at all on Christian commitment. Miles's first move was to introduce a militant atheist psychiatrist into the training programme and to refuse to terminate his involvement when instructed to do so. This failure to abide by mission policy led to his own dismissal. However, his supporters decided to carry on the battle to detach Life Line and their next move was to introduce a man of Jewish faith into the counselling programme. When Walker would not accept him (March 1973), the media levelled charges of antisemitism against the man who was Sydney's most consistent opponent of racism in all its forms. Walker was simply determined not to lose the battle to prevent the secularization of the CMM and believed it essential to insist that counsellors have "a declared commitment to Christian doctrine". Not all branches of Life Line observed the rule with equal strictness and in later years even the Sydney CMM put less stress on this aspect, though counselling was still to be in accordance with "Christian insights". Walker described this "backsliding" by Life Line as "the greatest disappointment of my ministry". He attributed it to the birth of Life Line at a time of "christological weakness" in the 1960s, when the "presence heresy" was prominent in the church's thinking.[17]

The final great innovative idea, and the one of which Walker remained most proud in later years, was Vision Valley, "the Christian country club for everybody". It appears that when Walker was overseas on long-service leave in 1968, he discovered interesting developments in Christian country renewal centres in the U.S.A. at Lake Junaluska and at Massanetta Springs. Soon after he returned, he reported on these at a Quarterly Meeting and had the whole concept thoroughly discussed. The outcome was a resolution that a fifty-acre property be purchased and a master plan developed. Sir Edward Hallstrom told Alan Walker of the location of a valley which would suit his needs and which was available. Twenty-five thousand dollars was provided by Ken Thomas of TNT for the purpose and other individuals and groups also assisted. Before the property was opened by Prime Minister William McMahon in June 1972, living quarters for more than one hundred, a dining-room, and chapels were built. Walking trails were created around the property and through neighbouring Crown land which the CMM was permitted to use for such recreational purposes. The state government also gave $10,000.

This costly venture had several purposes. It was an investment in peace and tranquillity and hence in the psychological stability of those who lived in the concrete jungle of Sydney. The affluent could provide their own way out through trips to the sea or country, the less fortunate needed to have an escape provided. As people from the various groups at the CMM went there for conferences, non-Christians attending would be brought into more extended contact with the Christians. The valley would become an extension of the

worship, fellowship, Christian education, and evangelical programmes of the mission. Two years after completion, Walker
indicated that an important "parallel ministry" was being
exercised at the valley. The value of Vision Valley was
threatened by the 1973 proposal to build a second airport for
Sydney at Galston and there was a strong protest from the
mission.

This was another aspect of the mission's programme which
drew extensive public support and considerable coverage in
the press, including all Sydney papers, the Melbourne *Age*,
and some rural papers. The valley continued to be well used
by the CMM and other church groups as well as by casual
visitors.[18]

The most innovative aspect of Walker's work at the CMM was
what he called his "prophetic ministry". This had its origin
directly in Niebuhr's theology of the Kingdom of God and of
Hebraic prophetism. One of the functions of the Christian
minister, as of the prophet of old, was to make pronounce-
ments on important developments in the secular world. The
church which was afraid to state its position on matters
regarded as vital to the well-being of mankind would quickly
become totally irrelevant. "Isaiah, Jeremiah, Amos — all
proclaimed a message of social redemption in national
politics and international affairs. They were fully involved
men of God." The first message delivered by Jesus in the
Nazareth synagogue proclaimed him to be Emancipator as
well as Redeemer; he was and is "the partisan of the poor".
The call for conversion and the search for social justice were
together the core of the Gospel.[19]

Before he had even arrived at the CMM, Walker had taken
a deliberate decision to transform the PSA, which he
regarded as a "Sunday afternoon entertainment" into a
"crusading platform" that would force people to think about
vital issues. Not that the PSA was the only place where
Walker took up major current issues: that also happened at
the Lyceum service from time to time. Nor would it be true
to say that the PSA (later known as the Lyceum Platform)
became no more than a political forum. Despite Walker's

views on 'Sunday afternoon entertainments", there were still occasional talks on "The Exciting World of Radio", "Cricket at the Crossroads", and "West Indies Prospects". There were many that were "religious" in the ordinary and narrower sense of that word: "Billy Graham Crusade", "Bible Sunday", "Discovering Christ Today'. Perhaps even more significant was the constant faithfulness with which Walker upheld the traditional Methodist social causes relating to alcohol and gambling. These were major themes in his ministry at the CMM, extending over its whole length. None of his battles was more diligently or perseveringly fought than those against the Sunday opening of hotels, the admission of eighteen-year olds to clubs, poker machines, and the legalization of casinos. It seems probable that he devoted more time to alcohol and gambling than any of his predecessors, though this was largely forced upon him by the changing nature of society and the increasingly liberal legislation on these subjects introduced by the various N.S.W. governments, but notably those of Sir Robin Askin and Neville Wran. The record of this activity, and the debate it sometimes raised with politicians and representatives of the liquor and gambling industries is scattered through twenty years of the secular press and the *Methodist.*

It was not these traditional Methodist issues which made Alan Walker the most dispute-prone parson in Sydney. As well, he tackled a list of subjects which is truly astonishing: the White Australia policy, nuclear testing, treatment of Aborigines, birth control and abortion, apartheid, child marriage, capitalism, economics, unemployment, state aid to education, religious instruction in state schools, the death penalty, conscription and the Vietnam war, U.S. bases in Australia, sex, the Russian invasion of Czechoslovakia, street violence, poverty, the dismissal of the headmaster of the Newington College, pensions, China, conservation, the Bill of Rights introduced by the Whitlam government and its Family Law Bill as well, Solzhenitsyn, Sir John Kerr, humanistic social legislation, and the principles to be kept in mind at various state and federal elections. Some of these topics were dealt with once or twice only, others cropped up regularly over a period of years and involved long-term campaigns: the Vietnam war campaign, for example, lasted for over a full decade.

There is nothing to be gained by studying each of these campaigns in detail, though brief reference must be made to two or three. Walker's opposition to racism in all its forms was longstanding and totally consistent as well as being firmly based in biblical teaching. He attacked the White Australia policy long before he went to the CMM and continued to do so from the Lyceum not only until important modifications were made in the late sixties, but as serious lapses occurred thereafter. The incident relating to Pacific Islanders, previously mentioned, is a good example of this. With this was always linked a concern for and a demand for aid to the Third World itself. His support for Aboriginal causes also extended over his whole period at the CMM and was expressed both in general terms and in relation to particular examples of prejudice as they arose. His firm, clear stand in this area gave greater point and validity to his regular attacks on apartheid in South Africa and his support for sporting bans on that country. His stand did not suffer from the weakness of the position taken by too many Australians who could readily enough be accused of concentrating on racism in South Africa while excluding from their minds that practised against the Aborigines at home. It was the coherence, consistency, and all-inclusiveness of his attitude on racism which perhaps made this the most attractively fought of all his religio-political causes.[20]

Conscription and the Vietnam war were bound to come under attack. These linked issues would lead him into more trouble than any of his other causes. The reason for this lay less in himself and in his approach to them than it did in the polarizing nature of the issues. Most commentators seem agreed that the Vietnam war divided Australians more deeply than any other issue, with the possible exception of conscription during World War I. Walker took a strong line against the war itself and against Australian involvement in it, against conscription and the use of conscripts in Vietnam, and against the injustice of demanding military service from only a minority selected by drawing marbles (with birth dates marked on them) from a Tattersalls' lottery barrel. Since his protest involved direct action, it was bound to draw on him the anger of the authorities as well as of those members of the church and general public who supported the war and conscription.

The most dramatic evidence of this opposition came on Sunday, 12 November 1967, when Canon D. B. Knox of the N.S.W. Council of Churches, ordered station 2CH, of which the council was the licensee, to cut an antiwar programme emanating from the Lyceum. If Knox's aim was to prevent the dissemination of antiwar ideas (and it was), he failed signally. The speeches had finished by the time the connection had been cut and, in any case, the action sparked headlines in the secular press: the *Sydney Morning Herald* hoarding on the Monday morning read "Anti-war Programme Taken off Air" and it gave its main front-page article to the subject.[21] In all his antiwar work, Walker confined himself to views supported by Methodist Conference resolutions and by the Australian branch of the World Council of Churches.

The state aid controversy, mainly 1961–66, was the least happy of the political causes taken up by Alan Walker. Partly this was because of the "dirty" political nature of the subject: the introduction of state aid for schools by Sir Robert Menzies in 1961 was clearly a ploy to exploit the Catholic vote. Later, the ALP also decided that expediency was to be preferred to principle and the CMM was caught in the crossfire of this unpleasant battle. The question inevitably involved some sectarian bitterness, especially during the Catholic school strike at Goulburn in 1962. More importantly, the issues were never as clear-cut as Walker at first imagined them: a divided system of education did not necessarily lead to a divided society. In any case, the CMM itself was actively seeking and accepting state aid for its childrens' and aged persons' homes. While there was certainly a difference between those areas and education, it was not a black-and-white one and some inconsistency was involved. The waters were muddied even further in 1964 when the Methodist Conference decided to accept aid for its schools and when action by the state ALP government appeared to Walker to endanger the religious education programme in state schools. These events finally led Walker to accept the concept of aid.

It had been an unhappy incident for both Alan Walker and the CMM.[22]

Walker annoyed many over the years. On 15 August 1962, the *Australian Church Record* commented: "Mr Walker has always been a controversial figure. He has developed the Central Methodist Mission's 'Pleasant Sunday Afternoon' meetings into little more than forums for the airing of social and political grouches." Other individuals expressed annoyance or disappointment as he opposed their chosen points of view, and Methodist presidents were themselves at times constrained to point out that he was not an official spokesman for the church. Much of the criticism was carping and beside the point, or sprang from conservative opposition to his consistently radical views: conservatives were used to winning in the Australian churches. Some outside the church thought that it should confine itself to worship and piety, a convenient line for an increasingly permissive society not anxious to be confronted by the voice of the church.

Within the mission there was some conservative resistance to his challenge to government policy, but most continued to attend. The few who did not were usually replaced by others. Some appear to have become inured by the frequency of his controversial statements. However, it might possibly be argued with success that the political colour of those who trod the Lyceum Platform was more varied than in any preceding superintendency. The past had seen few of radical tendency; Walker did invite a number of conservatives.

Mission officials apparently never questioned his right to speak out and express unpopular views on sensitive issues, even if his action elicited a public response and thus imposed some strain on the CMM itself. A case in point occurred on 27 June 1976 when Walker, in the context of an address on "National Unity and Righteousness", called on the governor-general, Sir John Kerr, to resign. His treasurers discussed the issue with him but made no demands, because they recognized that, like all Methodist ministers, he had "the freedom of the pulpit".[23] A failure of confidence on either side would have greatly inhibited Walker's prophetic ministry.

The real problem was not whether Walker should have involved himself as he did, or whether he was sometimes wrong in the views he expressed. A meeting of lay and clerical leaders at The Hague, years before, had defended the right of involvement in public affairs, provided the clergy were properly informed, but had argued that the church should not provide "a running commentary on the international newsreel".[24] In dealing with so many issues so frequently, Walker was in danger of being inadequately informed on some and also of weakening the impact of his efforts.

How successful the Lyceum Platform was in affecting the policies of governments must remain unclear. It is certainly likely that Sunday hotel trading and casinos would have been introduced much sooner but for the determined opposition of the churches which had a longstanding and accepted interest in such matters. Government policies on war, conscription, immigration, Aborigines, and many other issues also changed but it is not possible to prove a direct causal link. In any such protest, the CMM was usually joined by a strange assortment of allies and it is difficult to apportion credit (or blame). Sometimes changed policies in the U.S., or changed political and economic circumstances in Australia, also played their part. Yet it seems likely that the CMM also had its effect. It was a voice calling for change. It was often enough either the first voice to stir the Christian or the national conscience and it seems unlikely that either state or federal government could afford to turn a deaf ear. Beyond that it is impossible to go with certainty.

The late sixties and seventies were a period of financial strain at the CMM. Soaring costs in the homes and the heavy burden imposed by Wesley Centre after the fire were the main causes. The mission had only three sources of income: government subsidies which were reasonably liberal for aged persons' homes, meagre for child care, and nonexistent for other activities; payments by the people being served; voluntary donations which were a highly significant item.

The main problem lay in the inflation which increasingly afflicted the Australian economy as the years passed. In any year, some of the mission's institutions would show a substantial deficit and would have to be "carried" by others. Sometimes, as in mid-1967, Walker spoke of "deepening financial crisis", though this was done more to forestall anticipated trouble than to describe an existing state of affairs, since there was never an overall deficit in any year. The heavy funded debt on Wesley Centre remained a problem and in 1976 the Galston property was sold to enable a reduction of the interest burden which would otherwise have been beyond the capacity of the Lyceum Trust. There was nothing new about a problem which had caused Taylor so much agony eighty years before, after the opening of Centenary Hall. Ultimately a solution could be found only in the reduction of the interest burden.[25]

The 1960s and 1970s were a busy and turbulent time. That was bound to be the case: the rapid and increasing pace of change in Australian society made it inescapable. The discovery first of the needs of youth and later of those of the aged meant that the church would have to respond in new ways. The increasing secularism of society had a profound effect as did the existence of deeply divisive issues like the Vietnam war and conscription. It was proper for a great city mission church, facing greater problems and possessing larger resources than the ordinary local church, to act in experimental ways. The CMM had always done that: it had been a great experiment itself in its initial phase. All that had changed now was the degree and pace of innovation. The "prophetic ministry" was largely new for the CMM and was certainly the harbinger of controversy. This ministry sprang from the superintendent's own convictions and from his intellectual inheritance. Yet other clergy, world-wide, especially but not only in the Methodist church, were thinking about the great problems of peace and war, of racism, poverty, and the unequal distribution of this world's goods and were coming to similar conclusions. It is difficult to see how a minister of ability, vision, and sensitivity could have remained uninvolved in at least some of this activity at this particular period and in the circumstances in which the mission was placed. Indeed, it has been part of the argument of this work that it was the main weakness of the CMM in its earlier years that it became involved in the important controversies of everyday life only rarely. Too often it was content to do ambulance work and to refashion individuals while regarding the refashioning of society at large as outside its scope. Its inheritance from the nineteenth century sprang from the English philanthropic and evangelical traditions rather than from the American "social Gospel" tradition. Change came after 1958 as Walker consistently applied his view that "the Church cannot do other than plunge into the search for a new humanity".[26]   This "whole Gospel" approach involved fundamental changes and challenged the church as vigorously as it did the community.

Epilogue:
After the First Hundred Years

No attempt will be made to assess the work of the Wesley Central Mission, as it is now known, over its last few years, but a brief factual statement, culled from current reports, may be made.

The mission continues to function in all the areas of activity developed over the years and its aims, strengths, and problems remain largely the same, though a gradual development of methods continues to occur.

Under the leadership of the Rev. Gordon Moyes, formerly a Church of Christ minister at Cheltenham, Victoria, the mission has continued to put worship and evangelism at the heart of its work, in line with the view it has always expressed, that it must maintain its Christian character and not allow itself to be secularized by its host community. To this end, there are now daily services (except Saturday) in Wesley chapel and a total of thirty-nine services each week. Eight languages are used in these services and the work among Pacific Islanders and Chinese is particularly strong. There has also been a substantial revival of the practice, common in Taylor's day, of holding half-nights and whole-nights of prayer. The regular Sunday evening prayer meeting has become two, one in the John Lees chapel at 6.00 p.m. and another, a little later, below the Lyceum stage and incorporating all who are involved in any way in the conduct of the 7.00 p.m. service. That service maintains the evangelical thrust which it has had since 1884, though the form is now different as Moyes makes considerable use of audio-visual techniques, a method not previously employed.

The WCM still reaches out through street work and the Easter Mission. The Sunrise Service is now held on the steps

G. Moyes, CMM superintendent 1978– By courtesy of the Wesley Central Mission.

of the Opera House rather than at a suburban drive-in theatre, an appropriate move given the important place the new location has in the community life of Sydney. However, Moyes, like Walker, clearly believes that the media provide the modern equivalent of the open air. There are daily radio "spots" featuring the superintendent, a three-hour Sunday evening radio broadcast beginning with the Lyceum service and following with recorded interviews with leading Christian personalities, and a long talk-back session. The major component of the TV outreach is the programme "Turn Round Australia", shown weekly over sixteen channels in all states. An important new feature of this form of evangelism is that people hearing or watching the programmes are invited to telephone a central counselling point where trained counsellors are available to guide them to faith in Christ. The result of this is that while attendance at the WCM's weekly services are less than half the peak attendances of Taylor's time (assuming both counts to be accurate), the mission's message now has a potential audience far greater than ever before. The fact that "Turn Round Australia" is the highest rated religious TV programme and that the ratings for the Sunday evening radio session are also high indicates that at least a part of that potential is being realized.

Institutional care continues unabated. A new alcoholic rehabilitation programme involving three farms (known as the "Serenity Farms") and a halfway house at Milson's Point, is linked with the work of the Edward Eagar Lodge. This represents a more sophisticated and scientific revival of the work begun by Woolls Rutledge at the Medical Retreat late last century. The old Refuge in Francis Street has been used as emergency accommodation for thirty Vietnamese refugee orphans, while the facilities for the intellectually handicapped have reached maturity and now seek to train young people in the skills of independent living. Taylor's first love among his institutions, the Evangelists' Training Institute, has closed. Under the Uniting Church all such training has been centralized.

The WCM children's homes, like all such institutions, have struggled to survive and have only done so as a result of the money available from the Cottee Orchard, Australia's largest

orange orchard, gifted to the Dalmar homes by H. W. Cottee.
The more modern techniques of running the homes, pioneer-
ed in Walker's time, have been continued and improved upon.

Aged care continues through the various homes and
hospitals and the School for Seniors as well as a new visitation service, Do. (Domiciliary) Care, for the shut-in. Plans
are in hand for a senile dementia centre at Lottie Stewart
Hospital and there is to be an $18 million aged care centre
developed at Frank Vickery Village. As part of this, the
N.S.W. Housing Commission will pay the cost of providing
accommodation for thirty needy aged persons. Development
is also due to begin during the centenary year on a $25
million development on part of the Dalmar land (Carlingford)
which will involve aged care, child care, and handicapped
persons centres. The changing composition of the Australian
community, and of government policies in respect to welfare,
is likely to propel the WCM into ever greater involvement in
such areas.

The pastoral management of the mission's nine hundred
members continues difficult. Home bible study groups have
been established and eighty elders are involved in pastoral
visitation, but it is admitted that, as was the case a decade
earlier, this work is not uniformly effective.

Other aspects of the "in place" caring programme continue
to develop. Life Line, which has moved to Wesley Centre
from its original Darlinghurst home, receives sixty thousand
calls a year and now has associated with it the Youth Line
counselling service for the young and Ethnic Life Line, which
trains multilingual counsellors. A financial counselling
service, Credit Line, which helps six hundred families a
month, provides a new and important service in a time of
severe economic depression and unemployment.

The political and social issues which trouble Australia in
the 1980s are very different from those of the two preceding
decades. Moyes has taken a public stand on such matters as
casinos, unemployment, drug addiction, random breath testing, community violence, and humanitarian aid to North
Vietnam. His style has been more low-key than that of his
predecessor. Again, it must be emphasized that it is
impossible to estimate success in this area, let alone make
comparisons.

The financial turnover of the WCM has expanded enormously in the last five years. This is partly the result of the extremely high level of inflation experienced by the Australian economy throughout the period, but it goes beyond that. The financial base of the mission has broadened. The number of donors has increased significantly and the policy of seeking legacies has been successful to an increased extent. The Spring Fair, an annual event since just before the Great War, now raises almost $100,000 a year. An interesting new development has been in the area of entrepreneurial activity. The Cottee Orchard at Renmark, South Australia, has been mentioned. Nineteen eighty saw the opening of a Textile and Recycling Centre and in 1982 a Youth Line plant nursery was established.

The WCM will need all this money and more if it is to continue to expand its activities and to participate (with the N.S.W. Synod of the Uniting Church) in a possible $160 million redevelopment of the property between Pitt and Castlereagh Streets. Plans include a new theatre, enlarged Wesley chapel, several floors of facilities and of administrative offices for the mission and the Synod, and a thirty-four storey tower of income-producing office space. No final decision has been made on this at the time of writing.

Yet, as the Wesley Central Mission begins its second century, the real interest does not lie in facilities, offices, and institutions, for such appurtenances could never be more than a means to an end. The real interest will lie where it always has: in the continuing struggle by the mission to remain true to its own nature and in its attempt to cast over Sydney the "mantle of Christ".

Appendix A:

Some Life Line Statistics

Table A.1. Life Line Calls: Yearly Statistics, 1963–68

Year	Initial	Telephone Calls Subsequent	Total	Total Contacts	Trouble Teams
1963 (Mar–Dec)	7,203	–	7,203	9,386	113
1964	7,549	685	8,234	10,433	135
1965	7,326	759	8,085	10,478	151
1966	8,504	436	8,940	11,584	166
1967	9,961	1,554	11,515	14,083	221
1968	9,252	2,968	12,220	17,726	142

Source: UCA, CMM, box 16, folder 1, Life Line Director's Report, January 1969.

Table A.2. Life Line Movement, December 1968

Members	305
Phone counsellors – active	130
Phone counsellors – on leave	37
Caring division members – active	109
Caring division members – on leave	17

Source: UCA, CMM, box 16, folder 1, Life Line Director's Report, January 1969.

Table A.3. Life Line Calls for a Typical Period of Four Weeks During 1970

Marriage guidance	218	Furniture	5
Domestic guidance	138	Child care	30
General guidance	269	Unmarried mothers	36
Youth guidance	64	Adoptions	3
Homicide	3	Gambling	30
Medical	29	Legal	46
Psychiatric	378	Financial	5
Pastoral	215	Miscellaneous	141
Alcohol	62	Attempted suicide	17
Drug addiction	35	Threatened suicide	31
Live-in positions	18	Potential suicide	79
Food	88	Accommodation	103
Clothing	39	Employment	32
Money	21		

Source: Impact, December 1970, p. 3.

Appendix B:

Superintendents of the CMM

Taylor, William George, 1884—87
Bowring, James A., 1887—89
Taylor, William George, 1889—93
Bavin, Rainsford, 1893—96
Rutledge, W. Woolls, 1896—98
Taylor, William George, 1898—1913
Stephen, Patrick J., 1913—15
Hoban, Samuel J., 1915—21
Foreman, H. J. Clifton, 1921—31
Williams, Rupert J., 1931—38
Rayward, Frank H., 1938—58
Walker, Alan E., 1958—78
Moyes, Gordon, 1978—

Notes to Chapters

1

1. Josiah Strong, *The Challenge of the City* (New York: Eaton and Mains, 1907), p. 49.
2. M. B. Simey, *Charitable Effort in Liverpool in the Nineteenth Century* (Liverpool: University Press, 1951), pp. 5-6. See also C.H. Hopkins, *The Rise of the Social Gospel in American Protestantism, 1865-1914* (New Haven: Yale, 1961), p. 79.
3. Samuel L. Loomis, *Modern Cities* (New York: The Baker and Taylor Co., 1887), pp. 62-63.
4. K. J. Heasman, *Evangelicals in Action* (London: Bles, 1962), pp. 2-3.
5. Andrew Mearns in *The Bitter Cry of Outcast London*, ed. A.S. Wohl (New York: Humanities Press, 1883, reprinted 1970).
6. Except where otherwise stated, this section draws heavily on the factual material in the Introduction to K.S. Inglis, *Churches and the Working Classes in Victorian England* (London: Routledge and Kegan Paul, 1963).
7. Asa Briggs, *Victorian Cities* (Harmondsworth: Pelican, 1968), p. 63.
8. George Jackson, *Collier of Manchester* (London: Hodder and Stoughton, 1963), p. 37.
9. Aaron I. Abell, *The Urban Impact on American Protestantism, 1865-1900* (Hamden: Archon, 1962), p. 64.
10. Loomis, *Modern Cities*, p. 99.
11. Abell, *The Urban Impact*, pp. vii, 10, 26; C. Stelzle, *Christianity's Storm Centre, A Study of the Modern City* (New York: F.H. Revell Co., 1907), p. 59.
12. Abell, *The Urban Impact*, pp. 4, 7-8; Strong, *Challenge of the City*, p. 189; Josiah Strong, *Religious Movements for Social Betterment*, Monographs on American Social Economics, no. 14 (n.p., 1900), pp. 6-7.
13. Full details of the work referred to in the preceding three paragraphs, and much more, may be found in Heasman, *Evangelicals in Action*, chaps. 2 and 3, and in I. Bradley, *The Call to Seriousness* (London: Jonathon Cape, 1976), chap. 3.
14. Ibid., pp. 120, 122.
15. Abell, *Urban Impact*, p. 30.
16. Richard Allen, *The Social Passion: Religion and Social Reform in Canada, 1914-1928* (Toronto: University of Toronto Press, 1971), pp. 1-7.
17. Hopkins, *Rise of the Social Gospel*, p. 79; Abell, *Urban Impact*, p. 117.
18. Hopkins, *Rise of the Social Gospel*, pp. 250-51; Allen, *The Social Passion*, pp. 27-29.

19. Hopkins, *Rise of the Social Gospel.* chap. 9.
20. Heasman, *Evangelicals in Action*, chap. 4; Mearns, *Bitter Cry*, Introduction.
21. See Roger Standing, "When the Windows of Heaven Opened: Liverpool Methodist Mission 1875-1905", typescript, Liverpool, 1981; Ian Sellers "Nonconformist Attitudes in Later Nineteenth Century Liverpool", *Historical Society of Lancs and Cheshire: Transactions* 114 (1962): 215-39; W. J. Townsend, H. B. Workman, and George Earys, eds. *A New History of Methodism*, 2 vols. (London: Hodder and Stoughton, 1909), vol. 1, bk. 2. chap. 2.
22. H. P. Hughes, *Social Christianity*, 4th ed. (London: Hodder and Stoughton, 1890), p. viii.
23. J. Scott Lidgett, *My Guided Life* (London: Methuen, 1936), p. 61.
24. Townsend et al., *A New History of Methodism*, vol. 1, pp. 457-58.
25. Strong, *Challenge of the City*, pp. 243-52.
26. M. Kelly, *Nineteenth Century Sydney* (Sydney University Press in association with the Sydney History Group, 1978), p. 68.
27. Shirley H. Fisher, "Life and Work in Sydney, 1870-1890: Aspects of Social Development in a Nineteenth Century City" (Ph.D. thesis, Macquarie University, 1976), p. 49. Brisbane ward was bounded by Margaret, George, and Bathurst Streets and by Darling Harbour.
28. Ibid., p. 48.
29. J. D. Bollen, *Protestantism and Social Reform in NSW 1890-1910* (Melbourne: Melbourne University Press, 1972), pp. 28-29, quoting Rev. E. S. Hughes.
30. Census of N.S.W., 1891, pp. 544-45 in ibid., pp. 233-34. See also p. 230.
31. *Sydney Morning Herald* (*SMH*), 13 August 1884, letter by W. G. Taylor; A. Roberts, "City Improvement in Sydney: Public Policy 1880-1900", (Ph.D. thesis, Sydney University, 1977), p. 63; Kelly, *Nineteenth Century Sydney*, pp. 76, 80; G. Davison, "Sydney and the Bush: an Urban Context for the Australian Legend", *Historical Studies* 18, no. 71 (October 1978): 193.
32. Fisher, "Life and Work", pp. 224-25, 235, 237.
33. Ibid., pt. 3, especially chap. 4; Bunyip, "The Sewing Girls of Sydney", *The Australian* 4 (1880): 615-21; Florence Gordon, "The Conditions of Female Labour and the Rates of Women's Wages in Sydney", *The Australian Economist* 4, no. 7 (23 August 1894): 423-29; M. Cannon, *Life in the Cities* (Melbourne: Nelson, 1978), pt. 6, chap. 17.
34. N. Pidgeon, *The Life, Experience and Journal of Nathaniel Pidgeon, City Missionary* (Sydney: Mason and O'Connor, 1864); *Australian Dictionary of Biography (ADB)*, vol. 2.
35. L. Hoare, *Ten Decades — the History of the Sydney City Mission*, n.p., n.d., especially pp. 10-12, 19.
36. N. Gash, "A History of the Benevolent Society of NSW", (M.A. thesis, Sydney University, 1967).
37. For material in this section see especially N. D. McLachlan, "Larrikinism: an Interpretation" (M.A. thesis, University of Melbourne, n.d.); P. N. Grabosky, *Sydney in Ferment* (Canberra: ANU, 1977); Ambrose Pratt, " 'Push' Larrikinism in Australia", *Blackwood's Magazine* 1029 (July 1901): 27-40; "Ajax", "Larrikinism", *Sydney Quarterly Magazine* 1, no. 2 (January 1884): 207-15.
38. McLachlan, "Larrikinism: an Interpretation", p. 130.
39. See F. R. Swynny, "Sydney Circuit Prior to the Founding of the CMM", *CMM Jubilee Report 1884-1934*; J. E. Carruthers, "Memories of Old York

Street", *Methodist,* 6 March 1920; J. E. Carruthers, "Old York Street, 1840–1887", *Methodist,* 24 September 1927; Joseph Oram, paper delivered at a social reunion in connection with the closing service for York Street church, *Wesleyan Advocate (WA),* 20 November 1886; A. McCallum, "A Hundred Years of Methodism in Australia", *Age,* 4 August 1915.

40. W. Phillips, *Defending "A Christian Country"* (St Lucia: University of Queensland Press, 1981), p. 9.

41. *Christian Advocate and Weekly Record (CA&WR),* 1 December 1871; W.G. Taylor, *The Life Story of an Australian Evangelist* (London: Epworth, 1920), pp. 127-28. Curiously, in a slightly earlier contribution to another work Taylor had appeared to accept the sociological explanation, see J. Colwell, *A Century in the Pacific* (Sydney: W. H. Beale, 1914), p. 693.

42. *CA&WR,* 1 September, 2 December 1873; 1 April, 5 November 1874; 17 October 1876.

43. Minutes of Quarterly Meeting (QMM), 15 January 1875, Sydney Central Circuit.

44. *WA,* 26 August (quoting the *Christian Advocate*), 23 December 1882.

45. *SMH,* 22 May 1877.

46. W. Phillips, "James Jefferis in Sydney: his Ministry at Pitt Street Congregational Church, 1877–1889", *Church Heritage* 2, no. 2 (September 1981): 119–43.

47. F. B. Boyce, *Fourscore Years and Seven* (Sydney: Angus and Robertson, 1934), chap. 8.

48. Phillips, *A Christian Country*, p. 64; *WA,* 19 April 1884.

49. Barbara Bolton, *Booth's Drum* (Sydney: Hodder and Stoughton, 1980), especially pp. 14-20, 41, 60, 161-62; *WA,* 22 July 1882.

50. Ibid., see various issues after 10 June 1882, but especially 10 June, 14 October, 2, 9, 16, and 23 December 1882; 24 February 1883.

51. Phillips, *A Christian Country*, pp. 87-90, 113-15, 160-67.

52. Fisher, "Life and Work", p. 107.

2

1. *CA&WR,* 1 August 1871; *WA,* 2 and 23 February, 5 October 1878; 15 November 1879; 31 January, 21 August 1880; 8 October 1881.

2. Ibid., 5 and 12 August, 9 and 16 September, 4 November 1882; 3 February 1883.

3. Taylor, *Life Story*, p. 130; Carruthers, "Memories of Old York Street", *Methodist,* 6 March 1920.

4. *WA,* 28 July 1883.

5. *SMH,* 24 January 1884; *WA,* 15 March 1884; *Evening News,* 8 April 1884.

6. The following account is based on Taylor, *Life Story*, chap. 11; Colwell, *Century in the Pacific*, pt. 5, chap. 4 (by Taylor); J. E. Carruthers, *Lights in the Southern Sky* (Sydney: Methodist Book Depot, 1924), chap. 13; Carruthers, "Memories of Old York Street", *Methodist,* 6 March 1920; Carruthers, "Old York Street, 1840–1887", ibid., 24 September 1927; J. Colwell, *The Illustrated History of Methodism – Australia: 1812-1855 New South Wales and Polynesia 1856 to 1902* (Sydney: William Brooks, 1904), chap. 20.

7. The following account is based on Taylor, *Life Story*, 3-10; Carruthers, *Lights*, chap. 9; J. E. Carruthers, *Memories of an Australian Ministry* (London: Epworth, 1922), chap. 21.
8. *WA*, 17 and 24 June 1882.
9. Taylor, *Life Story*, Appendix C, pp. 345-46.
10. *WA*, 26 April 1884.
11. Ibid., 10 March 1883.
12. Ibid., 19 and 26 April, 3 and 24 May, 7 and 21 June, 19 July, 2 August 1884; *SMH*, 2 August 1884; Taylor, "Diary", 28 April 1884; *DT*, 19 May 1884.
13. *WA*, 21 June 1884.
14. Ibid., 23 August, 6 September 1884; *SMH*, 26 August 1884.
15. *WA*, 21 February 1885; Taylor, *Life Story*, pp. 135-39.
16. Taylor, "Diary", pp. 94-115.
17. *WA*, 22 August, 12 and 19 September, 28 November 1885; 15 May, all July 1886.
18. Ibid., 2 and 16 May 1885.
19. *SMH*, 3 February 1885; *WA*, 4 July 1885; 20 November 1886; 19 March 1887.
20. Ibid., 5 February, 7 May, 10 September, 1 October, 26 November 1887; 2 June 1888; 26 January 1889.
21. Ibid., 30 October 1886; 22 January 1887; *Minutes of the 14th New South Wales Annual Conference of the Australian Wesleyan Methodist Church, January 1887 (Conference Minutes, 1887)* (Sydney: Wesleyan Book Depot, 1887), p. 83.
22. *WA*, 11 February 1888.
23. Ibid., 20 and 27 October, 3 November 1888.
24. Ibid., 2 and 9 February 1889; *Conference Minutes 1889*, pp. 104-5.
25. *WA*, 6 April 1889.
26. Standing, "When the Windows of Heaven Opened", pp. 7-9; Colwell, *Century in the Pacific*, p. 692; Taylor, *Life Story*, p. 53; *WA*, 26 April, 21 June 1884.

3

1. *WA*, 27 April 1889.
2. J.D. Bollen, *Religion in Australian Society: an Historian's View* (Sydney: Leigh College, 1973), pp. 27-28.
3. *WA*, 4, 11, and 18 May 1889.
4. *Report of the CMM Committee (CMM Report)* to December 31 1889.
5. *WA*, 16 November 1889; 12 April 1890.
6. Ibid., 17 May 1890.
7. Ibid., 20 and 27 September, 4 October 1890.
8. Report at second annual meeting, *WA*, 4 April 1891.
9. *Methodist*, 16 January 1892.
10. Ibid., 19 and 26 March 1892.
11. "Saturday Night at the Centenary Hall", *WA*, 14 September 1889; "An Hour

at the Centenary Hall", ibid., 13 December 1890; *Methodist*, 24 September 1892.

12. *WA*, 7 December 1889; 12 April 1890.
13. Ibid., 24 and 31 October 1891.
14. W. G. Taylor, *Pathfinders of the Great South Land* (London: Epworth, n.d.), chap. 8; Taylor, *Life Story*, chap. 12.
15. *WA*, 4 September 1886; 6 March 1889; 8 March 1890; Taylor, *Pathfinders*, p. 92.
16. G. Kitson Clark, *The Making of Victorian England* (London: Methuen, 1962), p. 181.
17. Colwell, *Illustrated History*, p. 539; *WA*, 10 August, 7 September 1889; 12 July 1890.
18. Taylor, *Life Story*, pp. 196-97; *WA*, 14 September 1889; 4 April 1891; *CMM Report* to 31 December 1889.
19. Ibid.; *WA*, 10 August 1889.
20. D. P. Hughes, *The Life of Hugh Price Hughes* (London: Hodder and Stoughton, 1904), p. 201.
21. *WA*, 14 and 28 June, 5 and 19 July, 2 and 9 August 1890; *Gazette*, 5 July 1890.
22. *WA*, 28 June 1890; *Evening News*, 5 and 6 August 1890.
23. *Maitland Mercury*, 28 August, 23 September 1890; Abell, *Urban Impact*, pp. 194–95.
24. *WA*, 13 September 1890; *Methodist*, 26 March 1892.
25. Taylor, *Life Story*, pp. 210-11.
26. *Gazette*, 26 April, 5 July 1890; *WA*, 7 June, 26 July 1890; 13 June 1891.
27. Ibid., 2 August 1890; *Gazette*, 5 July 1890.
28. *WA*, 13 December 1890; 4 April 1891; UCA, CMM, box 7, Apartment Register, 1890.
29. *SMH*, 8 February 1890; *Gazette*, 26 April 1890; *WA*, 7 June 1890; 4 April 1891; *DT*, 2 February, 20 June 1891; *Methodist*, 26 March 1892.
30. *CMM Report*, to 31 December 1889; *Gazette*, 5 July 1890.
31. *WA*, 15 June 1889.
32. Ibid., 20 July, 3, 10, and 17 August 1889; *SMH*, 13 August 1889; Taylor's own account is in *Life Story*, pp. 226–28.
33. *WA*, 14 and 21 December 1889.
34. Ibid., 21 June 1890; *Gazette*, 5 July 1890; *SMH*, 5 July 1890; *Evening News*, 5 August 1890.
35. *WA*, 4 April, 15, 22, and 29 August 1891; *Methodist*, 26 March 1892.
36. UCA, CMM, box 9, Admissions Book.
37. Carruthers, "Memories of Old York Street", *Methodist*, 6 March 1920; *CMM Report*, 1904/05.
38. Bollen, *Religion in Australian Society*, pp. 28, 58.
39. *WA*, 14 February, 4 April 1891; UCA, CMM, box 10, balance sheets for 1891, 1892; *Methodist*, 26 March, 17 December 1892.
40. *Conference Minutes*, 1893, pp. 53, 86.
41. *Methodist*, 29 January 1898.

4

1. *Methodist*, 22 April, 18 November 1893; 10 November 1894; 16 March 1895.
2. *Gazette*, 1 June 1893; *Conference Minutes*, 1894; *Methodist*, 5 March 1898.
3. For the following account see *Methodist*, 29 January, 5, 12, 19, and 26 February 1898.
4. See report of Conference debate in ibid., 5 March 1898.
5. References for what follows are scattered throughout the *Methodist* for the period, but see especially 23 September 1893; 24 March 1894; 30 May 1896; 19 June 1897; 5 March 1898; *Gazette*, 1 June 1893; *SMH*, 18 June 1894.
6. UCA, CMM, box 21, folder 2, petition no. 4903 of 1927 before the Equity Court of N.S.W.; *Methodist*, 16 and 23 September, 14, 21, and 28 October, 4 November 1893; 20 May 1922.
7. UCA, CMM, box 7, unlabelled blank exercise book: see re Miss Seymour's case; ibid., box 28, Children's Home *Report*, 1894/5, 1895/6; *Methodist*, 8 December 1894; 6 June 1896; Taylor, *Life Story*, chap. 20.
8. *Methodist*, 27 February, 24 April, 8 May 1897; 16 January 1904; *DT*, 15 December 1897.
9. Ibid., 16 December 1897; *Evening News*, 16 December 1897; *Methodist*, 8 January 1898; 17 June, 4 November 1899; UCA, CMM, box 7, Medical Institute cash receipts and admissions book.
10. UCA, CMM, box 7, Medical Institute cash receipts and admissions book; *Methodist*, 8 January, 13 August 1898; 22 November 1902; 16 January 1904; *DT*, 15 December 1897; 9 January 1904.
11. W. G. Taylor, *The Central Mission Medical Retreat of NSW*, 1902 (a sixteen-page pamphlet to attract patients and explain the work).
12. Taylor, *Life Story*, p. 257.
13. A. J. Derrick, *The Story of the Central Mission* (Melbourne: Spectator, 1918), pp. 66-69.
14. *Methodist*, 25 August, 8 and 29 September, 13 and 20 October, 17 November 1894; 2 and 23 March, 6 and 27 April, 22 June, 10 August 1895.
15. Ibid., 30 April 1898; balance sheet to 31 December 1898 in *Conference Minutes*, 1899, pp. 174-77.
16. *Methodist*, 19 November, 31 December 1898; 7 January, 18 March, 1 April 1899.
17. Ibid., 11 November 1899; UCA, CMM, box 10, minutes of staff meetings, 3 July—14 August 1900.
18. *Methodist*, 14 June 1902; 1 August 1903.
19. *SMH*, 29 May 1905; *Methodist*, 16 September 1905.
20. Ibid., 10 March, 21 April 1906; 25 May 1907; 11 April 1908; *CMM Report*, 1908.
21. *SMH*, 29 May 1909.
22. *Methodist*, 12 June 1909; *SMH & DT*, 29 April 1913.
23. Taylor, *Life Story*, pp. 264-69.
24. *Methodist*, 5, 12, and 26 August 1905.
25. "Theatres, Public Halls, and other places of Public Concourse: report of the committee appointed to consider what steps should be taken to minimize the risk of fire and the danger of panic", Legislative Council of N.S.W., 6 December 1905, p. (vi) and Appendix.
26. UCA, CMM, box 15, Connexional Premises Committee Minute Book (CPCMB), 1906-16, 1, 4, and 16 May, 8, 15, 22, and 29 June 1906; ibid.,

1906-07, Hon. E. Vickery to Rev. J.G.M. Taylor (president of Conference), 26 July 1906, with entry for 15 August 1906, which also contains extracts from letters by Vickery to his son, E. Vickery, 29 June, 6 July 1906.

27. Ibid., 1906-07, Deed of Settlement, 14 March 1906, with entry for 18 February 1907; *Methodist,* 17 November 1906.

28. UCA, CMM, box 15, CPCMB, 1906-07, 7, 11, and 17 September, 9, 23, and 27 November 1906; 8 and 21 January, 18 February 1907; ibid., box 13, Lyceum Trust Minute Book (LTMB), 1906-38, 23, and 31 August, 3 and 13 September, 2 November 1906; 18 and 28 January, 15 February 1907; ibid., box 15, Trustees of the Lyceum Lease Minute Book (TLLMB), 1907-16, 30 January 1907; *Methodist,* 9 February 1907.

29. Ibid., 2 March 1907.

30. *SMH,* 13 April 1908; *Methodist,* 21 December 1907; 18 April 1908.

31. *SMH,* 21 August 1899; *Methodist,* 30 December 1899; 2 January 1904; 10 August, 14 December 1907; *CMM Reports,* 1908, 1911, 1913, 1914.

32. Ibid., 1913, 1914; *Methodist,* 9 and 23 July 1904; 3 August 1912; *SMH,* 3 November 1904.

33. Don Wright, "Alfred Deakin and Immigration, 1901-10", *ANU Historical Journal,* no. 5 (November 1968), pp. 41-50.

34. *Methodist,* 1 May 1909; 24 February, 23 March, 3 and 10 August 1912; 2 May 1914; *CMM Reports,* 1908, 1911; *Conference Minutes,* 1911; *SMH,* 1 May 1908.

35. *Methodist,* 23 July 1898; 16 September 1899; 11 December 1909; 23 March 1912.

36. Grabosky, *Sydney in Ferment,* pp. 81, 91-92.

37. *Methodist,* 8 October, 24 and 31 December 1898; 11 and 18 February 1899.

38. Ibid., 6 December 1902; 5 March 1904; 26 May 1906; 25 May 1912; *DT,* 21 May 1904 (article by "Una"); *Our Weekly Greeting (Greeting),* 28 May 1904; 11 August 1906; *CMM Report,* 1904/05, 1908, 1913, 1914.

39. *Methodist,* 6 August 1898; 14 March, 19 December 1903; 19 March 1904; 31 October 1914; *Dalmar Report,* 1902/03.

40. *Methodist,* 4 and 25 June, 29 October, 10 December 1898; 19 August, 30 September 1899; 27 January 1900; 15 March 1902; 18 May 1907; *CMM Report,* 1911, 1913; UCA, CMM, box 10, red covered memo book, dated 9 November 1901, authorizing Sister Nellie to collect for the social and rescue work of the CMM.

41. Bollen, *Religion in Australian Society,* p. 28.

42. *Methodist,* 19 June, 3 and 10 July 1897; 9, 16, 23, and 30 July, 6 August 1898.

43. Ibid., 10 September, 3 and 31 December 1898; 21 January, 25 February, 18 March, 8 April, 15 July, 5 August 1899; 24 March 1900; 11 March 1911; *Conference Minutes,* 1900; *SMH,* 2 March 1911.

44. Derrick, *Story of the Central Mission,* pp. 12-13; W.J. Palamountain, *A. R. Edgar: a Methodist Greatheart* (Melbourne: Spectator, 1933), pp. 145-49; Sir C.I. Benson, *A Century of Victorian Methodism* (Melbourne: Spectator, 1935), pp. 282-83.

45. Bollen, *Protestantism and Social Reform,* passim, but especially pp. 7-8, 25, 93.

46. *SMH,* 25 November 1899; 18 June 1894; 20 August 1906; *Methodist,* 22 September 1894; 13 June 1903; 16 January 1904; *DT,* 9 January 1899.

47. *SMH,* 8, 12, and 19 February, 18 August 1890; *DT,* 18 August 1890; 2 February, 20 June 1891; Bollen, *Protestantism and Social Reform,* p. 59; G.P. Walsh, "Factories and Factory Workers in NSW, 1788-1900", *Labour History* 21 (1969): 13-14.

48. *SMH & DT*, 20 November 1893; Bollen, *Protestantism and Social Reform*, p. 57;   P. J. O'Farrell, "The History of the NSW Labour Movement 1880–1910, a Religious Interpretation", *Journal of Religious History* 2, no. 2 (December 1962): 142.

49. *SMH*, 28 February, 1, 12, and 15 March, 11 June 1894; *Methodist*, 16 June 1894.

50. *SMH & DT*, 23 August 1897; *Methodist*, 28 August, 11, 18, and 25 September 1897.

51. *Methodist*, 28 February 1903.

52. *DT*, 10 and 13 October 1898; *SMH*, 11 and 13 October 1898; 9 September 1901; *Methodist*, 15 October 1898.

53. *Australian Dictionary of Biography*, vol. 6, pp. 333-34; R. Broome, *Treasure in Earthen Vessels* (St Lucia: University of Queensland Press, 1980), pp. 58-59.

54. Ibid., p. 127; O'Farrell, "History of the NSW Labour Movement", p. 139.

55. W. G. Taylor, *Restore the Fellowship of the Church* (notes of a sermon preached before the N.S.W. Methodist Conference on the 100th anniversary of the first class meeting in the Southern World, March 6th, 1912) (Sydney: Epworth, 1912), p. 10; *Methodist*, 20 December 1902; *CMM Report*, 1910, pp. 21-25, 35 (article by Stephen); 1914, p. 9.

5

1. M. McKernan, *Australian Churches at War* (Sydney and Canberra: Catholic Theological Faculty and Australian War Memorial, 1980), p. 1.

2. A. D. Gilbert, "The Churches and the Conscription Referenda, 1916-19", (M.A. thesis, ANU, 1967), pp. 195-96.

3. R. Ward, *Australia: a Short History* (Sydney: Ure Smith, 1975), p. 151.

4. *SMH*, 1 January 1923.

5. Donald E. Hansen, "The Churches and Society in NSW, 1919-1939: a Study of Church Activities, Socio-religious Issues, Community-Church and Inter-Church Relations" (Ph.D. thesis, Macquarie University, 1979), pp. 21-31.

6. Ibid., p. 45; Bollen, *Religion in Australian Society*.

7. Hansen, "Churches and Society in NSW", pp. 56-60, 88-90, 134-40.

8. F. T. Walker, *Towards Industrial Peace* (Sydney: Epworth, 1926).

9. F. Alexander, *Australia Since Federation* (Melbourne: Nelson, 1976), p. 113.

10. Phyllis Peter, "Social Aspects of the Depression in NSW, 1930-34" (Ph.D. thesis, ANU, 1964), chap. 4.

11. Hansen, "Churches and Society in NSW", pp. 203-205; see also R. Mendelsohn, *The Condition of the People* (Sydney: Allen and Unwin, 1975), p. 100.

12. *Methodist*, 11 October 1913.

13. *Greeting*, 4 and 18 September 1915; 1 and 15 January 1916; 19 September 1931; *Methodist*, 12 August 1916; 18 May 1918; *CMM Report*, 1934.

14. *SMH*, 5 August 1929; 24 May 1937.

15. *CMM Report*, 1922-27 inclusive; *Methodist*, 23 June 1923; 25 June, 9 July 1927; *SMH & DT*, 4 July 1927.

16. *Methodist*, 28 January, 8 December 1928; 16 August 1930; 29 June 1935; *CMM Report*, 1929ff; *Greeting*, 4 June 1932; *SMH*, 14 May 1935.

17. See *Greeting* accounts of Foreman's sermons 1927-30; see also *SMH*, 24 February, 7 and 14 April 1930.
18. Ibid., 16 November, 14 December 1931; 25 June, 23 July 1934; 25 February, 23 September, 1935; 9 August 1937.
19. Charlie Woodward, *The Story of My Conversion* (Sydney: Central Press, n.d.) (ca. 1918 from internal evidence, despite Mitchell Library dating of 1921).
20. *Methodist*, 11 July 1925; 6 March 1937; *CMM Report*, 1918-20, 1926-27, 1929; C. Woodward, *Out of the Depths* (Sydney: J.A. Packer, n.d.) (ca. 1922); C. Woodward, *The Burglar Captured* (Sydney: Newmarket Press, 1922); *Greeting*, 8 August, 5 September 1931; C. Woodward, *Peeps into Gaols, Police Courts, Opium Dens* (Sydney: J.A. Packer, n.d.) (ca. 1933).
21. *Methodist*, 12 May 1927; 4 February 1933; 3 November 1934.
22. Figures for the various years may be found in *Conference Minutes*. Comments on the nature of the congregation are in *Methodist*, 13 July 1929; 4 July 1936; *Greeting*, 7 October 1933; *CMM Report*, 1916, 1919, 1924, 1926.
23. UCA, CMM, box 21, folder 1, quarterly syllabus for Tuesday evening class meeting June-August 1916; *Methodist*, 18 November 1916; 28 June 1919; *Greeting*, 7 November 1931; *CMM Report*, 1920-21.
24. *Greeting*, 30 May 1931; *Methodist*, 23 May 1936.
25. Rev. F.H. Raward was colleague to H.C. Foreman in the 1920s and superintendent 1938-58. In the intervening years, he changed his name by deed poll to Rayward to overcome pronunciation difficulties. The latter spelling is used throughout.
26. Ibid., 25 April 1908.
27. For material on PSA, in addition to references given in text, see *Methodist*, 31 October 1908 and *CMM Report* for 1908 and 1911. Titles of addresses are scattered through thirty years of the *Methodist* and the *Greeting*.
28. For Green's address see *SMH*, 4 February 1929.
29. The most valuable material is to be found in UCA, CMM, box 28 and includes *Dalmar Reports* for the period and Dalmar Children's Home Trust Minutes, 6 March 1911 to 18 September 1934 (DCHTM, 1911-34); see also *Methodist*, 17 November 1917; 6 August 1921; 20 May 1922; 31 March 1923.
30. Ibid., 29 January 1927; 9 May 1936; UCA, CMM, box 28, DCHTM, 1911-34, 8 February, 24 June 1926; 7 May 1931; *CMM Report*, 1926-27; *SMH*, 27 April 1931.
31. Interview with Dr F.H. Rayward, 12 February 1981; *CMM Report*, 1916-23 inclusive; *Methodist*, 12 August 1916. On the general question of attitudes to women see A. Summers, *Damned Whores and God's Police* (Harmondsworth: Penguin, 1975), chap. 12.
32. *CMM Report*, 1917-21 inclusive, 1924.
33. Ibid., 1929.
34. *SMH*, 24 April 1929; *Methodist*, 30 November 1929; 16 November 1935.
35. UCA, CMM, box 13, LTMB, 1906-38, 17 and 21 December 1906; 3 April 1908 and newspaper clippings on p.16; ibid., box 15, TLLMB, 1907-16, 21 February 1907; 27 January 1909; 16 May, 22 June 1910, E. Frank Vickery to T.H. England, 19 May 1911; *Conference Minutes*, 1910, p.143; *Methodist*, 2 April 1910.
36. UCA, CMM, box 13, Minute Book of the Executive of the Lyceum Trustees (MBELT), 30 August 1916; ibid., box 22, folder of miscellaneous documents, Greater Union Theatres to Lyceum Trustees, 10 August 1917; *Con-*

ference Minutes, 1917, p.175 (cf. 1918, p.187 and 1919, p.193); *Methodist*, 27 July 1918.

37. Ibid., 24 March, 5 and 12 May 1923; 22 and 29 March 1924; 7 April 1934; UCA, CMM, box 13, MBELT, 21 June 1931: see also loose sheets inside back cover of same and signed P.N. Slade, 23 July 1923.
38. *Methodist*, 6, 20, and 27 November 1915.
39. Ibid., 6 August 1921; 16 February 1924; 21 March 1925; 10 September 1927; 23 April 1932; 3 February 1934; UCA, CMM, box 13, MBELT, 2 August, 26 September, 19 October 1928.
40. *SMH*, 8 March 1935; *Methodist*, 20 April 1935; UCA, CMM, box 13, LTMB, 1906-38, 10 June 1936 with attached letters, Geo. B. Vickery to secretary, Lyceum Trust, 10 June 1936 and E.F. Vickery to secretary, Lyceum Trust, 3 February 1938, unsigned letter (probably E.F. Vickery) to H.C. Foreman, 4 March 1938; ibid., box 15, City Church Committee Minute Book (CCCMB) including letter, P.N. Slade, to E.W. Hyde, 18 February 1938.
41. Gilbert C. Bradley to Editor, *Methodist*, 3 February 1934.
42. Material on Hoban's departure may be found in *Methodist*, 13 December 1919; 10 April, 12 June, 7 August, 18 September 1920; 19 February, 12 and 26 March, 2 April 1921; 1 October 1927; *SMH*, 4 May 1922.
43. Interview, 12 February 1981.
44. *SMH*, 4 November 1929; *Methodist*, 1 March, 19 July, 6 September 1930; UCA, CMM, box 21, folder 1, cutting from *Daily Guardian*, 9 February 1931; ibid., H.C. Foreman to president of N.S.W. Conference, 6 August 1930.
45. CMM Committee of Management (Executive Committee) Minutes 1936-59, 30 July 1937 to 21 February 1938, inclusive; interview with F.H. Rayward, 12 February 1981; *Methodist*, 12 March 1938.
46. Figures were obtained from *CMM Report*, 1916-38 inclusive and from UCA, CMM, box 14, cash statements, 1933-50.

6

1. Interview, 12 February 1981.
2. Ibid.; *Methodist*, 19 November, 13 December 1938; *CMM Report*, 1950.
3. *Methodist*, 14 and 28 May 1938; 29 June 1940; 19 July 1941.
4. Ibid., 11 March 1939; 31 August 1940; 18 January, 1 February 1947; 2 October 1954.
5. Ibid., 18 June 1938; 18 and 25 February 1939.
6. Ibid., 8 October 1938; 14 July 1945; 7 May 1949; interview 12 February 1981.
7. *Methodist*, 18 March 1939; 17 August 1940; 20 June 1942.
8. Ibid., 4 April 1942; membership statistics taken from *Conference Minutes*, 1938-57.
9. Executive Committee, 1936-59, 3 August 1949; *CMM Report*, 1924, 1934, 1949, 1950; *Methodist*, 16 January 1926; 16 October 1948; 8 October 1949; 18 November 1950; *Greeting*, 3 March 1934.
10. *Methodist*, 9 June 1951; 27 March, 23 October, 13 November 1954; 6 August 1955; 24 March, 7 July 1956; 16 February, 20 July, 5 October 1957; *CMM Report*, 1956-57.

11. *Methodist*, 30 July 1938; 24 October 1942; 4 December 1943; *CMM Report*, 1950.
12. Calculations are based on figures in 59th *Dalmar Report*, 1951/52 in UCA, CMM, box 28.
13. Executive Committee, 1936-59, 5 November 1947; 21 January, 30 June, 20 October, 2 December 1948; *Methodist*, 22 January 1949. The interviewee referred to must remain anonymous.
14. *Methodist*, 2 December 1950; 7 June 1952; 9 May 1953; 55th *Dalmar Report* in UCA, CMM, box 28; Rayward interview, 12 February 1981.
15. *Methodist*, 5 and 26 August 1939; 6 April 1957; 15 March 1958; UCA, CMM, box 15, QMM, 1945-61, 25 January, 18 April 1956.
16. *SMH*, 11 September 1944; *Methodist*, 28 August 1948; 6 May 1950; 12 November 1955.
17. *SMH*, 9 May 1944; Executive Committee, 1936-59, see minutes of various meetings from 28 June 1944 to 16 April 1947; 23 November 1955; 8 October 1958; UCA, CMM, box 15, QMM, 4 December 1945; *Methodist*, 31 January 1948; 11 October 1958.
18. Ibid., 16 March 1957; 11 and 18 October 1958; Memo, E. Frank Vickery to CMM Executive, 7 May 1958 and ibid., to H. S. McClelland, 11 June 1958 (documents in possession of Lottie Stewart Hospital).
19. See following documents in possession of Lottie Stewart Hospital: Stewart to minister for army, 24 April 1957; reply, 5 June 1957; Stewart to superintendent CMM, 14 June 1957; H. S. McClelland to Stewart, 11 September 1957; Stewart to McClelland, 23 September 1957; McClelland to Stewart, 3 October 1957, enclosing secretary of Hospitals' Commission to secretary Lottie Stewart Hospital, 23 August 1957; Stewart to McClelland, 7 October 1957.
20. Executive Committee, 1936-59, H. W. Waddell to H.S. McClelland, 29 May 1946; minutes meetings 4 May, 23 November 1955, and letter, F.H. Osborne MHR, to R.C. Coleman, 19 September 1955; *Methodist*, 3 July 1954; 6 July 1957.
21. Ibid., 22 June 1940; 22 February, 16 August 1941; 28 February, 31 October 1942; 7 and 11 August 1943; 17 and 24 March, 7 April, 26 May, 25 August 1945.
22. Ibid., 29 June 1940; 30 September 1950; 21 June 1952; *CMM Report*, 1940; *SMH*, 7 December 1951.
23. *Methodist*, 31 January 1942; 17 July 1943; 23 June, 28 July 1945; 23 January, 8 May 1954; *SMH*, 5 January 1942; 28 February 1949; 11 January 1954.
24. Ibid., 26 October 1946.
25. *Tribune*, 24 and 31 March, 3, 7, and 10 April, 15 and 26 May, 2 June 1948; *Methodist*, 10 April, 1, 22, and 29 May, 5 and 12 June 1948.
26. UCA, CMM, box 14, cash statements 1933-50; ibid., brown rhino binder, financial statements 1951-57; Rayward interview, 12 February 1981.
27. *Methodist* 11 June 1949; 13 January 1951; 12 and 30 April, 3 May 1958; Rayward interview, 12 January 1981; *SMH & DT*, 31 March 1958.
28. Executive Committee, 1936-59, 25 October, 8 November 1957; *SMH*, 25 February 1958.

7

1. See, for example, C. McGregor, *Profile of Australia* (London: Hodder and Stoughton, 1966), chap. 13.
2. C. McGregor, *People, Politics and Pop* (Sydney: Ure Smith, 1968), pp. 172–73; see also R.W. Connell and T.W. Irving, *Class Structure in Australian History* (Melbourne: Longman-Cheshire, 1980), p. 294; J. King, *Waltzing Materialism* (Sydney: Harper and Row, 1978), p. 129.
3. R. Ward, *Australia: a Short History*, rev. ed. (Sydney: Ure Smith, 1975), pp. 179–80.
4. D. Horne, *The Lucky Country* (Harmondsworth: Penguin, 1964) pp. 42, 67; McGregor, *Profile of Australia*, pp. 132–34.
5. McGregor, *People, Politics and Pop*, chap. 3.
6. P. Spearitt, *Sydney Since the Twenties* (Sydney: Hale and Iremonger, 1978), pp. 108–109; see also R. White, *Inventing Australia* (Sydney: Allen and Unwin, 1980), p. 167.
7. Wirth, "Urbanism as a Way of Life", pp. 12–13.
8. McGregor, *Profile of Australia*, pp. 344–45; Horne, *Lucky Country*, chap. 3; King, *Waltzing Materialism*, p. 131; C.M. Clark, *A Short History of Australia*, rev. ed. (New York: Mentor, 1969), p. 266.
9. H. Mol, *Religion in Australia* (Melbourne: Nelson, 1971), see generally, but especially pp. 13, 18, 22, 42, 54, 67–71, 89, 94.
10. Ivan Southall, ed. *The Challenge* (Melbourne: Lansdowne, 1966), especially chaps. 6, 8, 11, 12, 20, 24.
11. A. Walker, *The Whole Gospel for the Whole World* (London: Marshall, Morgan and Scott, 1958).
12. R. Niebuhr, *The Nature and Destiny of Man*, 2 vols. (London: Nisbet, 1941–43); H.E. Brunner, *Justice and the Social Order* (New York: Harper and Bros, 1945); W. Temple, *Christianity and the Social Order* (London: SCM, 1942); A. Huxley, *Ends and Means* (London: Chatto and Windus, 1957) (original edition 1937).
13. *DT & SMH*, 21 and 23 April 1958; *Methodist*, 19 and 26 April, 3 May 1958.
14. *SMH*, 6 April 1960; *Impact*, April 1960, p. 5.
15. *Methodist*, 19 March, 9 and 30 April 1960.
16. Ibid., 25 March, 22 April 1961; *SMH*, 3 April 1961; Sir Alan Walker, press cuttings (hereafter, WPC), vol. 1.
17. *Methodist*, 4 and 11 April 1964; 1 May 1965; 19 March 1966; 1 April 1967.
18. Ibid., 4 October 1958; 13 June 1959; 26 May 1962; *Sunday Mirror*, about May 1963 (from WPC, vol. 1); QMM, 1973–June 1977, 23 August 1973; UCA, CMM, box 21, folder 1, memo, Henderson to Walker et al., 28 February 1975, A. Walker, *Love in Action* (Glasgow: Collins, 1977), chap. 12. 1977), chap. 12.
19. Executive Committee, 1960-68, 9 May 1962; 18 April 1963; *SMH & DT*, 11 August 1962.
20. *Methodist*, 8 August 1959; 8 April, 25 June, 23 July, 13 August 1960; WPC, vol. 1; *Impact*, September 1960; UCA, CMM, box 17, folder 3, sermons and releases by Alan Walker.
21. *Methodist*, 25 March 1967; 10 April 1971; 11 March 1972; QMM, 1961-73, 8 August, 27 November 1968; Executive Committee, 1969-72, 12 March 1969; 11 March, 15 April 1970; WPC, vol. 3, "How the Methodists beat the Skinheads" by Adrian McGregor (ca. July 1970).
22. *Methodist*, 12 August 1961; WPC, vol. 1 (ca. February 1963), vol. 2 (ca. June/July 1965); *Sunday Telegraph*, 21 February 1965; interview with

Noreen Towers, 19 January 1982; A. Walker, *Now for Newness* (Melbourne: Methodist Publishing House, 1970), chap. 7.

23. *Impact*, April 1960, p. 9; August 1960, p. 3; April 1962, p. 5; *Honi Soit*, 17 April 1962, article by Kevin Price.

24. *Methodist*, 9 November 1968; 17 May 1969; *Impact*, June 1969, p. 2; *SMH*, 12 May 1969; UCA, CMM, box 17, folder 1, press releases by Alan Walker, "Call to Youth".

25. QMM, 1969-73, 17 December 1970; 27 May, 12 August 1971; *Impact*, August 1973, p. 7; *Methodist*, 6 and 13 February 1971.

26. John Edwards, "What's Wrong with our Youth Work?", *Methodist*, 17 April, 1 May, 5 June 1971; interview with Rev. A. Jackson, 10 December 1981.

27. UCA, CMM, box 15, Leaders' Meeting Minutes, 1958-64, 3 February 1959; *Methodist*, 4 August 1973; Walker, *Love in Action*, chap. 6; QMM, 1973—June 1977, 10 March 1977.

28. *Methodist*, 16 January 1960; 11 January 1969; 5 December 1970; 4 December 1971; *Impact*, March 1972, p. 2; UCA, CMM, box 16, folder 2, "The Jesus Commune Completes First Year" by Fred Nile; ibid., Christian Training College brochure for 1976; Executive Committee, 1973-75, 9 July 1975; Walker, *Love in Action*, chap. 10; Community Service Division, Position Paper, November 1978.

29. Interview, 10 December 1981.

30. Executive Committee, 1936-59, 17 June 1959; *Methodist*, 29 August 1959; 18 December 1965; UCA, CMM, box 21, folder 1, *Dalmar Report*, 1962; *Impact*, January 1966, p. 4, January 1973, p. 6.

31. *Methodist*, 15 December 1962; 24 July 1971; *Impact*, February 1969, p. 7; April 1972, pp. 2-3; August 1972, pp. 6, 10; QMM, 1961-73, 28 March 1963; UCA, CMM, box 1, "Methodist Church City Missions 1971-75", folder: Reports to Conference, *CMM Report*, 1973.

32. CMM Homes Committee Minutes, November 1958—June 1963, 7 October 1959; *Impact*, October 1972, p. 2; Executive Committee, 1945-61, 12 July 1961; WPC, vol. 1.

33. QMM, 1961-73, 8 May 1969; 18 October 1972; 28 June 1973; Executive Committee, 1973-75, 13 June 1975.

34. Ibid., 12 March 1975; *Conference Minutes*, 1975, pp. 96-97; *Impact*, November 1974, p. 6; April 1975, p. 1; July 1975; interview with R. Rae, chief executive officer, 21 January 1982.

35. Executive Committee, February 1976—June 1977, 9 February, 9 March, 11 May, 8 June, 13 July, 10 August, 9 November 1977; CMM Homes Committee Minutes, July 1963—November 1968, 16 August 1967; QMM, 1973—June 1977, 11 September 1975; interview with A. Walker, 10 June 1983.

36. Interview with Noreen Towers, 19 January 1982; *Methodist*, 15 April 1967; 19 June 1971; QMM, 1961-73, 21 May 1970; Executive Committee, 1969-72, 16 December 1970.

37. Ibid., 8 March, 12 April 1972; ibid., 1973-75, 10 July 1974; 14 May 1975; *Impact*, April 1972, p. 5; March 1975, p. 2; Finance and Administrative Committee Minutes, January 1975—December 1976, 30 July 1975; *Methodist and Congregationalist*, 14 August 1976.

38. Interview with Noreen Towers, 19 January 1982.

39. Executive Committee, 1969-72, 7 May 1969; 11 February, 11 March 1970; ibid., 1973-75, 12 December 1973; QMM, 1973—June 1977, 23 August 1973; 6 June 1974; 17 April 1975; 10 March 1977; Treasurers' Minutes, 1 December 1976; 26 October 1977; *DT*, 16 May 1972.

40. Finance and Administrative Committee minutes, January 1975—December 1976, 19 March, 30 July, September (n.d.) 1975.

8

1. Alan Walker, "To Serve the Present Age", *Methodist*, 29 October 1960; UCA, CMM, box 17, sermons and press releases by Alan Walker, address at the first "Newness NSW" Mission at Parramatta, 1 November 1970.

2. Homes Committee minutes, November 1958—June 1963, 10 and 18 December 1958; 21 January, 4 March 1959; Executive Committee, 1960-68, 27 April 1960; 28 February 1961; *Impact*, May 1960, p. 9.

3. *Methodist*, 21 June 1958; *Impact*, February 1960, p. 11; September 1961, p. 10; February 1975, p. 2; QMM, 1961-73, 26 October 1967; 30 September 1976; interview with A. Jackson, 10 December 1981.

4. UCA, CMM, box 15, Sydney Christian Community Centre, August 1966—September 1970, undated meeting June/July 1968; QMM, 1961-73, 23 February 1972; Executive Committee, February 1976—June 1977, 9 November 1977; *SMH*, 16 and 17 May 1977.

5. Interview with A. Walker, 10 December 1981.

6. *DT*, 10 and 25 September 1958; *Methodist*, 19 July, 6 and 20 September 1958; 25 July 1959; *Impact*, February 1959, p. 7; *Daily Mirror*, 17 July 1959; WPC, vol. 1 (clippings from several papers, including *SMH*); *Australian Women's Weekly*, 19 April 1961.

7. *Impact*, March 1962, p. 8; March 1965, p. 4; QMM, 1961-73, 5 March 1964.

8. WPC, vol. 2, contains clippings re fire from *SMH, DT, Sun, Mirror*, and other papers; UCA, CMM, box 13, "Daily Record of the Lyceum Fire" (author unknown); ibid., *LTEMB*, 1940-65, 26 February, 3 and 18 March 1964; interview with Rayward, 12 February 1981.

9. *Methodist*, 16 May 1964; interview with A. Walker, 10 December 1981.

10. *DT*, 6 June 1966 (see also *SMH*); *Methodist*, 18 June 1966.

11. UCA, CMM, box 15, Sydney Christian Community Centre, August 1966—September 1970, Draft Constitution; also meetings 2 February, 7 December 1967; 19 March, 2 May 1968; Executive Committee, 1969-72, 11 July 1973; WCM Executive Committee, 19 July 1977—December 1978; QMM, 1961-73, 8 November 1978.

12. *Methodist*, 22 February 1969; *Impact*, November 1969, p. 2; December 1971, p. 6; WPC, vol. 3; Aged Care Division Report, November 1978; Walker, *Love in Action*, pp. 28-29.

13. Interview with A. Jackson, 10 December 1981; *Impact*, April 1974, p. 7; WPC, vols. 3 and 5.

14. UCA, CMM, box 21, folder 2, "Life Line and the Central Methodist Mission", by H. R. Henderson; *Methodist*, 18 March 1961; *Impact*, November 1965, p. 4; QMM, 1961-73, 7 June 1962.

15. UCA, CMM, box 21, Henderson, "Life Line"; ibid., "A Factual Summary of the Nature and Purpose of Life Line"; *Impact*, June/July 1965, p. 5.

16. *Methodist*, 7 December 1963; 28 March 1964; 22 January 1966; *Impact*, September 1966, p. 1; WPC, includes clippings from all Sydney dailies, *Australian Women's Weekly, Hamilton Spectator*; Walker, *Love in Action*, pp. 65-66.

17. *Methodist*, 19 August, 16 September 1967; 16 March 1968; 24 March 1973; *Impact*, September 1967, p. 1; Executive Committee, 1969-72, 11 February 1970; 8 November 1972; 7 January 1973; interviews with A. Walker, 10 December 1981 and 10 June 1983.

18. QMM, 1961-73, 20 February 1969; *Methodist*, 6 May 1972; *Sun*, 28 April 1971; Executive Committee, 1973-75, 12 September 1973; WPC, vol. 3

contains clippings from early May 1970; April 1972, 2, 3, and 4 June 1972, August 1972, from a variety of papers.

19. A. Walker, *The Promise and the Power* (Nashville: Discipleship Resources, 1980); Niebuhr, *Nature and Destiny of Man*.

20. See for example, *Methodist*, 11 October, 29 November 1959; 26 August 1961.

21. *SMH*, 13 and 15 November 1967; *Anglican*, 16 November 1967; see other clippings in WPC, vol. 3. On Vietnam generally see *Methodist*, 10 July 1965; 13 May 1967.

22. *DT*, 11 September 1961; 21 October 1964; *Methodist*, 30 September 1961; 11 August 1962; 27 June 1964; 28 September 1974; *Impact*, August 1962, p. 2; WPC, vols. 1 and 2; UCA, CMM, box 17, folder 3, undated release on "The Church, the State and the Schools".

23. *SMH*, 28 June 1976; *DT*, 6 July 1976; meetings of superintendent and treasurers, 1975—May 1977, 30 June 1976; interview with A. Walker, 10 June 1983.

24. *Methodist*, 29 April 1967.

25. *Impact*, March 1965, p. 6; Executive Committee 1969-72, 8 July 1970; 14 July 1971; ibid., 1973-75, 11 June 1975, Summary of Financial Results for 12 months to 31 December 1974; ibid., February 1976—June 1977, 8 December 1976; UCA, CMM, box 21, folder 1, Financial Review by Alan Walker; Homes Committee Minute Book, July 1963—November 1968, 23 May 1967; UCA, CMM, box 14, Collection Journal, 26 April, 1962—9 May 1971; WCM Finance and Administrative Committee minutes, February 1977—December 1978, 2 March 1977; 5 April 1978.

26. UCA, CMM, box 17, folder 3, "Three Lives of a Church" by A. Walker (1969).

Bibliography

Archival

Held at the Uniting Church Archives

(Material relating to the York Street Circuit and the CMM is grouped under the heading "Sydney CMM")
Apartment register
Appeal letters 1967 (Life Line appeal)
Balance sheets (various years)
Circuit Schedule Book, Sydney Circuit, 1851-62, 1862-71
City Church Committee Minute Book
Collection journals, 1870-95
Committee of Management minutes, 1945-61
Connexional Premises Committee Minute Book, 1906–16
Daily record of the Lyceum Fire
Evangelists' Minute Book
Evangelists' Training Scholarship Fund
Executive of the Lyceum Trustees Minute Book
Financial statements, 1951-57
Glebe Christian Community Centre, letters, minutes, and notes
Leaders Meeting Minute Book, 1958-64
Life Line reports, 1966-70
Lyceum Trust Executive Minute Book, 1940-65
Lyceum Trustees Letter Book
Lyceum Trust Minute Book, 1906-38
Membership list, January 1970
Press releases and sermons (Rev. Alan Walker)
Quarterly Meeting Minute Book, 1945-54
Staff Meeting Record, 1972 (H. R. Henderson)
Sydney Christian Community Centre Board Minutes, 1966-70
Trustees of the Lyceum Lease, Cash Book
Trustees of the Lyceum Lease, Minute Book, 1907-16
York Street Circuit members' roll book
Young People's Society of Christian Endeavour Minute Book

Held at the Wesley Central Mission

Committee of Management Minutes (Executive Committee), April 1936—December 1978

Finance and Administration Committee Minutes, March 1973—December 1978

Homes Committee Minutes, June 1967—December 1972

Homes and Finance Committee Minutes, August 1967—June 1971

Meetings of the Officers of the Wesley Central Mission, June 1977—December 1978

Meetings of the Superintendent and Treasurers, January 1975—May 1977

Lyceum Property Trust Committee Minutes, June 1972—April 1980

Property Committee Minutes, June 1971—December 1978

Quarterly Meeting Minutes, May 1961—June 1977

Various unnamed parcels and folders of documents containing a variety of unorganized records.

Reports

Central Methodist Mission, Annual Reports (incomplete)

Dalmar Children's Home, Annual Reports (incomplete)

Legislative Assembly of N.S.W., *Votes and Proceedings*, 1875-76. vol. 6, pp. 845-61

Report of the Select Committee on Common Lodging Houses

Legislative Council of N.S.W., *Theatres, Public Halls, and other Places of Public Concourse*, 6 December 1905

Methodist Conference of N.S.W. (including the Wesleyan Methodist Conference of N.S.W.), Minutes, 1880-1976

Proceedings of the Second Oecumenical Methodist Conference, London: Kelly, 1892.

Newspapers and Journals

Australian Christian Commonwealth, The (odd issues)

Central Mission Gazette, The (only a few issues remain)

Christian Advocate and Wesleyan Record, June 1858—March 1877

Christian Weekly and Methodist Journal, The (Adelaide), 18 June 1897; 8 September 1899

Co-operator, The (1916-19) (Also known as *Men's Own*)

Daily Telegraph

Evening News

Forward
Impact
Methodist, The
Methodist and Congregationalist
Newspaper cuttings, vol. 25 (Mitchell Library)
Newspaper cuttings of Sir Alan Walker
Newspaper cuttings on Methodism in Australia
    (assembled by G. Nicholson)
Old NSW: Newspaper cuttings, vol. 1, 1898–1903,
    (compiled by C.J.)
Our Weekly Greeting (only a few issues remain)
Sydney Morning Herald
Tribune (Sydney)
Weekly Advocate, The

Monographs

Abell, Aaron I. *The Urban Impact on American Protestantism 1865–1900*. Hamden, Connecticut: Archon, 1943/1962.

Alexander, Fred. *Australia Since Federation*. Melbourne: Nelson, 1976 (new enlarged edition).

Allen, Richard. *The Social Passion: Religion and Social Reform in Canada, 1914-28*. Toronto: University of Toronto Press, 1971.

Benson, C. Irving. *A Century of Victorian Methodism*. Melbourne: Spectator, 1935.

Birch, A., and Macmillan, D.S., eds. *The Sydney Scene 1788-1960*. Melbourne: Melbourne University Press, 1962.

Bollen, J.D. *Protestantism and Social Reform in New South Wales 1890-1910*. Melbourne: Melbourne University Press, 1972.

———.*Religion in Australian Society: an Historian's View*. Sydney: Leigh College, 1973.

Bolton, Barbara. *Booth's Drum*. Sydney: Hodder and Stoughton, 1980.

Booth, Charles. *Life and Labour of the People in London*. Vol. 7. New York: A.M.S., 1970 (reprint of 1902-04 edition).

Boyce, Francis B. *Fourscore Years and Seven: the Memoirs of Archdeacon Boyce*. Sydney: Angus and Robertson, 1934.

Bradley, Ian. *The Call to Seriousness*. London: Jonathon Cape, 1976.

Briggs, Asa. *Victorian Cities*. Harmondsworth: Pelican, 1968.

Broome, Richard. *Treasure in Earthen Vessels: Protestant Christianity in New South Wales Society 1900-1914*. St Lucia: University of Queensland Press, 1980.

Brunner, H. Emil. *Justice and the Social Order*. New York: Harper and Row, 1945.

Caiger, George. *The Australian Way of Life.* Melbourne: Heineman, 1953.

Cannon, Michael. *Life in the Cities.* Vol. 3. Melbourne: Nelson, 1978.

Carruthers, J. E. *Lights in the Southern Sky.* Sydney: Methodist Book Depot, 1924.

————.*Memories of an Australian Ministry.* London: Epworth, 1922.

Central Methodist Mission. *The Central Mission Medical Retreat of NSW.* Sydney, 1902.

Clark, G. Kitson. *The Making of Victorian England.* London: Methuen, 1962.

Clark, C. M. *A Short History of Australia.* Rev. ed. New York: Mentor, 1969.

Coghlan, T. A. *Labour and Industry in Australia.* 4 vols. Melbourne: Macmillan, 1969.

Colwell, James. *A Century in the Pacific.* Sydney: W.H. Beale, 1914.

————.*The Illustrated History of Methodism, Australia: 1812 to 1855, New South Wales and Polynesia: 1856 to 1902.* Sydney: William Brooks and Co., 1904.

Colwell, John. *Progress and Promise.* London: T. Woolmer, 1887.

Connell, R. W. and Irving, T. H. *Class Structure in Australian History.* Melbourne: Longman-Cheshire, 1980.

Crowley, Frank, ed. *A New History of Australia.* Melbourne: Heineman, 1974.

Derrick, Albert J. *The Story of the Central Mission.* Melbourne: Spectator, 1918.

Edwards, Maldwyn. *Methodism and England: a Study of Methodism in its Social and Political Aspects During the Period 1850–1932.* London: Epworth, 1944.

Ellul, Jacques. *The Meaning of the City.* Grand Rapids, Michigan: William B. Eerdmans, 1970.

Gane, Douglas M. *New South Wales and Victoria in 1885.* London: Sampson, Low, Searle and Rivington, 1886.

Glynn, Sean. *Urbanisation in Australian History, 1788–1900.* Melbourne: Nelson, 1970.

Gould, Nat. *Town and Bush.* London: Routledge, 1896.

Grabosky, Peter N. *Sydney in Ferment.* Canberra: ANU, 1977.

Greenwood, G., ed. *Australia: a Social and Political History.* Sydney: Angus and Robertson, 1955.

Heasman, Kathleen. *Evangelicals in Action.* London: Geoffrey Bles, 1962.

Henderson, Harold R. *Reach for the World.* Nashville: Discipleship Resources, 1981.

Hoare, L. *Presenting Ten Decades: the History of the Sydney City Mission.* N.p., n.d.

Hoban, S. J. *The Great Realities.* London: Epworth, 1927.

Hopkins, C. H. *The Rise of the Social Gospel in American Protestantism 1865-1915.* New Haven: Yale, 1961.

Horne, Donald. *The Lucky Country.* Harmondsworth: Penguin, 1966.

Hughes, Dorothea Price. *The Life of Hugh Price Hughes.* London: Hodder and Stoughton, 1904.

Hughes, Hugh Price. *Social Christianity.* 4th ed. London: Hodder and Stoughton, 1904.

Huxley, Aldous. *Ends and Means.* London: Chatto and Windus, 1957.

Inglis, K. S. *Churches and the Working Classes in Victorian England.* London: Routledge and Kegan Paul, 1963.

Jackson, George. *Collier of Manchester.* London: Hodder and Stoughton, 1923.

James, J. S. *The Vagabond Papers.* Melbourne: Melbourne University Press, 1969, abbreviated from original 1877-78 edition published by George Robertson.

Judd, Bernard C. *He That Doeth: the Life Story of Canon R. B. S. Hammond.* London: Marshall, Morgan and Scott, n.d.

Kelly, Max, ed. *Nineteenth Century Sydney.* Sydney: Sydney University Press in association with the Sydney History Group, 1978.

King, Jonathon. *Waltzing Materialism.* Sydney: Harper and Row, 1978.

Lidgett, J. Scott. *My Guided Life.* London: Methuen, 1936.

Loomis, Samuel L. *Modern Cities and their Religious Problems.* New York: The Baker and Taylor Co., 1887.

McGregor, Craig. *People, Politics and Pop.* Sydney: Ure Smith, 1968.

————.*Profile of Australia.* London: Hodder and Stoughton, 1966.

McKernan, Michael. *Australian Churches at War, Attitudes and Activities of the Major Churches 1914-18.* Sydney and Canberra: Catholic Theological Faculty and Australian War Memorial, 1980.

McLeod, A. L., ed. *The Pattern of Australian Culture.* Melbourne: OUP, 1963.

Mearns, Andrew. In *The Bitter Cry of Outcast London,* edited by Anthony B. Wohl. New York: Humanities Press, 1883, reprinted 1970.

Mendelsohn, R. *The Condition of the People, Social Welfare in Australia 1900-1975.* Sydney: George Allen and Unwin, 1979.

Menzies, R. G. *The Measure of the Years.* Melbourne: Cassell, 1970.

Mol, Hans. *Religion in Australia, a Sociological Investigation.* Melbourne: Nelson, 1971.

"Moocher, The". *Scenes in Sydney by Day and Night.* Parramatta: G. C. Baker, 1887.

Niebuhr, Reinhold. *The Nature and Destiny of Man, a Christian Interpretation.* 2 vols. London: Nisbet, 1941 reprinted 1949, 1943 reprinted 1956).

Oeser, Oscar A., and Hammond, Samuel B. *Social Structures and Personality in the City*. London: Routledge and Kegan Paul, 1954.

Palamountain, W. J. *A. R. Edgar: a Methodist Greatheart*. Melbourne: Spectator, 1933.

Phillips, Walter. *Defending "A Christian Country"*. St Lucia: University of Queensland Press, 1981.

Pidgeon, Nathaniel. *The Life, Experience and Journal of Nathaniel Pidgeon, City Missionary, 1857–64*. Sydney: Mason and O'Connor, 1864.

Roe, Jill. *Twentieth Century Sydney*. Sydney: Hale and Iremonger in association with the Sydney History Group, 1980.

Simey, Margaret B. *Charitable Effort in Liverpool in the Nineteenth Century*. Liverpool: University Press, 1951.

Southall, Ivan, ed. *The Challenge*. Melbourne: Lansdowne, 1966.

Spearritt, P. *Sydney Since the Twenties*. Sydney: Hale and Iremonger, 1978.

Standing, Roger. "When the Windows of Heaven Opened, Liverpool Methodist Mission 1875–1905". Liverpool: typescript, 1981.

Stelzle, Charles. *Christianity's Storm Centre. A Study of the Modern City*. New York: F. H. Revell Co., 1907.

Strong, Josiah. *The Challenge of the City*. New York: Eaton and Mains, 1907.

―――. *Religious Movements for Social Betterment*. Monographs on American Social Economics no. 14. N.p., 1900.

Summers, A. *Damned Whores and God's Police*. Harmondsworth: Penguin, 1975.

Taylor, William George. *Dalmar Children's Homes on the Heights of Carlingford Near Ryde, Sydney*. Sydney: Epworth, n.d.

―――. *Life Story of an Australian Evangelist*. London: Epworth, 1920.

―――. *Pathfinders of the Great South Land*. London: Epworth, n.d.

―――. *Restore the Fellowship of the Church*. Sydney: Epworth, 1912.

Temple, William. *Christianity and Social Order*. London: SCM, 1942, repr. 1955.

―――. *Malvern 1941*. London: Longmans Green, 1941.

Townsend, W. J., Workman, H. B., and Eayrs, George. *A New History of Methodism*. 2 vols. London: Hodder and Stoughton, 1909.

Udy, James S., and Clancy, Eric G., eds. *Dig or Die*. Sydney: World Methodist Historical Society, Australian Section, 1981.

Walker, Alan. *God, the Disturber*. Waco: World Books, 1973.

―――. *Love in Action*. Glasgow: Fontana, 1977.

―――. *The New Evangelism*. Belfast: Christian Journals, 1977.

―――. *Now for Newness*. Melbourne: The Methodist Publishing House, 1970.

————. *The Promise and the Power*. Nashville: Discipleship Resources, 1980.

————. *The Whole Gospel for the Whole World*. London: Marshall, Morgan and Scott, 1958.

Ward, R. *Australia: a Short History*. Rev. ed. Sydney: Ure Smith, 1975.

Wesley Central Mission. *This Amazing Mission*. Sydney: WCM, n.d.

Whitby, Kath and Clancy, Eric G. *Great the Heritage*. Mascot: E. H. Enterprise Holdings, 1975.

White, Richard. *Inventing Australia*. Sydney: Allen and Unwin, 1980.

Wilson, Bryan R. *Religion in a Secular Society*. Harmondsworth: Penguin, 1969.

Woodward, Charlie. *A Burglar Captured*. Sydney: Newmarket Printing House, 1922.

————. *Out of the Depths*. Sydney: J. A. Packer, n.d.

————. *Peeps into Gaols, Police Courts and Opium Dens*. Sydney: J.A. Packer, n.d.

————. *Story of my Conversion*. Sydney: Central Press, n.d.

Articles

Ajax. "Larrikinism". *Sydney Quarterly Magazine* 1, no. 2 (January 1884):207-15.

Bunyip. "The Sewing Girls of Sydney". *The Australian* 4 (1880):615-21.

Colwell, J. "The Passing of a Great Philanthropist". Manuscript tribute to Hon. E. Vickery on his death (Mitchell Library).

Davison, G. "Sydney and the Bush: an Urban Context for the Australian Legend". *Historical Studies* 18, no. 71 (October 1978):191-209.

Gerathy, Greta. "Sydney Municipality in the 1880s". *Journal of the Royal Australian Historical Society* 58, no. 1 (March 1972):23-54.

Gordon, Florence. "The Conditions of Female Labour and the Rates of Women's Wages in Sydney". *The Australian Economist* 4, no. 7 (23 August 1894):423-29.

Harrison, B. "Philanthropy and the Victorians". *Victorian Studies* 9, no. 4 (June 1966):353-74.

Howe, Renate. "Social Composition of the Wesleyan Church in Victoria during the Nineteenth Century". *Journal of Religious History* 4, no. 3 (June 1967):206-17.

Mansfield, Bruce and Hope, Desmond. "Protestant Australia Today". *The Bulletin*, 10 June 1961, pp. 12-14.

North, Frank Mason. "City Missions and Social Problems". *Methodist Review* 75 (1893):228-39.

O'Farrell, Patrick J. "The History of the NSW Labour Movement 1880-1910, a Religious Interpretation". *Journal of Religious History* 2, no. 2 (December 1962):133-51.

Phillips, Walter. "James Jefferis in Sydney: His Ministry at Pitt Street Congregational Church, 1877-1889". *Church Heritage* 2, no. 2 (September 1981):119-43.

Pratt, Ambrose. " 'Push' Larrikinism in Australia". *Blackwood's Magazine* 1029 (July 1901):27-40.

Sellers, Ian. "Nonconformist Attitudes in Later Nineteenth Century Liverpool". *Historical Society of Lancs and Cheshire: Transactions* 114 (1962):215-239.

Walker, R.B. "Growth and Typology of the Wesleyan Methodist Church in New South Wales, 1837-1900". *Journal of Religious History* 6 (1970-71):331-47.

Wirth, Louis. "Urbanism as a Way of Life". *American Journal of Sociology* 44, no. 1 (July 1938):1-24.

Wright, Don. "Alfred Deakin and Immigration, 1901-10". *ANU Historical Journal* no. 5 (November 1968):41-50.

Unpublished Theses

Fisher, Shirley. "Life and Work in Sydney, 1870-1890", Ph.D. thesis, Macquarie, 1976.

Gilbert, A.D. "The Churches and the Conscription Referenda, 1916-19". M.A. thesis, ANU, 1967.

Hansen, Donald E. "The Churches and Society in NSW, 1919-1939: a Study of Church Activities, Socio-religious Issues, Community-church and Inter-church relations". Ph.D. thesis, Macquarie, 1979.

Hicks, Neville. "The Establishment of a Central Methodist Mission in Adelaide". B.A. thesis, Adelaide, 1966.

MacLachlan, N.D. "Larrikinism: an Interpretation". M.A. thesis, Melbourne, n.d.

Meredith, Phillip. "The Evolution of a Social Concept: Aspects of Canabis Prohibition in Australia, 1960-1970", B.A. thesis, Newcastle, 1982.

Peter, Phyllis. "Social Aspects of the Depression in NSW 1930-1934". Ph.D. thesis, ANU, 1964.

Roberts, Alan. "City Improvement in Sydney: Public Policy 1880-1900". Ph.D. thesis, Sydney, 1977.

Interviews

Foreman, Miss L., 11 February 1981
Jackson, Rev. Alan, 10 December 1981
Rayward, Rev. Dr F., 12 February 1981
Staines, Mrs J. and Williams, Mr R (jointly), 11 February 1981
Towers, Deaconess Noreen, 19 January 1982
Walker, Rev. Sir Alan, 12 December 1981 and 10 June 1983

Index

Numbers in **bold** type refer to photographs

of debate re York Street church
by, 27-28; appointed to William
Street (1888), 39; attitude of to
proposed appointment to York
Street (1884), 28; autobiography,
89; background of, 29-30; burden
on, 77-78; concern of for sailors,
31; Conference aims in appoint-
ing to York Street, 29; criticism
of, 35; dissatisfaction of with
state of CMM, 77-78; and early
closing movement, 93; early services of at York Street, 32-33;
energies of sapped by burden of
debt, 88; on financial situation at
CMM, 69; and Garrett, 44; as
naval chaplain, 107; plans of for
operation of York Street, 31; as
president of NSW Conference,
67; and purchase of the Lyceum
Theatre, 80; reaction of York
Street stewart to proposed
appointment of, 28; reasons for
success of, 99; retirement of
(1913), 99; return to CMM (1898),
77; reviews first year's work at
York Street, 35; seeks reinstate-
ment at CMM (1898), 70; and
sisters of the people, 55, 57; and
social issues, 93, 97; on "sweating", 96; and unemployment, 93;
and unionism, 96; on urban
decline of Wesleyan Methodist
church, 19; visits Great Britain
(1887), 38; visits Great Britain
and the USA (1893), 67-69; work
of at the Glebe, 30. See also
Sydney CMM; evangelism
Teenage Cabaret, 64, 184-87; attendance at, 184-85; criticism of, 186-
87; decline of, 185; effectiveness
of in outreach, 186; media
interest in, 185; move of to
Wesley Centre, 185; nature of
programme of, 186. See also
ABC Television; *Australian
Women's Weekly*; Cinesound
News
telephone counselling service, 204,
213. See also Life Line
Temperance Hall, 58
Temperance Society: at CMM, 36,
73; at Glebe, 30
temperance work, 73, 93
Temple, William, 176
ten-day mission: 1884, 34; 1886, 36

ten-day prayer meeting, 1891, 50.
See also prayer
Textile and Recycling Centre, 229
theatre services, 69, 79
Theatres and Public Halls Act,
contravention of, 162
Theatres Inspection Committee,
condemns Centenary Hall and
criticizes Lyceum Theatre, 81-82
Third World, aid to, 219
Thomas, Ken, 216
Thompson, Peter, 9, 10
Thompson, Richard, 168
Time, 212
Towers, Noreen, 57, 197, **199**;
expands Life Line church, 198;
ministry of to Pacific Islanders,
205; plans new refuge develop-
ment, 199. See also alcoholism;
homeless men
Town Hall corner, 118, 181. See also
open-air services
"Turn Round Australia", 227
Two-up School Mission, 84

UN Delegation (Australian), 174
unemployed, march to CMM of
(1893), 94
unemployment, 218; attitude of
Wesleyan church to, 94-95;
churches lack interest in, 105;
growth of in 1970s, 171; Taylor
and, 58-59, 93
unionism: compulsory, 163; supported by Stephen, 95; of tailoresses
supported by Taylor, 96
United Charities Organisation, 124
United Licensed Victuallers Association, 148
University of Sydney, 181
urban churches, decline of, 20,
22-23

Vaughan, Archbishop Roger, 26
V.E. Day, 161
venereal disease, 101
Vickery, Ebenezer, 64; defends
capitalism, 97; financial support
of CMM by, 89-90; influence on
Taylor of, 97; loans home for
sisters, 54-55, 56; and Lyceum
pictures, 127; provides house for
children's home, 73; purchase of
Lyceum Theatre by, 80-81;
refuses to exchange Lyceum